Microsoft®
Office 2003

Nancy D. Lewis

C000176645

Contents

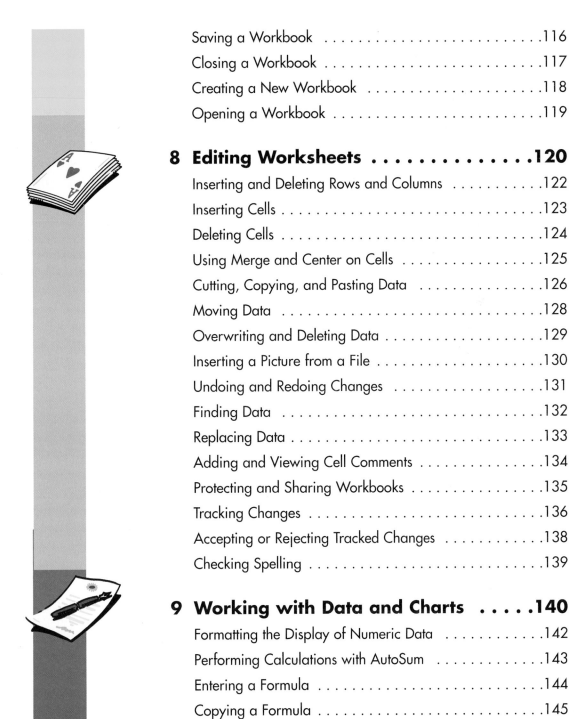

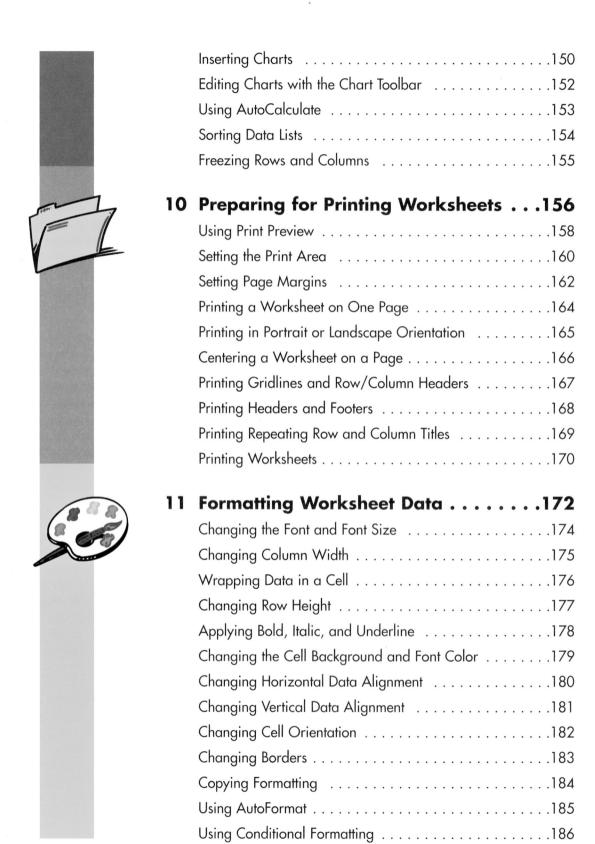

14 Getting Started with Outlook 228

15 Advanced Office and Web Features . .256

Easy Microsoft® Office 2003

Copyright © 2004 by Que Publishing

International Standard Book Number: 0-7897-2962-8

Library of Congress Catalog Card Number: 2003103669

Printed in the United States of America

First Printing: September 2003

06   05   04   03   4   3   2

Que Publishing offers excellent discounts on this book when ordered in quantity for bulk purchases or special sales. For more information, please contact

U.S. Corporate and Government Sales

1-800-382-3419

corpsales@pearsontechgroup.com

For sales outside the U.S., please contact

International Sales

1-317-581-3793

international@pearsontechgroup.com

Trademarks

Warning and Disclaimer

Associate Publisher
Greg Wiegand

Acquisitions Editor
Michelle Newcomb

Development Editor
Kate Welsh

Managing Editor
Charlotte Clapp

Project Editor
Tonya Simpson

Production Editor
Megan Wade

Indexer
Ken Johnson

Proofreader
Linda Seifert

Technical Editor
Bill Bruns

Team Coordinator
Sharry Gregory

Interior Designer
Anne Jones

Cover Designer
Anne Jones

About the Author

Nancy D. Lewis is a freelance writer, editor, and computer training consultant. Her books focus on computers, business, and real estate; while her teaching focuses on computer users of all ages who want to learn the tricks (as well as the ins and outs) of the Office products' trade.

Dedication

To Sid ....

Acknowledgments

A special thanks to Michelle Newcomb for working so patiently with me and being a terrific acquisitions editor! In addition, I would like to thank Kate Shoup Welsh for all her hard work and great suggestions; as well as Tonya Simpson, Megan Wade, and Bill Bruns for their edits.

We Want to Hear from You!

As the reader of this book, *you* are our most important critic and commentator. We value your opinion and want to know what we're doing right, what we could do better, what areas you'd like to see us publish in, and any other words of wisdom you're willing to pass our way.

As an associate publisher for Que, I welcome your comments. You can email or write me directly to let me know what you did or didn't like about this book—as well as what we can do to make our books better.

Please note that I cannot help you with technical problems related to the *topic* of this book. We do have a User Services group, however, where I will forward specific technical questions related to the book.

When you write, please be sure to include this book's title and author as well as your name, email address, and phone number. I will carefully review your comments and share them with the author and editors who worked on the book.

Email: feedback@quepublishing.com

Mail: Greg Wiegand
                Que Publishing
                800 East 96th Street
                Indianapolis, IN 46240 USA

For more information about this book or another Que title, visit our Web site at www.quepublishing.com. Type the ISBN (excluding hyphens) or the title of a book in the Search field to find the page you're looking for.

It's as Easy as 1-2-3

Each part of this book is made up of a series of short, instructional lessons, designed to help you understand basic information that you need to get the most out of your computer hardware and software.

2 Each task includes a series of quick, easy steps designed to guide you through the procedure.

3 Items that you select or click in menus, dialog boxes, tabs, and windows are shown in **bold**.

1 Each step is fully illustrated to show you how it looks onscreen.

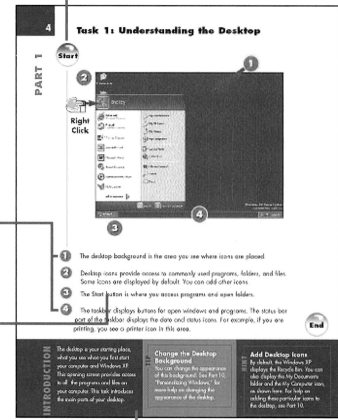

4 Task 1: Understanding the Desktop

1 The desktop background is the area you see where icons are placed.

2 Desktop icons provide access to commonly used programs, folders, and files. Some icons are displayed by default. You can add other icons.

3 The Start button is where you access programs and open folders.

4 The taskbar displays buttons for open windows and programs. The status bar part of the taskbar displays the date and status icons. For example, if you are printing, you see a printer icon in this area.

INTRODUCTION The desktop is your starting place, what you see when you first start your computer and Windows XP. This opening screen provides access to all the programs and files on your computer. This task introduces the main parts of your desktop.

Change the Desktop Background You can change the appearance of this background. See Part 10, "Personalizing Windows," for more help on changing the appearance of the desktop.

Add Desktop Icons By default, the Windows XP displays the Recycle Bin. You can also display the My Documents folder and the My Computer icon, as shown here. For help on adding these particular icons to the desktop, see Part 10.

Tips and Hints give you a heads-up for any extra information you may need while working through the task.

drag

How to Drag:
Point to the starting place or object. Hold down the mouse button (right or left per instructions), move the mouse to the new location, then release the button.

 Next Step:
If you see this symbol, it means the task you're working on continues on the next page.

End Task:
Task is complete.

Selection:
Highlights the area onscreen discussed in the step or task.

drop

Click:
Click the left mouse button once.

Right-click:
Click the right mouse button once.

Click & Type:
Click once where indicated and begin typing to enter your text or data.

Double-click:
Click the left mouse button twice in rapid succession.

Pointer Arrow:
Highlights an item on the screen you need to point to or focus on in the step or task.

Introduction to *Easy Microsoft Office 2003*

Easy Microsoft Office 2003 will help you learn to work efficiently and effectively in Microsoft Office 2003 applications. More specifically, you will learn about each of the following software applications:

- **Word**—This word processing application has features that enable you to create documents such as a one-page memo, a newsletter with graphics, a mass mail merge, or a 500-page report.

- **Excel**—This powerful yet easily managed spreadsheet application can be used to generate impressive financial statements, charts, lists of data, and graphs.

- **PowerPoint**—This presentation application enables you to create exciting slides and printouts that will help you give an informative and memorable presentation.

- **Outlook**—This application provides an electronic mail program, daily planner, calendar, contacts list, and to-do list that helps you manage your time and projects.

Because Microsoft Office 2003 is an integrated suite, you will find that many of the tasks you learn in this book apply to other applications in the suite. In addition, check out the section on Office 2003 and the Web to open documents on the Internet; browse Web documents; jump to other documents, objects, or pages using hyperlinks; or even share your documents on the Web.

Getting Started with Office

You need to know some fundamental things about Microsoft Office before you start working with its applications. The tasks in this part will introduce you to the basics of Microsoft Office 2003 and are common to all Microsoft Office applications. If you learn how to perform these tasks in one Office application, you can perform them the same way in all Office applications.

Before you begin, click the **Start** button on your Windows desktop and select **All Programs** to ensure that Microsoft Office is installed on your hard disk (you should see a Microsoft Office command in the menu, which opens a sub-menu containing the various Office programs you installed).

Using Office Applications

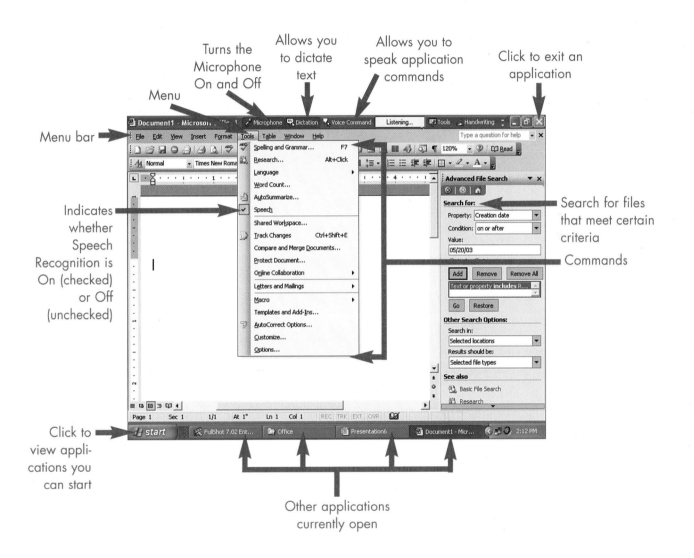

Turns the Microphone On and Off

Allows you to dictate text

Allows you to speak application commands

Click to exit an application

Menu

Menu bar

Indicates whether Speech Recognition is On (checked) or Off (unchecked)

Search for files that meet certain criteria

Commands

Click to view applications you can start

Other applications currently open

Starting Office Applications

Start

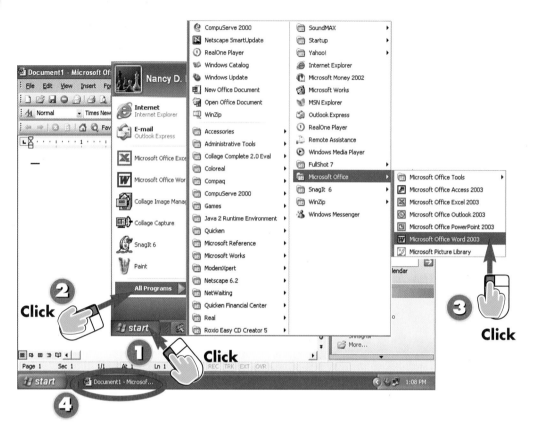

Click

Click

Click

Click

1 Click the **Start** button.

2 Click the **All Programs** command (check out the multitude of applications available to you on your computer, many of which you might not even know you have).

3 Click the application you want to start—for example, **Microsoft Word**—from the Microsoft Office submenu.

4 The Word window opens with a blank document, and a Word button appears on the taskbar.

End

You start Microsoft Office applications in the same way you do most other applications in Windows XP: using the Start menu. If you recently used a particular Office application, that application command might be visible on the first pane of the Start menu as well as in its normal location, in the All Programs submenu.

Using Desktop Shortcuts
Depending on your computer's setup, you might have a shortcut icon for various Office applications on your Windows desktop. If you do, you can double-click an application's shortcut icon to start the application.

Opening a File
Another way to start an application is to double-click an existing file that was created using that application—for example, one in your My Documents folder. Windows will start the application and open the file you double-clicked.

Working with Menus

Start

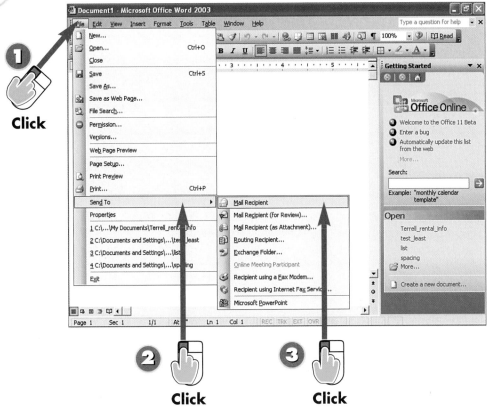

Click

Click   **Click**

---

1 Click the **File** menu and review the commands available to you.

2 Move the mouse pointer to the **Send To** command. The small black arrow next to the command denotes a submenu, which appears when the command is highlighted.

3 To execute a command in the submenu, move the mouse pointer to the command you want (in this example, **Mail Recipient**) and press the left mouse button.

End

TIP

Using Your Keyboard to Issue Commands
If you want to use your keyboard instead of your mouse to issue a menu command, press the **Alt** key and then press the letter that's underlined in the menu name. For example, press **Alt+F** to view the File menu.

TIP

Menu Commands Followed by an Ellipsis
If an ellipsis (...) appears next to a menu a command, it means a dialog box will open when you choose the command, giving you more options.

Using Shortcut Menus (the Right Mouse Button)

Start

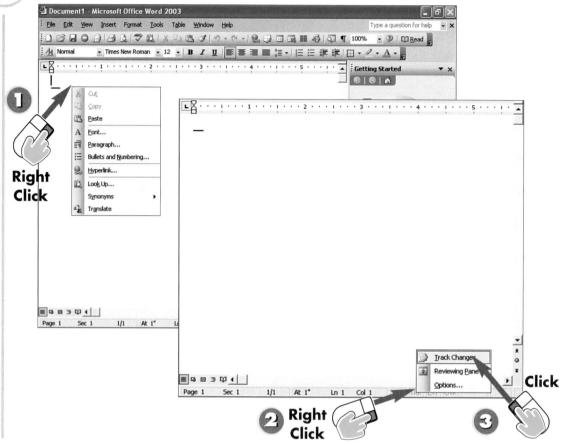

Right Click

2 Right Click

Click

3

1. Right-click anywhere in a document to see a shortcut menu.

2. Right-click the **TRK** command on the application's status bar, for example, to see a different shortcut menu.

3. Click a command on the shortcut menu—for example, **Track Changes**. The action is performed, and the shortcut menu disappears.

End

When you right-click an item in your workspace, a *shortcut menu* (also known as a *pop-up* or *context menu*) appears. The commands in shortcut menus vary, depending on your selection; that is, shortcut menus include the commands used most often for whatever object is selected—text, cells, graphics, and so on. If you open a shortcut menu that doesn't contain the command you want to use, exit the menu by pressing the **Esc** key or clicking elsewhere on the desktop.

TIP

Using Traditional Menus
The commands available on shortcut menus are also available on traditional menus (refer to the previous task). For example, you could issue the Track Changes command by opening the Tools menu and selecting the Track Changes command.

Working with Toolbars

Start

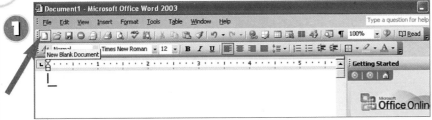

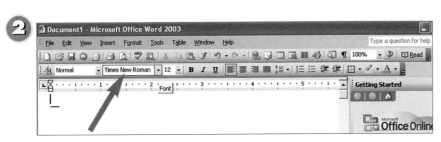

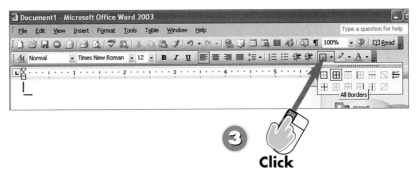

3 Click

① Move the mouse pointer over each button on the Standard toolbar, pausing momentarily over each button to see a descriptive ScreenTip.

② Move the mouse pointer over each button on the Formatting toolbar, again pausing for a second to see the descriptive ScreenTip.

③ Click a button to perform the corresponding action. For example, click the down arrow next to the **Borders** button to choose from the 12 border options (notice the ScreenTip).

End

Switching Between Office Documents and Applications

Start

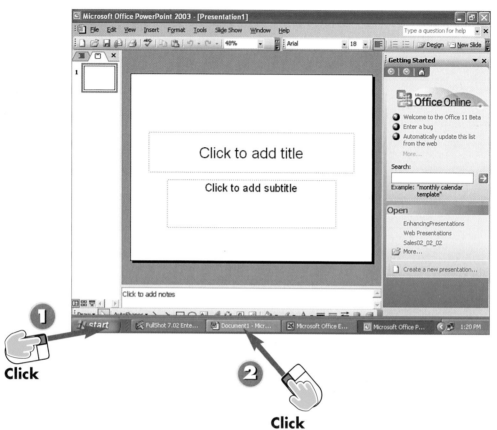

1 Click

2 Click

1 Open multiple Office applications by clicking the **Start** button—for example, start Word, Excel, and then PowerPoint.

2 Click the taskbar button for the application you want to make active—for example, **Microsoft Word**.

End

INTRODUCTION

You can have multiple Office applications and documents open at the same time and switch between them whenever you want. For example, you might use data in Excel to help create a report in Word and a presentation in PowerPoint, which you want to immediately send to your manager using Outlook.

TIP

Resizing Application Windows
If your application windows aren't maximized, you can resize them to view multiple windows on the desktop. Do so by placing the mouse pointer on the window border, where the pointer turns into a double-headed arrow. Then press and hold down the left mouse button and drag the window until it's the desired size. If your windows are maximized, you must first click the Restore Down button on the application window before dragging the window's edge.

Using the Task Pane

Using the Task Pane

Start

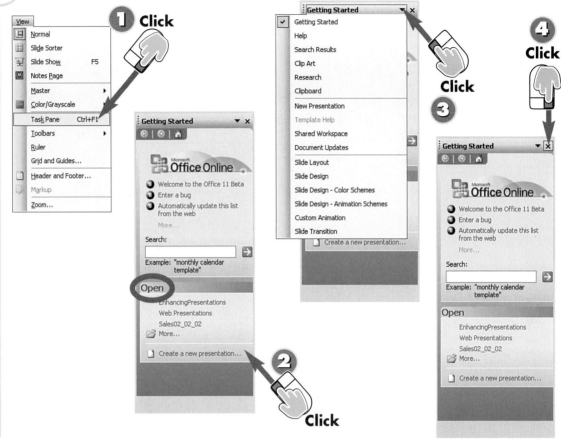

1. **Click**
2. **Click**
3. **Click**
4. **Click**

1. If the task pane isn't already visible in your application window, open the **View** menu and select **Task Pane** to display it.

2. The Open section of the task pane contains links to files you've recently worked on. Click a filename link to open it or click the **Create a New** link.

3. Click the down arrow at the top of the task pane to view the other available task panes.

4. Click the task pane's **Close** button, located at the top of the pane, to close it.

End

INTRODUCTION

If you recently installed Office, the task pane might be displayed when you start an Office application. The task pane simply offers additional ways for you to quickly perform common tasks, get help, find files, and much more. As you work in Office, additional task panes become active depending on which tasks you are performing.

TIP

Resizing the Task Pane
You can decrease the size of a task pane to increase your work area. Simply move the mouse pointer over the leftmost edge of the task pane; when the pointer changes to a two-pointed arrow, click and drag it to the left or right.

HINT

Available Task Panes
Performing certain actions in Office activates a particular task pane. For example, if you copy data, a Clipboard task pane will be activated. If you insert clip art into an Office document, the Clip Art task pane will appear.

Exiting an Application

Start

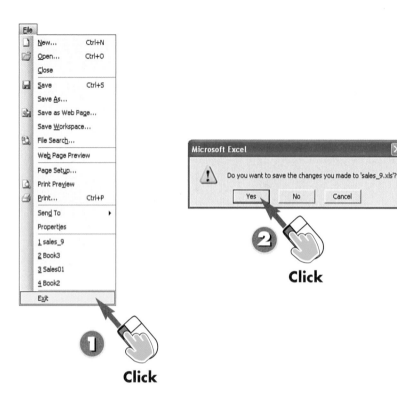

Click

Click

1. Open the **File** menu and select **Exit**. If you have made changes to the document without saving your work, the application asks whether you want to save it.

2. Click **Yes** to save your work; click **No** if you don't want to save it; click **Cancel** to return to working in the document without saving or exiting.

End

INTRODUCTION

When you no longer want to work in an application, you can exit it and return to the Windows desktop. The best practice is to save your work in each application and then exit all the applications before you turn off your computer.

TIP

Taskbar
Notice that after you close an application, the taskbar no longer displays a button for that application.

TIP

Quick Closing
There is a trick to quickly closing all open documents without exiting the specific Office application: Press the **Shift** key and select **File**, **Close All**.

Getting Help

Start

Click

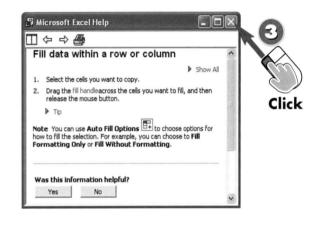

Click

① Type a question in the **Type a Question for Help** list box. For example, in Excel, type **how do I repeat similar items**.

② When you press Enter, the Search Results task pane opens and displays a list of possible answers from Microsoft.com. Click the link that seems like the best match.

③ Read the information in the Help window; then click its **Close** button. If necessary, click additional links in the Search Results task pane until your question is answered.

INTRODUCTION

Microsoft lets you easily get help in Office—even if you don't know exactly what type of help you need. In addition to typing a question in the Type a Question for Help search box found in each application's window, you can also use the Help task pane and other Help resources to get on track.

TIP

Helping Yourself
If none of the search results adequately answers your question, scroll to the bottom of the Search Results task pane and click the **Tips for Better Search Results** link for tips on conducting more effective searches.

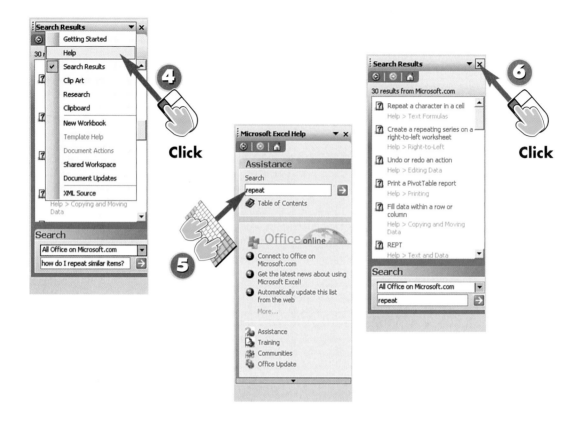

Click

Click

4 To use the Help task pane to get help, click the down arrow at the top of the Search Results task pane and select **Help** from the list that appears.

5 In the **Search** field, type a term relating to the task you need help with, and then press **Enter** or click the green arrow. Repeat steps 2 and 3 when the search results appear.

6 Click the Search Results task pane's **Close** button, located at the top of the pane, to close it.

Using Microsoft.com

In the Help task pane, you can click links to go directly to specific Web sites that offer assistance and training. In addition, you can download information and software fixes at Office Update. Finally, the Help task pane's Spotlight area provides direct access to Microsoft.com, where you can get the latest news about using Microsoft Office.

Finding Files

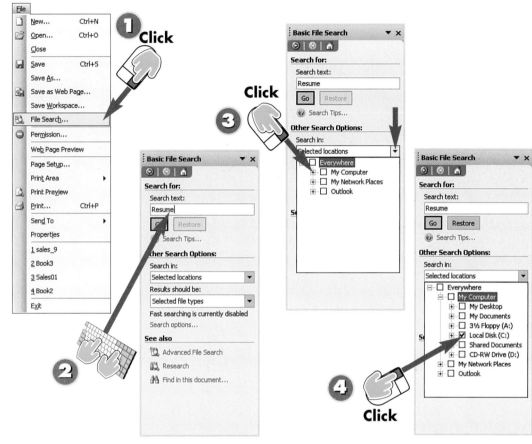

1. Open the **File** menu and select **File Search** to open the Basic File Search task pane.

2. Type all or part of the name of the file you are searching for (in this case, **Resume**). This searches the text of the documents as well as the filename.

3. Click the down arrow next to the **Search in** field, and then click the plus sign (**+**) next to **My Computer** to display a list of your computer's contents.

4. Click the check box next to the folders and drives you want to search, and uncheck any you want to bypass. When you're ready, click the down arrow to exit the list.

The more files you create and save in Office, the harder it can be to locate them all. Fortunately, if you haven't kept all your files organized in folders according to project, date, or task, Office can help you find your files.

Search Tips

For help with searching for files, click the **Search Tips** link below the Go button. Microsoft Help will show you how to indicate search text, help you with where to search, help you with finding specific document types, and even help you set up advanced search condition—for example, if you are trying to locate a file you know that you created on Monday, March 10, 2003.

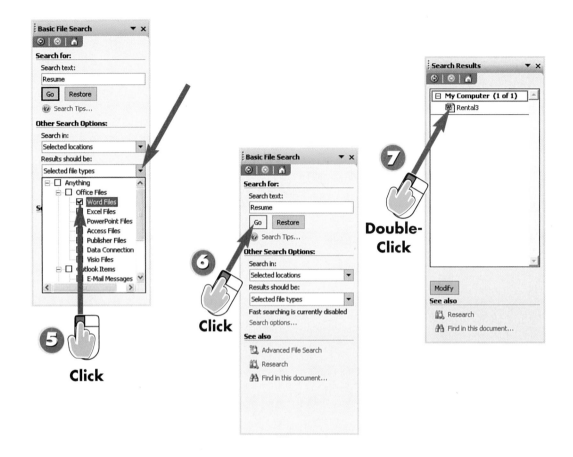

5 Click the **Results Should Be** field's down arrow and check or uncheck the boxes in the list for the desired type of file; then click the down arrow again to exit the list.

6 Click the **Go** button to initiate the search.

7 Double-click the file after it is found to open it and begin working.

End

Setting Up Speech Recognition

Start

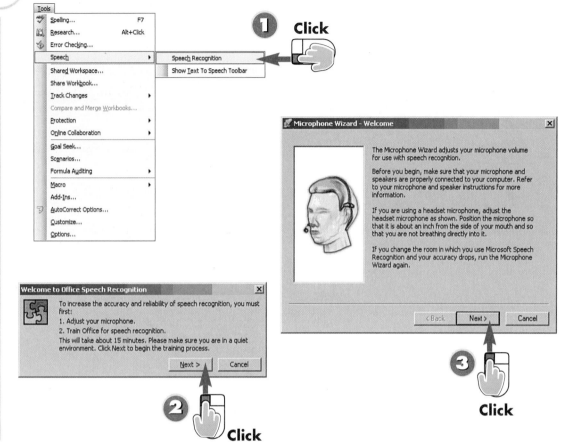

1 Click

2 Click

3 Click

1 In your open Office application, select the **Tools** menu and select **Speech**, **Speech Recognition** (or select **Tools**, **Speech** in some Office applications).

2 Read the information in the Welcome to Office Speech Recognition dialog box and click **Next**.

3 The Microphone Wizard Welcome page opens, providing useful information about adjusting your microphone. Read it, and click **Next**.

INTRODUCTION

If you like to dictate letters and memos, you'll be pleased to learn that Office supports speech recognition in all its applications. Before you can use this feature, however, you must set it up. You can do so in any Office application or by double-clicking the Speech icon in the Windows XP Control Panel. (In this task, you'll set it up from within Excel.) Before you begin, you'll need to connect a microphone and some speakers to your PC (refer to the instructions that came with those components for help).

TIP

Adjusting the Microphone's Sensitivity
Double-click the **Volume** icon in the system tray (on the far right end of the taskbar, to the left of the time) to open a window that enables you to increase or decrease the microphone's sensitivity.

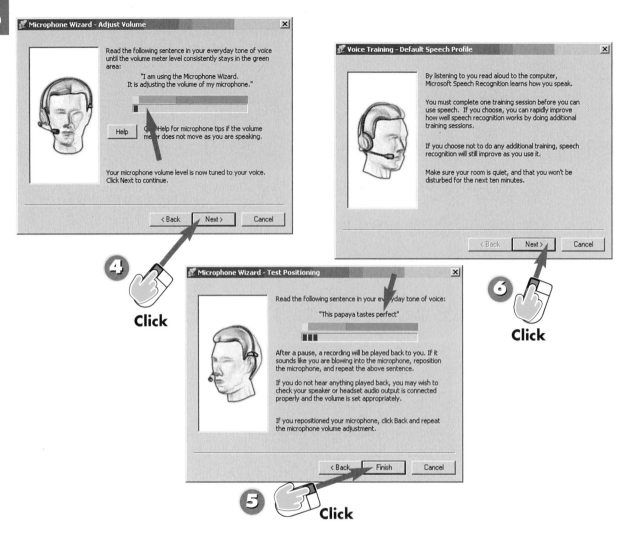

Click

Click

Click

4 Repeat the text featured in the Adjust Volume page in a normal tone of voice until the volume meter level is consistently in the green. When you're finished, click **Next**.

5 Read the Test Positioning sentence aloud. If the playback recording sounds distorted, reposition the mic, click **Back** and repeat; otherwise, click **Finish**.

6 The Voice Training Default Speech Profile page opens and says that you must complete at least one training session before using the Speech Recognition feature. Click **Next**.

HINT

Mistakes and Stops

If Office stops highlighting text while you are reading, you probably missed a word, read too quickly, or pronounced something incorrectly. Simply take a couple of breaths and begin again where the highlighting left off. If you don't recognize a word in the text or aren't sure how to pronounce it, you can skip it by clicking the Skip Word button. To stop for a moment (for example, to answer the phone), click the **Pause** button. (A Resume button appears for you to click when you are ready to continue.)

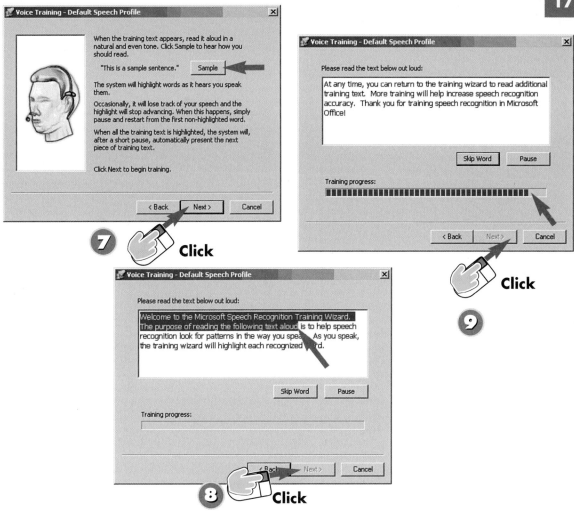

7 The Voice Training Wizard coaches you to read the training text in subsequent pages in a clear, natural tone. Click **Sample** to hear an example, and then click **Next**.

8 Read the displayed text aloud; the text you've read will become highlighted as you go. When finished, click the **Next** button that activates.

9 Continue to read the displayed text aloud, moving through each passage. (Notice that the Training Progress bar moves as you proceed.) Click **Next**.

Getting More Training
Click the **More Training** button in the screen in step 11 to read additional passages aloud, which will make the speech-recognition feature more accurate.

Setting Up Multiple Speech Profiles
Other people who use your computer can set up their own speech-recognition profiles. To do so, they must select Tools, Speech to activate the Language bar, click the Tools button in the Language bar, and select Options from the list that appears to open the Speech Properties dialog box. There, they click the New button to initiate a new speech profile. After multiple speech profiles are set up, you can choose your own by selecting Tools, Current User, and the appropriate username.

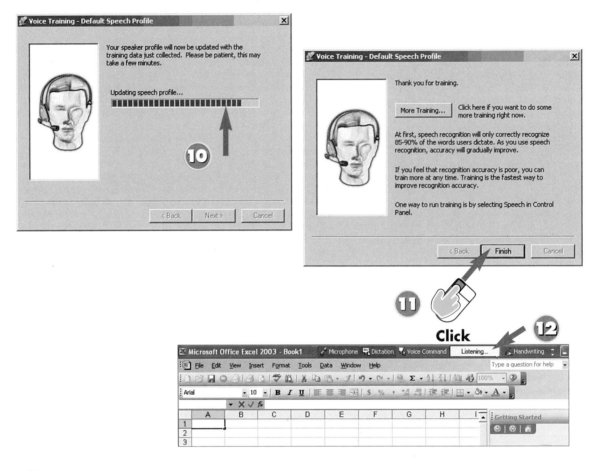

10 After you finish reading all the passages, your speech profile is updated.

11 Click the **Finish** button.

12 The Voice Training Wizard closes. A Language bar is added to the active application window's title bar, which you can click and drag to other locations on your desktop.

End

Displaying the Language Bar

If the Language bar isn't visible, open the **Tools** menu and select **Speech**. If the Tools button on the Language bar isn't visible, click the **Options** button in the Language bar and select **Speech Tools**.

Adding Words

To add a word to the Speech Recognition dictionary, select **Tools**, **Add/Delete Word(s)** from the Language bar. Type the word, click the **Record Pronunciation** button, and say the word to add it to the dictionary. Click the **Close** button when finished.

Dictating Your Text and Data

Start

1 Click

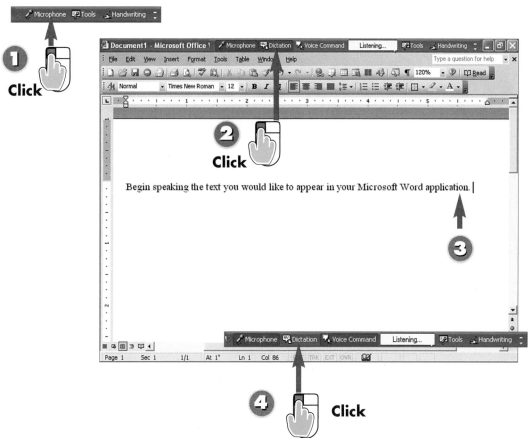

2 Click

3

4 Click

---

1 Click the **Microphone** button on the Language bar. (If the Language bar isn't displayed, open the **Tools** menu and select **Speech**.)

2 Click the **Dictation** button on the Language bar.

3 Say the words you want to appear in your document.

4 To stop dictating, click the **Dictation** button; then click the **Microphone** button (or say "microphone") to turn off the microphone.

End

INTRODUCTION

The whole point of using Office's Speech Recognition feature is so you can speak into your microphone, rather than typing, to input data into the various Office applications. In Excel, for example, say the numbers or words you want to enter into a cell and say "enter."

TIP

Adding Punctuation and Nonprinting Characters
To add punctuation to your document, simply say the name of the mark you want to add. For example, to add a comma, say the word "comma." To move to a new line, say "new line"; to begin a new paragraph, say "new paragraph" or "enter." You can also issue the following self-explanatory commands: "tab," "space," "up," "down," "left," and "right."

Using Voice Commands

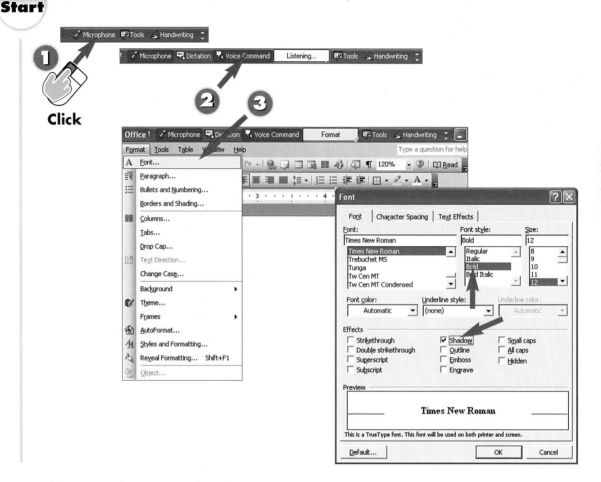

Start

① Click

Microphone ✏ Tools ✎ Handwriting

② ③

① If the microphone is not already in use, click the **Microphone** button on the Language bar to activate it. (If the Language bar isn't displayed, select **Tools**, **Speech**.)

② Click the **Voice Command** button on the Language bar (or say "voice command").

③ Say the name of the menu you want to open—for example, "Format." Then, say the name of the command you want to issue, such as "Font."

④ In the Font dialog box, say the name of the tab you want to use. Then, say the name of the option you want to activate (for example, "Shadow" and "Bold").

INTRODUCTION

Use the Voice Command feature in Speech Recognition to select buttons from toolbars, commands from menus, options from dialog boxes, and links on the task pane. This task demonstrates using selection commands for a menu and dialog box; read the tips in this task to learn how to select toolbar buttons and links on a task pane.

TIP

Talking to the Task Pane
You can choose commands on a task pane by saying the full name of the desired link. For example, in the New Document task pane in Word, you could say "from existing document" to create a new document from an existing document.

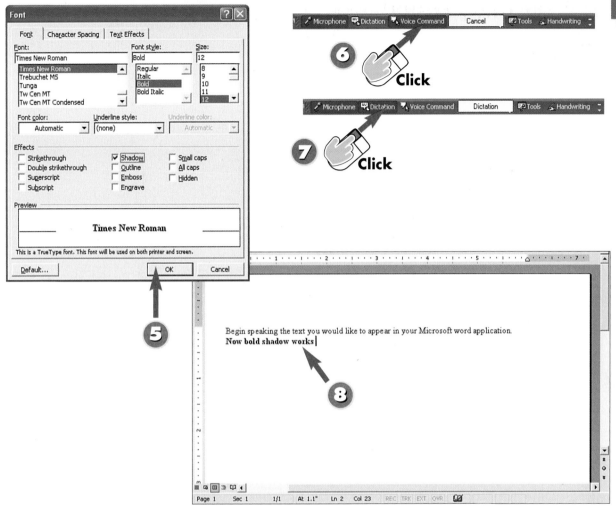

Say "OK" to process your commands, or "Cancel" to cancel them.

6 To turn off the Voice Command feature, click the **Voice Command** button.

7 To resume dictating, click the **Dictation** button (or simply say "dictation").

8 As you dictate, changes you made using the Voice Command feature will be active. Notice the newly dictated text appears with bold and shadow effects.

TIP

Talking to the Toolbar

To access buttons on a toolbar, you must know the exact name of each button. Move the mouse pointer over each toolbar button to become familiar with them. When you are ready to access a toolbar button, click the **Voice Command** button (or say "voice command") and say the name of the button. For example, to begin typing underlined text, say "underline," then say "dictation," and then say the words you want to appear underlined in your document. If you make any errors, you can switch back to the Voice Command feature and say "undo."

Getting Started with Word

When you first start working in Microsoft Word, you will begin by entering and inserting text. When you begin to create documents that you can move around in, you will need to save and close those documents. Eventually, you will need to know how to reopen the documents you create and perhaps move text around, insert new text (or other items you will learn about in Parts 3, 4, 5, and 6), and even change the view of the document.

If you need to switch between two documents on which you are working, Word makes that a simple task. Then, when you have saved your documents again—because you know you should save frequently—this part will show you how to preview and print your documents.

Opening and Saving Documents

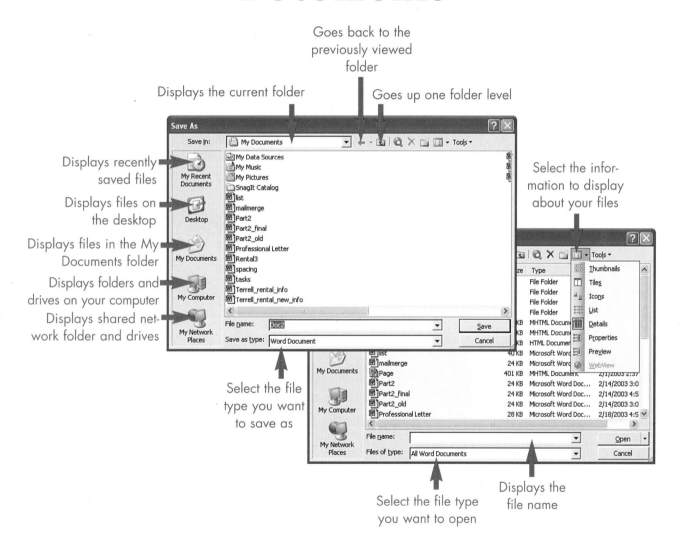

Goes back to the previously viewed folder

Displays the current folder

Goes up one folder level

Displays recently saved files

Displays files on the desktop

Displays files in the My Documents folder

Displays folders and drives on your computer

Displays shared network folder and drives

Select the information to display about your files

Select the file type you want to save as

Select the file type you want to open

Displays the file name

Entering and Inserting Text

Start

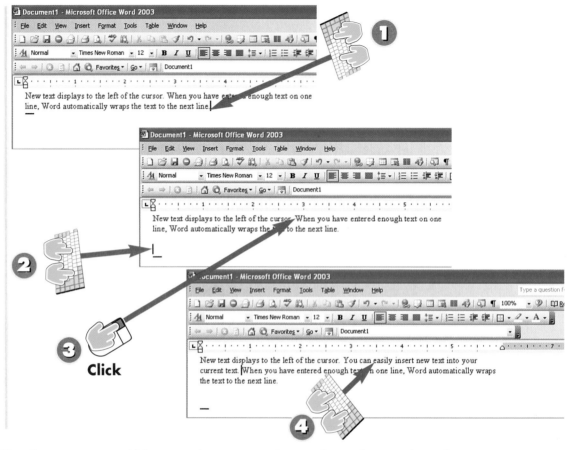

Click

1. Type some text. When you have entered enough text for one line, the cursor automatically wraps (moves) to the next line.

2. Press the **Enter** key a couple of times to insert new paragraphs.

3. Click once at the location where you want to insert new text.

4. Type the text you want to insert. Word slides over the existing text and inserts the new text.

End

INTRODUCTION

When you open Word, you can immediately begin entering text in a new default document called **Document1**. The insertion point, or *cursor*, "blinks" at the top of the document where the text you are typing will be displayed.

TIP

Paragraphs
You can split a paragraph by moving the cursor to where you want to divide the paragraph and pressing the Enter key.

TIP

Insert and Overtype
The Insert key toggles Insert mode and Overtype mode on and off (OVR displays in the Word status bar). When you type in Overtype mode, your typing replaces the current text.

Moving Around in Documents

Start

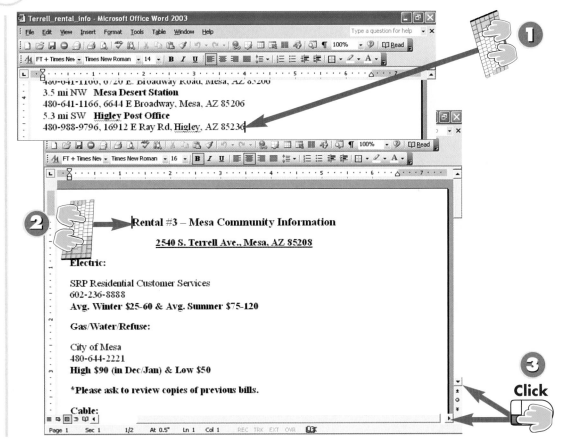

Click

End

① Press the **arrow** keys on your keyboard to get the feel of how the cursor moves. Also press the **Page Up** and **Page Down** keys.

② Press the **Ctrl+Home** keys to move the cursor to the beginning of the document.

③ Click the scrollbar arrows to move the document view up or down or to the left or right.

INTRODUCTION
Sometimes you'll want to move through your document, placing the cursor in different locations to add text. You can click the scrollbars to change which part of the document is shown, or you can press the arrow keys on the keyboard to move the cursor through the document.

TIP
Roller Button Mouse
If you have a roller button on your mouse, you can use it to scroll up and down through the document.

TIP
Switching Between Multiple Documents
You can use the Window menu to switch between multiple documents you have open. Select the document name from the Window menu, and that document becomes the active document window.

Selecting Text

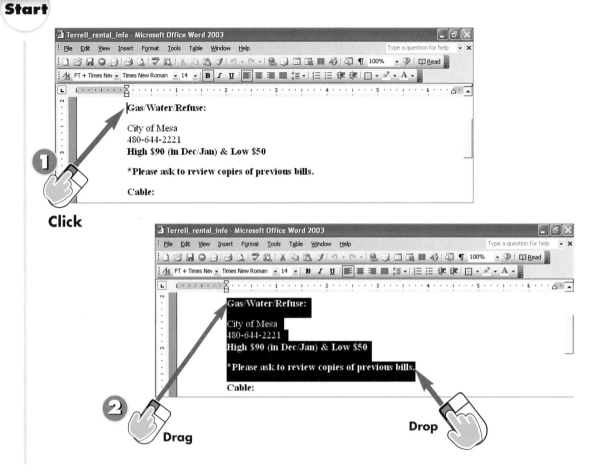

Start

Click

Drag

Drop

1 Click at the end or beginning of the text you want to select.

2 Press and hold down the left mouse button while you drag the pointer over the text you want to select. When all the desired text is selected, release the mouse button.

End

TIP

Selecting All
A fast way to select an entire document is to triple-click in the left margin. You can also press Ctrl+A to select the entire document.

TIP

Selecting with Shift
Another way to select specific text is to click once at the beginning of the text selection, press the Shift key, and click at the end of the desired selection.

Moving Text

Start

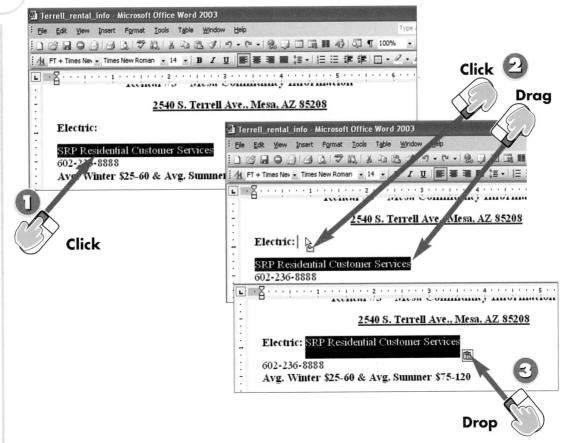

Click ②

Drag

Click

Drop

① Select the text you want to move.

② Press and hold down the left mouse button over the selected text; then drag the pointer to the new location.

③ Release the mouse button to drop the text in the new location.

End

INTRODUCTION

You can reorganize text in a Word document by moving items as you work. The method shown here is faster than cutting and pasting text. For example, if you are working on a report, you can use this technique to quickly play around with the order in which you present information.

Undoing Actions

TIP

If you accidentally release the mouse button before you place the insertion point at your desired location, click the **Undo** button to remove the inserted text. Then try the move operation again.

Moving Objects

TIP

You can move objects the same way you move text. For more information about inserting and moving objects, see Part 3.

Saving a Document

Start

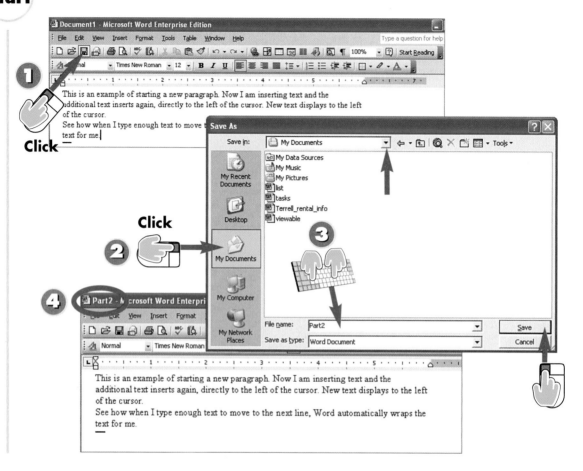

Click

Click

1
2
3
4

1 Click the **Save** button on the Standard toolbar; the Save As dialog box opens with a default name for the file.

2 Click the **My Documents** icon on the Places bar, or use the **Save in** drop-down list to move through the folder structure to save the file where you want.

3 Type a name for the document in the **File Name** field (initially, the filename defaults to the first line of text in the document) and click the **Save** button.

4 The document is saved; the filename you assigned now appears in the title bar.

End

INTRODUCTION

Until you save the document you are working on, it is not stored on disk. For this reason, it's a good practice to save your documents frequently as you work on them. After you save a document, you can retrieve it later to work on it again. You can save a document as many times as you like, even under another name.

TIP

Saving As a New Name
If, after you've saved a file, you need to save the document with a different name, open the **File** menu, and select **Save As** to open the Save As dialog box. Type a new filename in the **File Name** field and click **Save**. You now have two documents.

TIP

Converting File Formats
If you need to share a document with someone who uses a different word processor (or an older version of Word), click the **Save As Type** drop-down list box and select the alternative file type to convert your document.

Closing a Document

Start

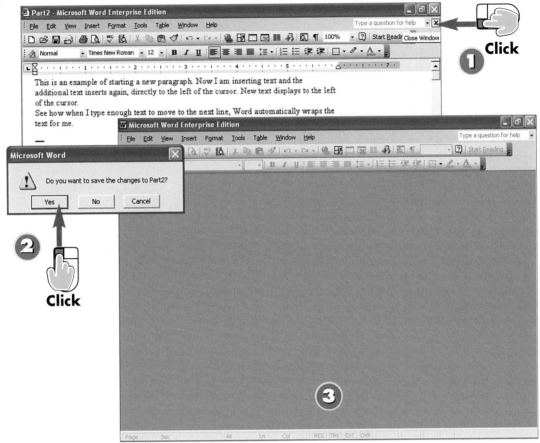

Click

Click

---

1 Click the **Close** (×) button in the document window. If you have edited the document since saving it last, Word asks whether you want to save it.

2 Click the **Yes** button to save your changes.

3 Word closes the document.

End

INTRODUCTION

When you finish working on a document, you can close it and continue to work on other documents. You can close a file with or without saving changes. If you have been working in a document and you try to close it, Word asks you whether you want to save the document before it closes.

TIP

Grayed-out Buttons
When Word has no documents open, only a few buttons are available on the Standard toolbar. The other buttons are *grayed out*, meaning their features are not currently available.

TIP

No Save
Click **Cancel** to continue working in the document. Otherwise, click **No** if you want to close your document but don't want to save your changes; in this case the document reverts to the previously saved version.

Creating a New Document

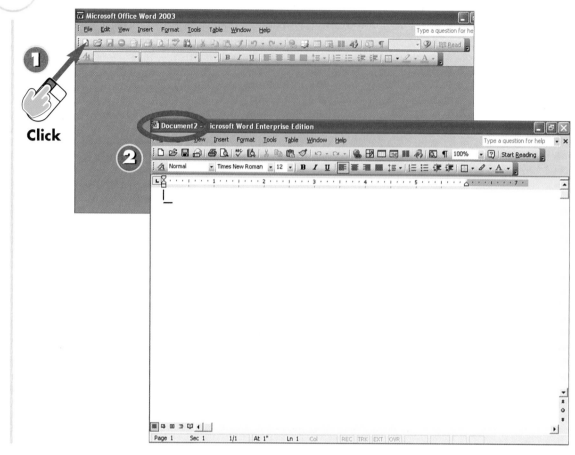

1️⃣ Click the **New Blank Document** button on the Standard toolbar.

2️⃣ Word opens a new document.

Word presents a new, blank document each time you start the application. You can create another new document at any time. For example, after you save and close one document, you might want to begin a new one.

Default Document Names
The default filename for each new document increases sequentially (**Document1**, **Document2**, **Document3**, and so on). After you exit and restart Word, the numbers begin at 1 again.

Sample Documents
For more options, open the **File** menu and select **New**. Then, peruse the options in the New Document task pane. Click the link of the type of new document or template you want to create.

Opening a Document

Start

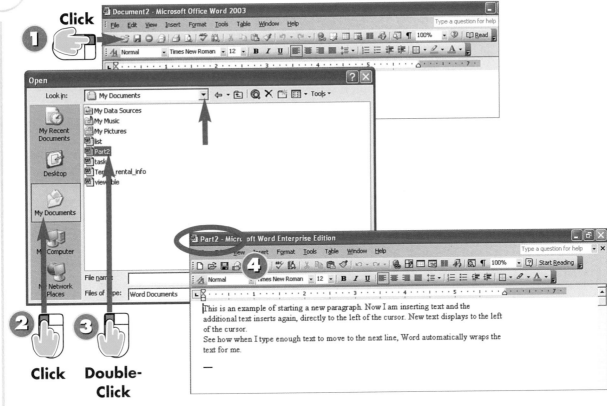

Click
①

② **Click** **③** **Double-Click**

① Click the **Open** button on the Standard toolbar. The Open dialog box appears.

② Click the **My Documents** icon on the Places bar, or use the **Look in** drop-down list to move through the folders to find the file you want.

③ Double-click the file you want to open.

④ Word opens the document.

End

INTRODUCTION

Each time you want to work with a document, you need to open it first by using the Open dialog box. The Open dialog box includes a Places bar with icons that immediately take you to recently saved history files, personal files, files on your desktop, files in your Favorites folder, and Web folders.

Dialog Box Views

You can change the information listed about a document in the Open dialog box by clicking the **Views** button on the dialog box's toolbar and selecting Thumbnails, Tiles, Icons, List, Details, Properties, Preview, or WebViews.

Alternative Look-in Locations

To move up a folder level, click the **Up One Level** button on the Open dialog box's toolbar. If necessary, click the **Look in** drop-down arrow and select the desired folder from the list.

Changing the Document View

Start

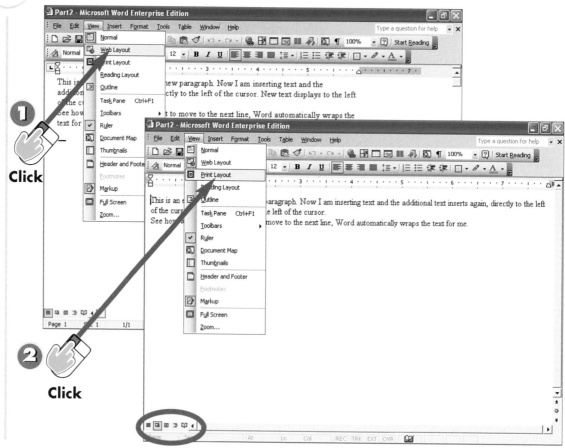

Click

Click

① Open the **View** menu and select **Web Layout** to switch from the current view (in this case, Normal, the default) to Web Layout view.

② The document displays in Web Layout view. Open the **View** menu and select **Print Layout** to see how objects will appear on a printed page. Notice the different view buttons.

INTRODUCTION

Word provides many ways to view documents, and each view has its purpose. The two most common views are Normal and Print Layout, but Reading Layout view is nice because it increases the size of the text so you can read it more easily onscreen. Normal view (Word's default view) shows text formatting in a simplified layout of the page so you can type and edit quickly.

Alternative View Buttons

TIP Instead of using the View menu, you can also select the various views from the view buttons to the left of the horizontal scrollbar.

32

PART 2

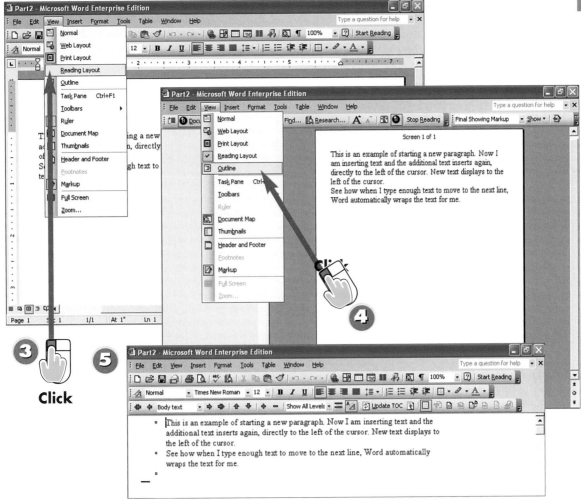

Click

③ The document is displayed in Print Layout view. Open the **View** menu and select **Reading Layout** to switch to the Reading Layout view.

④ The document is displayed in Reading Layout view. Open the **View** menu and select **Outline** to switch to Outline view.

⑤ The document is displayed in Outline view. Use the Outlining toolbar to manipulate the text levels.

End

Print Layout View

If you are in Print Layout view, you can double-click the cursor at any point in the new document and Word will insert carriage returns and a tab before the new location. Begin adding text on the page wherever you like.

Using the Window Menu

The Window menu options let you switch between document windows. Select **Arrange All** to resize all open documents onscreen, and select **Compare Side by Side** to compare two documents at a time (you will be asked which documents to compare if you have more than two open). Select **Split** to place a split in the document so you can, for example, scroll down to information on page 45 and compare it with information on page 2.

Previewing a Document

Start

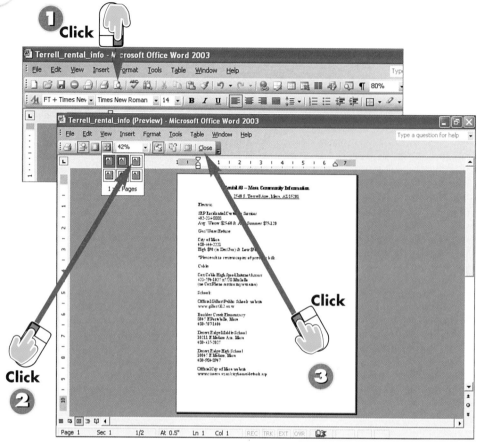

① Click the **Print Preview** button on the Standard toolbar to display the document in Print Preview mode.

② Click the **Multiple Pages** button on the Print Preview toolbar to select the number of pages you want to view at a time.

③ Click the **Close** button on the Print Preview toolbar to return to the document's Normal view.

End

INTRODUCTION

Print Preview enables you to see document pages onscreen as they will appear printed on paper, displaying page numbers, headers, footers, fonts, font sizes and styles, orientation, and margins. Previewing your document is a great way to catch formatting errors such as incorrect margins. You also save paper and time by previewing your documents before you print. You can even zoom in on a document with the mouse pointer. When it becomes a magnifying glass with a minus sign (–), click in the document to zoom in; when it becomes a plus sign (+), it zooms out. Press the **Page Up** and **Page Down** keys on your keyboard, or click the up and down scrollbar arrows to navigate through your document.

TIP

Editing in Print Preview
You don't need to go back to Normal or Print Layout view to fix typos. Click the **Magnifier** button on the Print Preview toolbar to stop magnifying the document; then click in the previewed document and make your edits.

Printing a Document

Start

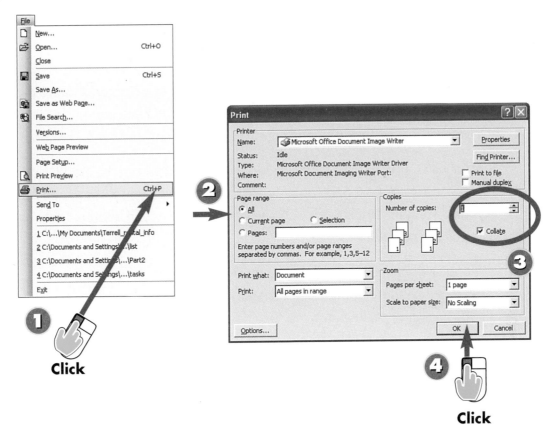

Click

Click

End

1. Open the **File** menu and select **Print** to open the Print dialog box.

2. Type or select printing **Page Range** options: **All** pages is the default option; the other options are described in the tip on this page titled "Print Range Options."

3. Select from the **Number of Copies** list and whether you want the copies to **Collate** (which means to print in the current page order).

4. Click the **OK** button, and the document pages print. You can tell Word is printing the document because of the Printing Job indicator on the status bar.

INTRODUCTION

Word makes printing a document easy and enables you to select the printer and font settings. You can print the whole document, a single page, specific page ranges, specific separate pages, or selected text. You can also specify the number of copies to print and collate the copies as you print.

TIP

Print Range Options
Type specific pages in the **Pages** box (for example, 1-3, 5), or select **Current Page** (the page with the cursor). To print only a certain portion of a document, first select the text; then select **File**, **Print**; and select the **Selection** option.

HINT

Canceling a Print Job
If you need to cancel a print job you sent to the printer, double-click the **Printing Job** indicator on the status bar to open the Printer job window. Right-click the document name, and select **Cancel** from the shortcut menu.

Editing Documents

There are many ways you can edit your documents, and Word makes it as easy as possible. You can cut, copy, or paste text or objects, or you can simply overwrite them. And if you make a mistake, Word lets you undo your changes; that way, if you change your mind again, you can redo the changes.

Another commonly used editing feature is Word's Search and Replace, which you can use to find and replace text. This enables you to make changes in your document quickly, instead of one at a time while searching through the document yourself.

Along with checking the spelling and grammar in your documents, you can use Word's thesaurus to find just the right word to convey your meaning or to avoid using a particular word too many times in the same sentence.

Last, but not least, you can add passwords to share your documents with others as well as compare documents and use revision marks to keep track of edits and changes that everyone makes. Then, of course, you get to review any changes and determine which ones you want to keep and which ones you want to delete.

Making Document Changes

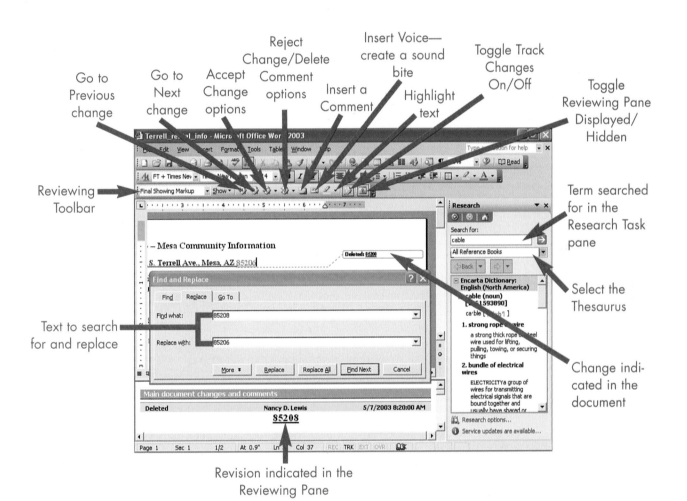

Go to Previous change

Go to Next change

Accept Change options

Reject Change/Delete Comment options

Insert a Comment

Insert Voice—create a sound bite

Highlight text

Toggle Track Changes On/Off

Toggle Reviewing Pane Displayed/Hidden

Reviewing Toolbar

Term searched for in the Research Task pane

Text to search for and replace

Select the Thesaurus

Change indicated in the document

Revision indicated in the Reviewing Pane

Cutting, Copying, and Pasting Text

Start

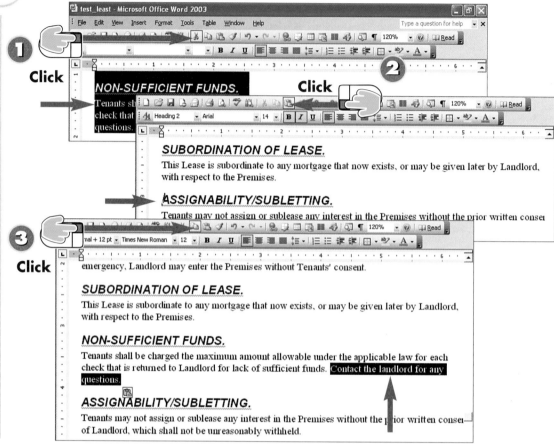

Click

Click

Click

1 Select the text you want to cut, and click the **Cut** button.

2 Click in the document where you want to paste the cut text, and click the **Paste** button.

3 The cut text appears in the new location. Select the text you want to copy and click the **Copy** button.

You can save the time and trouble of retyping duplicate information in a document by cutting or copying text and pasting it. In addition to the cut, copy, and paste commands, use the Office Clipboard task pane to work with multiple items known as *scraps*. For example, if you need to copy two different selections of text from the beginning of a document to two different locations toward the end of a document, you can use the Clipboard to perform the procedure in fewer steps than if you were to copy and paste each separately.

Cutting Versus Copying

When you want to move (rather than copy) text from its current location and place it in a new location, click the **Cut** button on the Standard toolbar instead of the Copy button. The Cut option removes the selection from the old location.

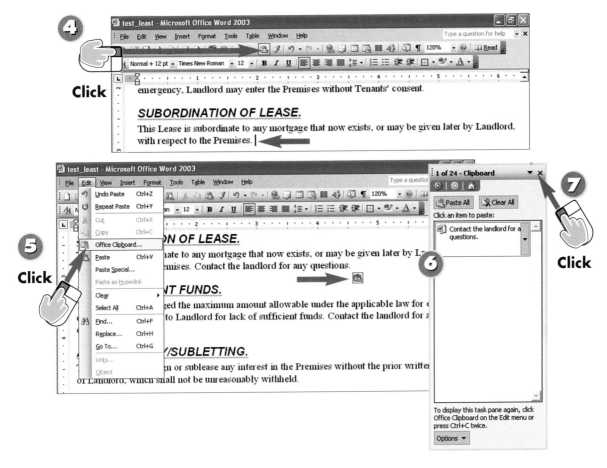

4 Click in the document where you want to paste the copied text, and click the **Paste** button.

5 The copied text is pasted in the new location. Unless it's already displayed, open the **Edit** menu and choose **Office Clipboard**.

6 Notice the copied data is displayed on the Clipboard. Additional cut or copied items will display on the clipboard; click each "scrap" to paste them.

7 Click the **Close (x)** button on the Clipboard Task pane when finished.

End

Performing a Single Cut/Copy/Paste Operation
You can use the Copy or Cut and Paste buttons on the Standard toolbar when you want to perform a single cut/paste or copy/paste. The Clipboard task pane appears only when you click the Copy or Cut button multiple times before clicking the Paste button.

Using the Clipboard
To clear all the items copied to the Clipboard, click the **Clear All** button; to paste all the items saved to the Clipboard in one location, click the **Paste All** button. If you no longer want to use the Clipboard task pane, click the **Close** (x) button.

Overwriting and Deleting Text

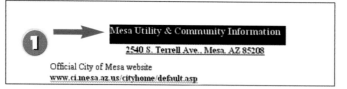

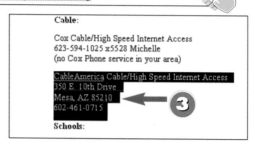

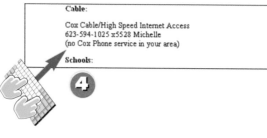

1. Select the text you want to overwrite.

2. Type the text that you want to replace the selected text.

3. Select the text you want to delete.

4. Press the **Delete** key on your keyboard to remove the text.

End

Sometimes you will need to alter or delete text in a document. You can do this in many ways in Word. A couple of the easiest ways are to overwrite text and to delete it with the Delete command. *Overwriting* replaces the existing text with new text as you type; *deleting* completely removes the text from the document.

Backspace and Delete

If you make a mistake when typing text, either press the **Backspace** key to delete characters to the left of the insertion point or press the **Delete** key to delete characters to the right of the insertion point.

Undoing and Redoing Changes

Start

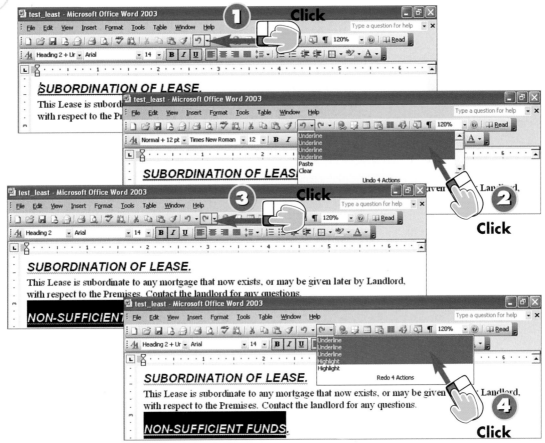

1. To undo your most recent action, click the **Undo** button on the Standard toolbar. Continue clicking the **Undo** button to undo more of your recent actions.

2. To undo multiple actions, click the down arrow next to the **Undo** button and select the number of actions to undo.

3. If you undo an action in error, click the **Redo** button on the Standard toolbar to redo the action. Continue clicking the **Redo** button to redo more actions.

4. To redo multiple actions, click the down arrow next to the **Redo** button and select the number of actions to redo.

End

INTRODUCTION

Suppose you've made a change to your document but decide you don't want the change after all. Instead of starting over, you can undo and redo your changes. The Undo and Redo options are convenient when you want to see how your document looks with and without a change.

Keyboard Undo

A quick and easy way to undo an action is to use the **Ctrl+Z** shortcut key; you can redo an action using **Ctrl+Y**.

No More Undo

When you close a document, its Undo/Redo "memory" is cleared, so be sure you are happy with any changes before you save and close your document.

Checking the Word Count

Start

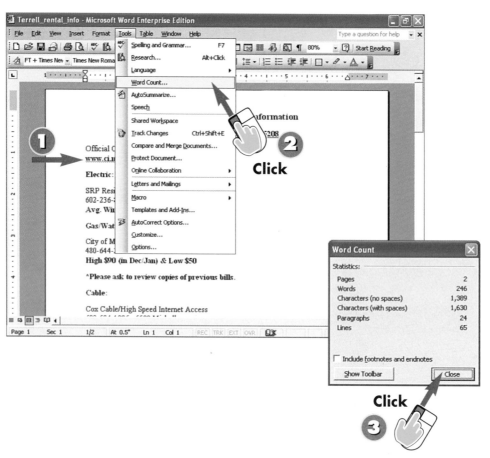

Click

Click

3

1. Select the text in which you want to count the words or characters. If you don't select anything, it defaults to tallying the entire document.

2. Open the **Tools** menu and select **Word Count**. The Word Count dialog box opens, displaying the number of pages, words, characters, paragraphs, and lines.

3. Click the Word Count dialog box's **Close** button to return to your document.

End

INTRODUCTION

Sometimes you might be asked to create documents with particular length specifications. For example, your boss might ask you for a 200-word project summary, or the newspaper in which you want to run an ad for your garage sale might limit the ad to three lines with 30 characters per line—including spaces. Instead of counting each character, space, word, line, paragraph, or page, let Word do the work for you. In addition, to track the word count as you work, click the **Show Toolbar** button in the Word Count dialog box. If you add or remove any text, click the **Recount** button on the Word Count toolbar.

Space Characters
The words count calculates only the number of words in the selected text, whereas the characters count tallies up each letter, numeral, space (if desired), and punctuation mark.

Finding Text

Start

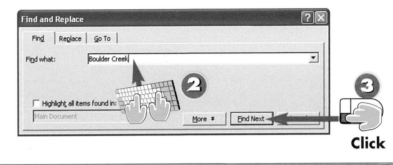

2

3

Click

1

Click

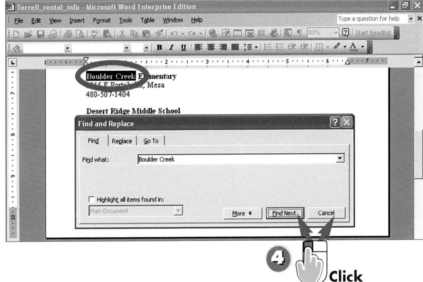

4

Click

1 Open the **Edit** menu and select **Find** to open the Find and Replace dialog box with the Find tab displayed.

2 Type the text you want to locate in the **Find What** text box.

3 Click the **Find Next** button. If Word finds a match, the match is highlighted.

4 Continue clicking **Find Next** to look for more matches (if there are none, Word will let you know), or click **Cancel** to cancel the search.

End

INTRODUCTION

You can use Word's Find feature to locate text, characters, paragraph formatting, or even special characters. For example, if you want to determine where your document refers to a specific name or date, you can search for that text and Word will take you to the location in the document.

Narrowing Your Search

Click the **More** button on the Find and Replace dialog box to display additional search options you can use to narrow the scope of your search. For example, if the word you're looking for is in all caps, type the word in all caps in the **Find What** text box and select the **Match Case** check box in the Search Options area. If Word cannot find the text you are searching for, a message appears telling you the search item was not found. Click **OK** to resume working on the document.

Replacing Text

Start

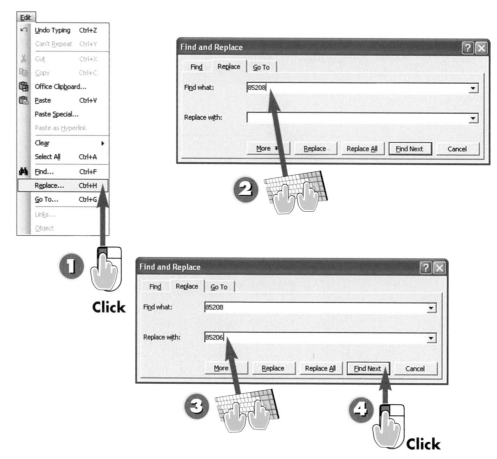

Click

Click

1 Open the **Edit** menu and select **Replace** to open the Find and Replace dialog box with the Replace tab displayed.

2 Type the text you want to locate in the **Find What** text box. (The Find What text box might contain text from a previous search, which you'll need to type over.)

3 Click in the **Replace with** text box (or press the **Tab** key), and type the text that you want to replace the Find What text with.

4 Click the **Find Next** button.

You use Word's Replace command to have Word search for and replace all occurrences of a particular bit of text, character or paragraph formatting, or special character. For example, if you entered a number incorrectly throughout a document, you can search for the number and replace it with the correct number. You can begin a find-and-replace operation from any location in a document, not just from the beginning.

Special Characters

If you need to search for special characters in your document, click the **More** button to view additional search options and then click the **Special** button. You can select the special character (for example, a Tab character) from the pop-up list.

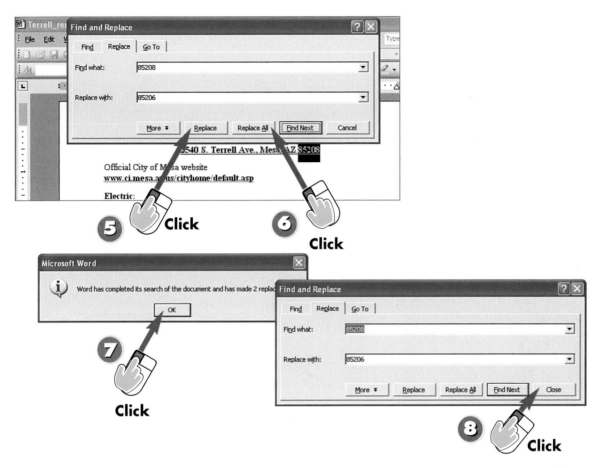

5 Click

6 Click

7 Click

8 Click

5 Word highlights the first occurrence of the Find What text. To replace it, click the **Replace** button; to skip it without making the change, click **Find Next**.

6 To replace all instances of the Find What text in one fell swoop, click the **Replace All** button.

7 Click the **OK** button when Word tells you how many replacements were made.

8 Click the **Close** button to close the Find and Replace dialog box.

End

Using the Find and Replace Dialog Box
You can search and replace through a document one occurrence at a time by clicking the Replace button. If you don't want to replace a specific occurrence, click the **Find Next** button to move on.

Using More
You can click the More button in the Find and Replace dialog box to narrow the scope of your search options. For example, if you need to replace all references to *and* with the ampersand (&), select the **Find Whole Words Only** search option. This way, the search skips over any references that contain *and* in any form—such as *candy* or *android*—and finds only the whole word *and*.

Inserting a Picture from a File

Start

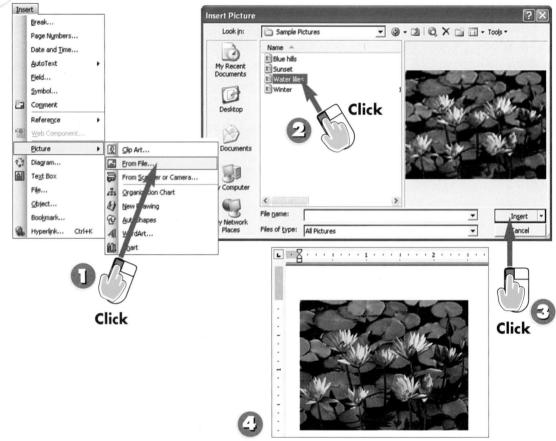

Click

Click

Click

End

① Open the **Insert** menu and select **Picture, From File** to open the Insert Picture dialog box.

② Locate the file you want to use, and click it to see a preview (you might need to select **Preview** from the dialog box **Views** button).

③ Click **Insert**.

④ The image is inserted into your worksheet.

As using digital images becomes more popular, there will almost certainly be times when you'll want to insert in your document a picture file you have saved on your computer. You can easily insert all types of graphics files: Windows Metafiles, JPEG files, PNGs, Macintosh PICT files, Kodak Photo CD, and many more.

Picture Filenames

TIP

If you don't see the picture filenames as thumbnail images, click the down arrow next to the **Views** button in the dialog box's toolbar and select **Thumbnail** or **Preview**.

Using the Picture Toolbar

TIP

When you insert a picture, the Picture toolbar appears. It contains tools you can use to crop the picture, add a border to it, or adjust its brightness and contrast. See the next task for details about resizing and moving graphic objects such as pictures.

Resizing and Moving Objects

Start

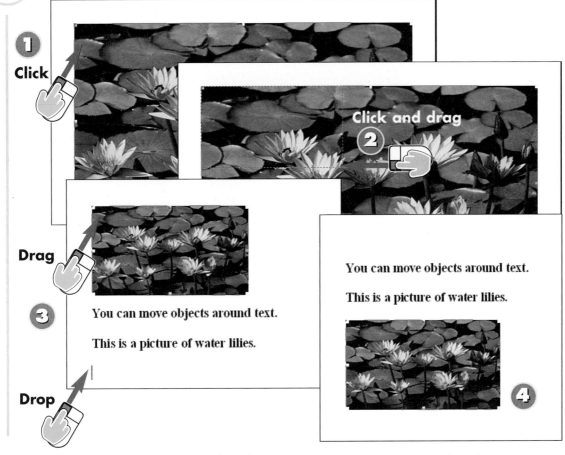

1 Click

Click and drag **2**

Drag **3**

You can move objects around text.

This is a picture of water lilies.

You can move objects around text.

This is a picture of water lilies.

4

Drop

---

1 To resize an object, first click the object you want to resize. Sizing handles appear around the edges of the object.

2 Click and drag one of the handles inward to make the object smaller or outward to make it bigger; then release the mouse button.

3 To move an object, click the object and drag it to the spot where you want it to appear. Release the mouse button to drop the object in its new location.

4 The object is moved.

End

INTRODUCTION

You can easily move or resize objects—such as pictures, clip art, charts, tables, text, and more—in your document, or you can move them to another location altogether. In addition to resizing and moving objects, you can cut, copy, and paste them.

TIP

Keeping the Same Proportions
Use the corner sizing handles to resize an object to increase or decrease the object's horizontal and vertical measurements proportionately. If you use the side border handles, you increase the horizontal and vertical size separately, possibly making the object look out of proportion.

Using AutoCorrect Options

Start

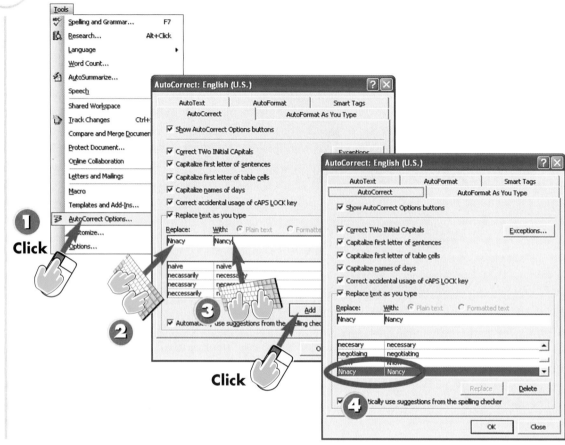

Click

Click

---

1 Open the **Tools** menu and select **AutoCorrect Options** to open the AutoCorrect dialog box with the AutoCorrect tab selected.

2 Review the correction options. To add a word to the list of words that are corrected automatically, click in the **Replace** box and type the misspelled version of the word.

3 Click in the **With** box and type the word you want AutoCorrect to insert as the replacement text. Then, click the **Add** button.

4 The word is added to the list of words that AutoCorrect corrects automatically.

The AutoCorrect options in Word, including AutoCorrect and AutoText (discussed here), are quite clever and can save you a lot of time. AutoCorrect makes corrections to your text as you type. For example, if you forget to capitalize the first word in a sentence, Word's AutoCorrect feature will do it for you automatically. AutoText, on the other hand, automatically enters designated text as you type in your document. For example, if you are working on a document in which you must type the same name repeatedly (for example, **Nancy D. Lewis**), you can instruct Word to automatically complete the name as soon as you enter the first few characters (that is, you type **Na** and press **Enter** and the entire name appears).

TIP

Altering the Defaults
If errors are on the AutoCorrect tab that you don't want to automatically fix, uncheck the appropriate box. If any words are on the AutoText tab that you don't want to automatically complete as you type, select the entry and click **Delete**.

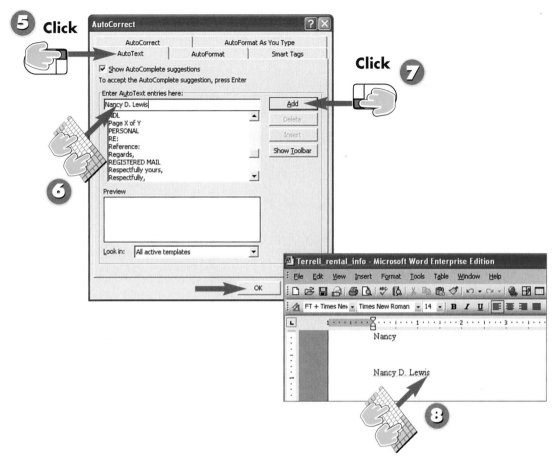

5 Click the **AutoText** tab and scroll through the list of AutoComplete entries.

6 Type the text of a word or phrase you want AutoText to automatically complete in the **Enter AutoText Entries Here** box.

7 Click the **Add** button to add the new text as part of the default AutoText settings; click the **OK** button when you are finished making changes to the AutoCorrect dialog box.

8 Type the AutoCorrect text and press the **spacebar**; the error is corrected. Then, type the beginning of the AutoText phrase. When the ScreenTip appears, press **Enter**.

End

Checking Spelling and Grammar

Start

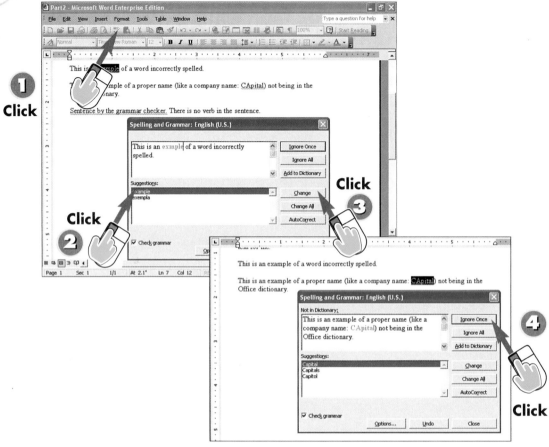

Click ①

Click ②

Click ③

Click ④

① Click the **Spelling and Grammar** button on the Standard toolbar to open the Spelling and Grammar dialog box.

② The first spelling or grammatical error in your document appears, as well as suggestions for fixing the problem. If an option in the **Suggestions** list is correct, click it.

③ Click the **Change** button to change this instance, or click **Change All** to change it throughout the document. Word makes the change and moves to the next error.

④ If word is incorrectly flagged, click **Ignore Once** to ignore this instance or **Ignore All** to ignore it throughout the document. Word moves to the next error.

Word shows red wavy lines under any words it thinks are misspelled and shows green wavy lines under any sentences it finds grammatically problematic. This enables you to immediately see whether a word you typed is misspelled or a sentence is not grammatically correct.

Not in Dictionary
Sometimes, the correct spelling for a misspelled word is not listed among the options in the Suggestions list. If so, select the word in the **Not in Dictionary** text box, type the correct spelling over it, and click the **Change** or **Change All** button.

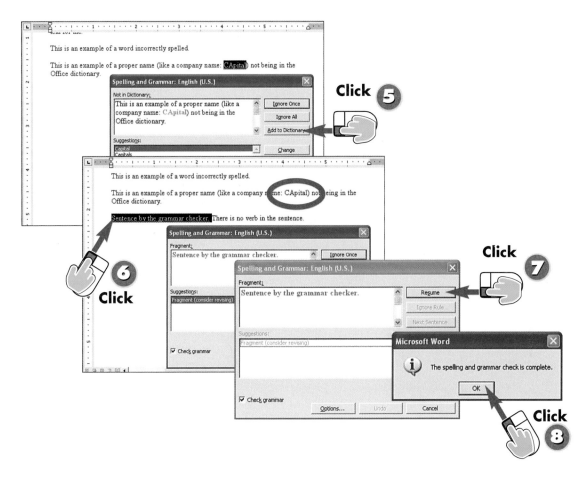

5 If Word incorrectly flags a word you use frequently, click the **Add to Dictionary** button to add the word to the dictionary Word uses to check your spelling.

6 If Word flags a grammatical problem but no usable suggestions appear in the Suggestions list, click and type the change in the document to correct the problem.

7 Click the **Resume** button in the Spelling and Grammar dialog box to continue checking the document.

8 After Word has reviewed all the inaccuracies in your document, it displays a message telling you the spelling and grammar check is complete. Click **OK**.

End

From the Beginning
You don't have to be at the beginning of a document when checking spelling and grammar. If you start in the middle of a document, Word checks until it reaches the end and then asks you whether you want to continue checking at the beginning.

Checker Errors
Keep in mind that Word's spelling and grammar check isn't perfect. For example, it might think a slang word or sentence is an error. Fortunately, you can ignore Word's spelling and grammar suggestions. Furthermore, Word's spelling and grammar check doesn't catch everything, so you still need to proofread your documents.

Researching with the Thesaurus

Start

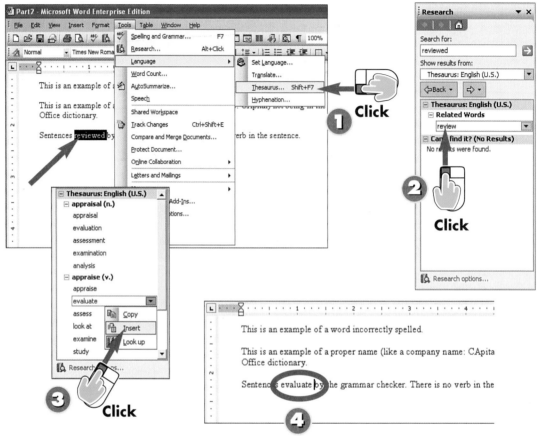

Click

Click

Click

End

1. Select the word you want to replace, and select **Tools, Language, Thesaurus** to open the Research task pane.

2. If your selection is not a root word, the task pane will require you to select a word from the **Related Words** list to focus the search (otherwise, go to step 3).

3. The Related Words list expands to show synonyms of the selected word. To replace the word, click the synonym and select **Insert** from the drop-down list.

4. The word is replaced with the synonym you chose.

Word's thesaurus is a convenient tool that helps you replace words with more suitable ones. For example, if you find yourself using a certain word too often, you can substitute another word so your text doesn't sound redundant. The thesaurus is not usually part of the default Office installation; the first time you try to run it, Word might ask whether you want to install the feature. If so, click **OK** and proceed through the installation steps.

Show Results from List
You can use the **Show Results from** drop-down list to review thesauruses from other languages or even find translations (in case the word is, for example, a French word).

Sharing Documents with Others

Start

Click

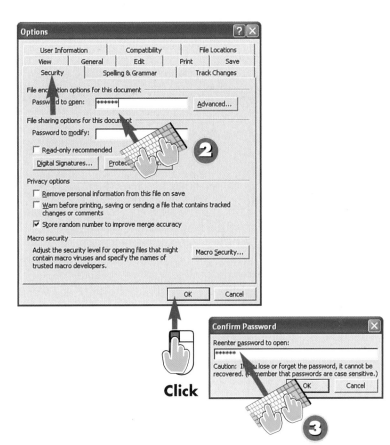

Click

End

1 Open the **Tools** menu and select **Options** to open the Options dialog box.

2 Click the **Security** tab and type a password in the **Password to Open** field (any time you try to open this document, you must enter the same password); then click **OK**.

3 Reenter the password in the Confirm Password dialog box and click **OK** to return to the document. When others attempt to open the file, a password will be required.

INTRODUCTION

Word allows you to share your files with others. When you share files with multiple users, however, you might want to protect your documents. You can do so either by restricting access to the document or by preventing changes being made within each particular document. The three file-sharing options are password to open (covered here), password to modify, and read-only recommended. The Track Changes feature is turned on automatically when you protect a document (see the task "Tracking Document Changes" later in this part for more information). Don't forget the password you assign to your documents. If you forget or misplace the password, you will not be able to access the document.

TIP

File-sharing Options
Password to Modify: You can read the document but must know the password to make any changes. Read-only Recommended: You can suggest the document be opened as read-only, but you can't require it.

Comparing Documents

Start

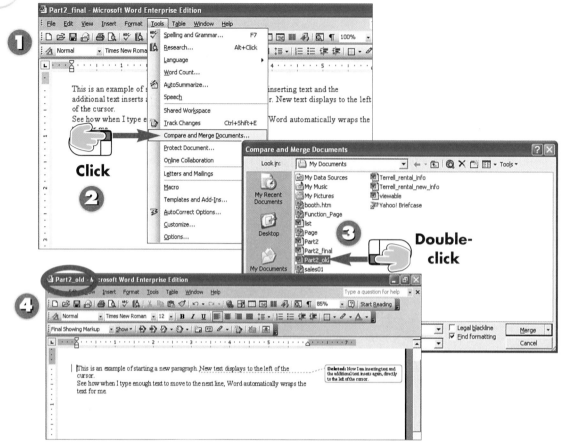

Click

Double-click

1. Open the most recent version of the document you want to compare.

2. Open the **Tools** menu and select **Compare and Merge Documents** to open the Compare and Merge Documents dialog box.

3. Locate and double-click an earlier version of the file you opened in step 1 to compare the two versions.

4. Review the differences that the compare reveals. The details are in the comment bubble.

End

When you make changes to your documents, you should keep copies of older versions of them in case you need to determine which changes have been made. A quick way to find the differences between older and newer versions of a document is to do a *document compare*. After you compare the documents, depending on the current document view (for example, Normal view), new text appears in one color with underline and old text appears in a different color with strikethrough (known as *revision marks*).

Accepting or Rejecting Changes

See the next two tasks to learn how to specify which tracked changes you want to keep and which you want to reject.

Tracking Document Changes

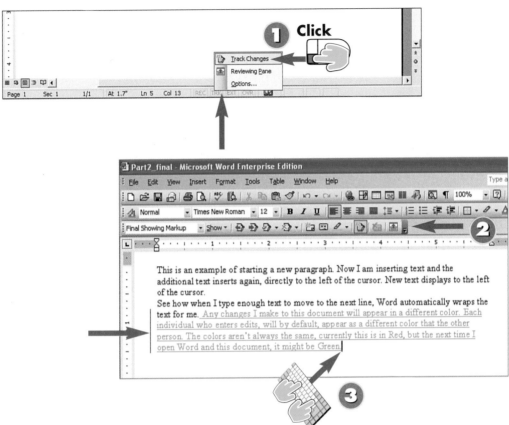

1 Right-click the grayed-out **TRK** text on the status bar and select **Track Changes** from the shortcut menu that appears. (Alternatively, double-click the **TRK** text.)

2 The Reviewing toolbar appears. Move the mouse pointer over the buttons on the toolbar to see which commands are available.

3 Type some new text in the document. The new text is underlined and is a different color. Changes are also flagged by a vertical line in the margin.

End

INTRODUCTION

Suppose you're editing another person's document or are working on a report in a team environment. If so, it's a great idea to track the changes to the document through the use of *revision marks*. That way, other people can easily see what changes have been made to the document, and by whom.

Disabling Document Tracking
You can quickly turn off Word's document-tracking feature by double-clicking **TRK** on the status bar.

Tracking Names
When you place the mouse pointer over a revision mark, the username of the person who made the edit is displayed in a ScreenTip.

Accepting or Rejecting Tracked Changes

Start

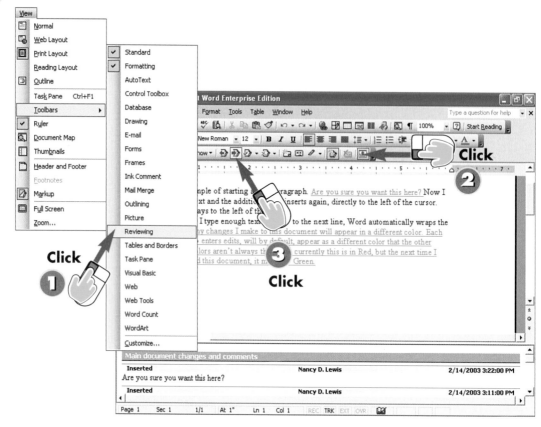

1 Open the **View** menu and select **Toolbars**, **Reviewing** to open the Reviewing toolbar in a document that contains revision marks.

2 Click the **Reviewing Pane** button on the Reviewing toolbar to see extra information about the various changes, edits, and comments in the edited document.

3 The Reviewing pane opens at the bottom of the screen. Click the **Next** button on the Reviewing toolbar to locate a change in the document.

When you are ready to finalize any tracked changes in a document, you need to determine which changes to accept and which to reject. If you accept a change, Word keeps the text change and removes the revision marks. If you reject a change, Word deletes the new text and restores the old.

The End of the Document

If you begin reviewing tracked changes at the end of a document, you might see a message box that asks if you want to continue searching for changes from the beginning of the document. Click the **OK** button if you do; click the **Cancel** button if you want to stop searching for changes. You can start reviewing revision marks at any point in your document.

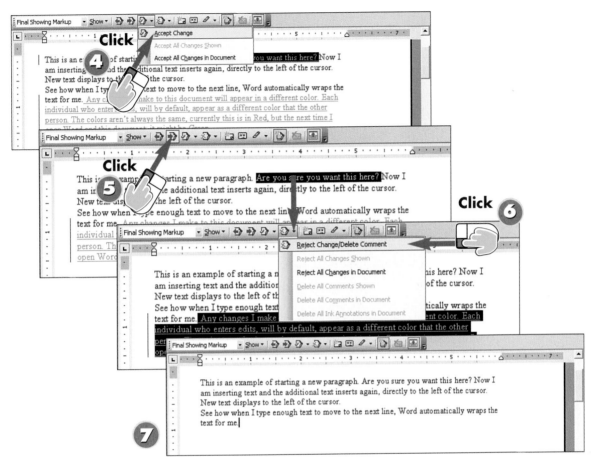

Click the **Accept Change** button on the Reviewing toolbar to accept the change. Alternatively, click the **down arrow** next to the button to see other options.

Click the **Next** button to move to the next tracked change.

Click the **Reject Change/Delete Comment** button to reject the tracked change. Alternatively, click the **down arrow** next to the button to see other options.

When finished, your document should have no more tracked change indicators and the Reviewing Pane (not visible in this figure) will display **(none)**.

End

Using the Reviewing Toolbar

If you want to accept or reject all changes at once, click the **Accept All Changes in Document** or **Reject All Changes in Document** option in the Accept or Reject drop-down list boxes on the Reviewing toolbar. If you don't want to accept or reject a change but want to leave the revision mark intact, click the **Next** button to move to the next revision mark.

Formatting Text

There are many types of ways you can format your documents in Microsoft Word. For example, you can change the font, font size, and font color; highlight the text; add a border; or perhaps even shade the background.

Then there are the old standbys for formatting your documents, such as adding bulleted lists, numbered lists, and tabs, and indenting text. This part even shows you how to make a short document look longer than it really is. How, you ask? By increasing the space between the lines and between the text characters and realigning the text. And what if you format a block of text exactly the way you want it, but now you want your entire document to look that way? Just copy the formatting. You don't even have to go through all the steps to format the text again!

Formatting Text Options

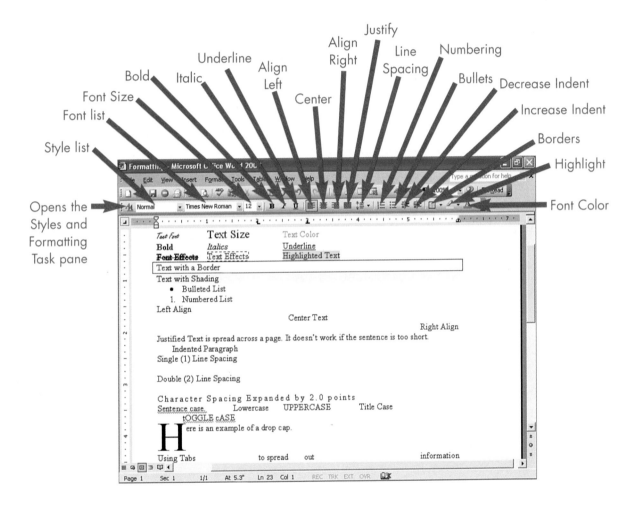

Changing Text Font, Size, and Color

Start

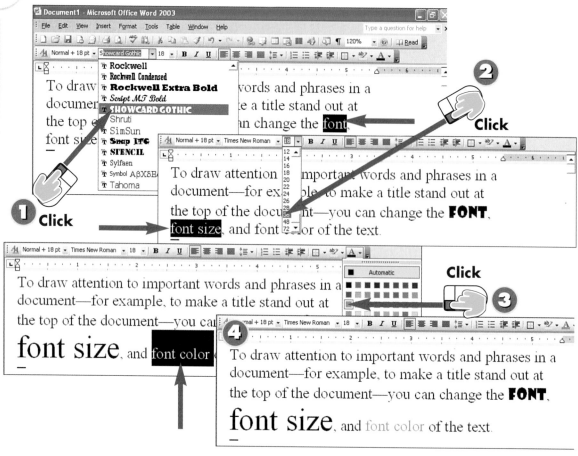

Click

Click

Click

1. Select the text in which you want to change the font, click the **Font** drop-down arrow, and select the font from the list.

2. Select the text in which you want to change the font size, click the **Font Size** drop-down arrow, and select the size from the list.

3. Select the text in which you want to change the font color, click the **Font Color** drop-down arrow, and select the color from the list.

4. The font, font size, and font color are applied to the selected text.

End

INTRODUCTION

To draw attention to important words and phrases in a document—for example, to make a title stand out at the top of the document—you can change the font, font size, and font color of the text. If you make a word large, it has a pretty good chance of being read. On the other hand, you might want to make text smaller so you can fit more information on a page. Colors can also emphasize items in documents. For example, if you are creating a report to show an expense, you might want key information to be in red. To change the font, font size, and color as you type, simply choose the appropriate option before you begin typing. Alternatively, you can format existing text, as outlined here.

TIP

Serif Versus Sans-Serif Fonts

The two categories of fonts are *serif* and *sans-serif*. Characters in serif fonts, such as Times New Roman and Courier, have little "tails," whereas characters in sans-serif fonts, such as Helvetica and Arial, do not.

Applying Bold, Italic, and Underline

Start

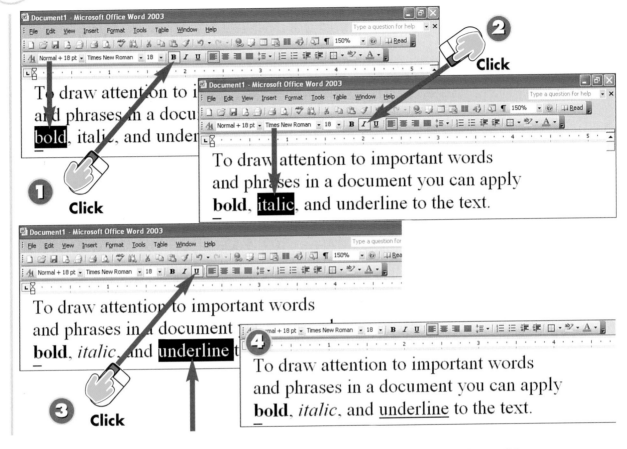

Click

Click

Click

1 Select the text in which you want to apply bold formatting, and click the **Bold** button.

2 Select the text in which you want to apply italic formatting, and click the **Italic** button.

3 Select the text in which you want to apply underline formatting, and click the **Underline** button.

4 The bold, italic, and underlining are applied to the selected text.

End

INTRODUCTION

To apply bold, italic, or underline to text as you type, simply click the appropriate button before you begin typing. Alternatively, you can format existing text as outlined here. You can also apply all the formatting options to the same text.

TIP

Removing Formatting

If you decide you don't want certain text to be bolded, italicized, or underlined, you can select the text and click the appropriate button on the Formatting toolbar again to remove the formatting. Alternatively, you can open the **Edit** menu and select **Clear**, **Formats**; however, this clears all formatting on the selected text, including font selections and the like.

Applying Font Effects

Start

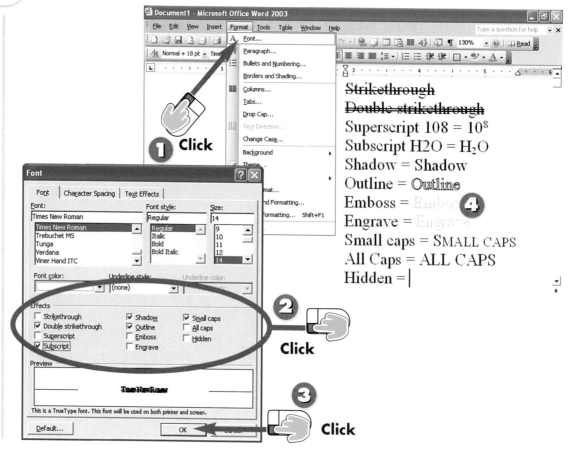

1 Click

2 Click

3 Click

4

Strikethrough
Double-strikethrough
Superscript 108 = 10^8
Subscript H2O = H_2O
Shadow = Shadow
Outline = Outline
Emboss = Emboss
Engrave = Engrave
Small caps = SMALL CAPS
All Caps = ALL CAPS
Hidden = |

1 Open the **Format** menu and select **Font** to open the Font dialog box. (Click the **Font** tab if it's not already displayed.)

2 Select from the **Effects** area options: Strikethrough, Double-strikethrough, Superscript, Subscript, Shadow, Outline, Emboss, Engrave, Small Caps, All Caps, and/or Hidden.

3 Click **OK**.

4 Begin typing. The font effects you chose in step 2 are applied to the text you type. (This figure shows the various font effect options available.)

End

Effects you apply to your font can draw attention to important information. For example, if you wanted to indicate deleted text (without using revision marks), you could apply a strikethrough or double-strikethrough to your text. If you needed to display a power of 10 to the eighth, you could apply a superscript effect to the 8 to present it as an exponent (10^8); likewise, to display the water molecule as text, you could apply a subscript effect to lower the 2 in H_2O. You can also apply any number of eye-catching effects. To apply font effects as you type, click the appropriate check box in the Font dialog box before you begin typing (as shown here). Alternatively, you can format existing text by selecting it and then choosing the desired options.

Effect Options

Consider using the Small Caps option to indicate time, as in 2PM. All Caps are good for EMPHASIS. Consider using Hidden when you don't want anyone to view what you have typed, so it is "for your eyes only."

Highlighting Text

Start

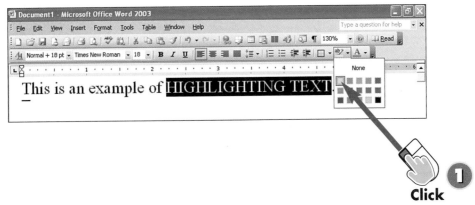

Click **1**

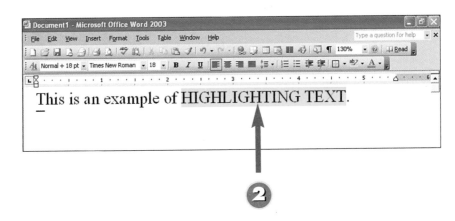

2

1 After you select the text you want to highlight, click the down arrow next to the **Highlight** button on the Formatting toolbar and select a color from the list that appears.

2 The selected text is highlighted.

End

INTRODUCTION

When you want to draw attention to important text, you can highlight it, just like you use a highlighter when reading books or articles to note the important parts. Highlighting is different from applying a text color, however, because highlighting alters the color of the text's *background*, not the text itself.

Typing Highlighted Text

Instead of highlighting text after it is typed, you can select a highlight color and then begin typing. Anything you type will be highlighted in the color you selected until you change it back to **None** (the default highlight color).

Highlighting Options

You can display or hide highlighting on the screen and in the printed document by opening the **Tools** menu and selecting **Options**. In the Options dialog box, select the **View** tab, and uncheck the **Highlight** check box.

PART 4

Adding a Border to Text

Start

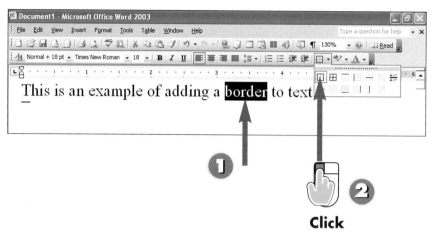

Click

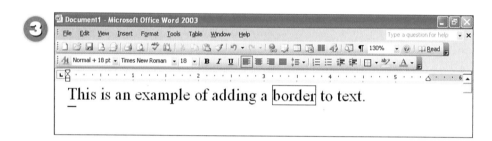

1 Select the text or click anywhere within a paragraph in your document around which you want to add a border.

2 Click the down arrow next to the **Border** button on the Formatting toolbar and select the type of border you want to apply from the list that appears.

3 The border is applied around the text.

End

You can add a border to any or all sides of a paragraph or selected text in Word. Borders can accentuate portions of your text, add a clean frame to your entire document, or even divide sections of a document.

More Border Options
For more border options, open the **Format** menu and select **Borders and Shading**; then review the options on the **Borders** tab of the dialog box that appears.

Page Border
You might add a border around the contents of an entire page; for example, to "frame" an awards certificate. Open the **Format** menu and select **Borders and Shading**; select the **Page Border** tab and choose some options.

Adding Shading to Text

Start

PART 4

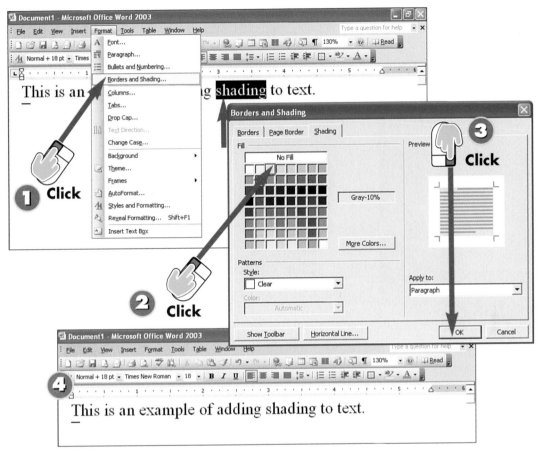

① **Click**

② **Click**

③ **Click**

④

1 Select the text to which you want to apply a shading effect, open the **Format** menu, and select **Borders** and **Shading**.

2 On the Borders and Shading dialog box that appears, click the **Shading** tab and review the available colors in the **Fill** area.

3 Click the fill color you want to apply to the background of the selected text—for example, **Gray-10%**—and click the **OK** button.

4 The shading is applied.

End

Shading your text is similar to highlighting it, in that the text you select ends up with the selected shading in the background. When you apply shading, however, you can choose from specific patterns and various shading coverage percentages (although this task focuses on the colors available in the Fill section of the Shading tab).

TIP

More Colors
Click the **More Colors** button on the Shading tab to choose from more color options on the Colors dialog box. There are also additional colors on the **Standard** tab, or you can create your own colors on the **Custom** tab.

Changing Text Alignment

Start

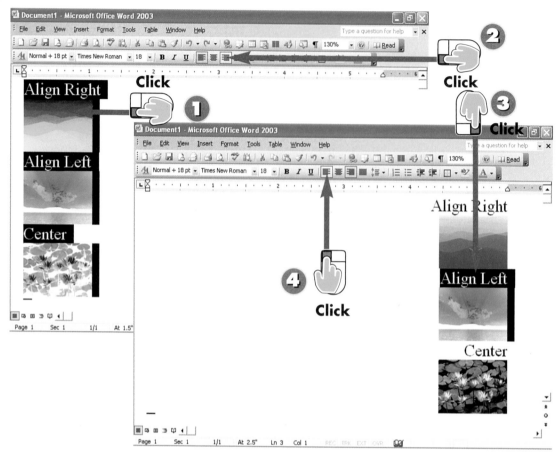

Click

1

Click

2

Click

3

Click

Align Right

Align Left

Center

Click

4

Click

Align Right

Align Left

Center

1 Select the text (and/or objects) to align to the right.

2 Click the **Align Right** button on the Formatting toolbar.

3 The selection is made flush with the page's right margin. Now select the text (and/or objects) to align to the left.

4 Click the **Align Left** button on the Formatting toolbar.

INTRODUCTION

When you enter text into a document, the text automatically aligns flush (even) with the left margin. However, you can change the *alignment* of text at any time, before or after you have entered the text. You can center text, make it flush with the right margin, or justify it (make it flush with both margins).

67

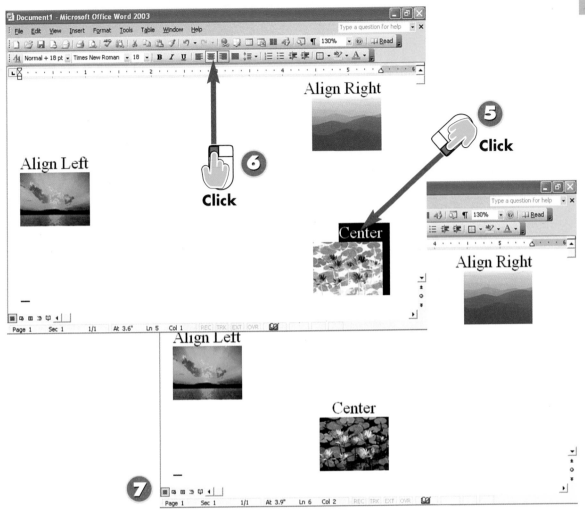

5 The selection is made flush with the page's left margin. Now select the text (and/or objects) to center.

6 Click the **Center** button on the Formatting toolbar.

7 The selection is centered between the page's margins.

End

Justifying Text
If you select text and click the Justify button on the Formatting toolbar, the text becomes flush left *and* flush right. The Justify option doesn't work on single words or sentences, only on text in a paragraph that wraps to another line.

Adding Numbers and Bullets

Start

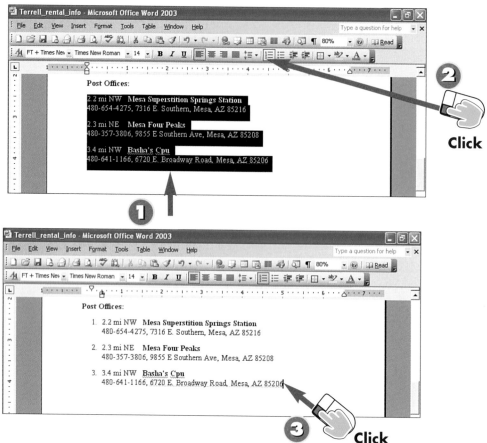

Click

Click

① Select the text you want to make into a numbered list.

② Click the **Numbering** button on the Formatting toolbar.

③ Move through the document and place the cursor at the end of the last numbered paragraph.

If you type a list of, say, three items, you can have Word add bullets or numbers to the items automatically. Numbered lists are useful for presenting a set of items or steps that must be in a particular order, whereas bulleted lists are useful for presenting a series of items when order doesn't matter.

TIP

Creating Multilevel Lists
You can automatically create multilevel bulleted and numbered lists. When typing text into a list, press the **Tab** key to automatically indent the list to a new level. A numbered list sequences like an outline (1, 2, a, b, i, ii, and so on); a bulleted list uses different kinds of bullet symbols at each level.

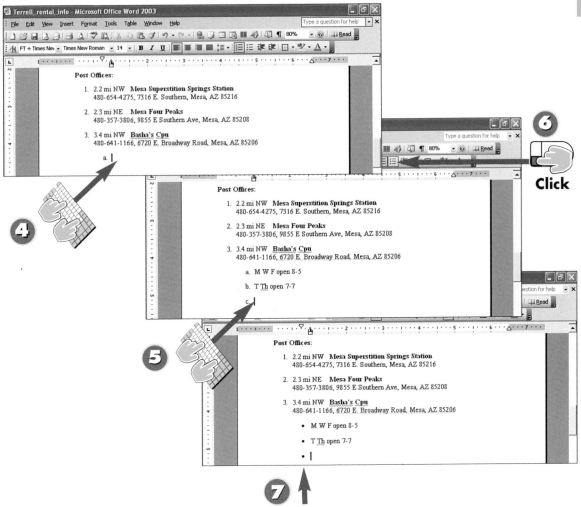

Click

④ Press the **Enter** key and then the **Tab** key. Word automatically numbers the new line, switching from numbers to letters, assuming you're moving down one outline level.

⑤ Type your text and press the **Enter** key at the end of each line to move to the next line.

⑥ Click the **Bullets** button on the Formatting toolbar to make the indented entries a bulleted list instead of a numbered list.

⑦ The entries are preceded by bullets.

End

TIP

Creating a New List
If you haven't yet created the list you want to make into a numbered or bulleted list, click the **Numbering** or **Bullets** button on the Formatting toolbar and then start typing the information. When you press Enter to start a new line, Word adds the number or bullet automatically. To stop adding bullets or numbers, press the **Enter** key more than once.

Indenting Paragraphs

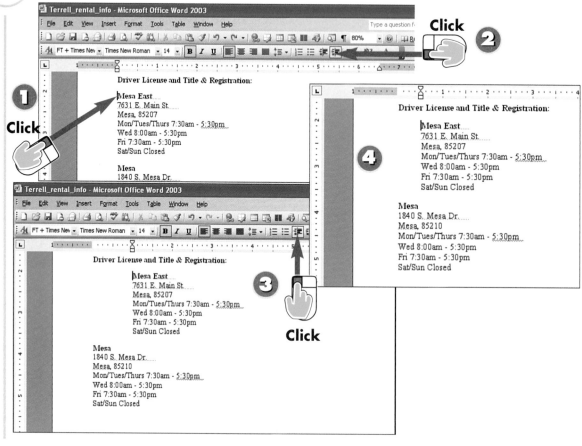

1 Click anywhere in the paragraph you want to indent.

2 Click the **Increase Indent** button on the Formatting toolbar twice. The paragraph is indented by two tab spaces.

3 Again, click anywhere in the paragraph you want to indent, and then click the **Decrease Indent** button once.

4 The indented paragraph moves to the left one tab space.

End

You can indent an entire paragraph to the right of the left margin (or left of the right margin) to make it stand out. For example, if you are creating a contract, you might want to indent certain paragraphs to make them subordinate to other text.

Adding Hanging Indents

When you're creating a resume, you might find it convenient to use *hanging indents*. With a hanging indent, all but the first line of a paragraph is moved to the right, giving a clean presentation of information with the emphasis on the first line. To create a hanging indent, click anywhere in the paragraph to which you want to apply the indent. Then open the **Format** menu and select **Paragraph**. In the Paragraph dialog box, click the **Indents and Spacing** tab and select **Hanging** from the **Special** drop-down list.

Changing Line Spacing

Start

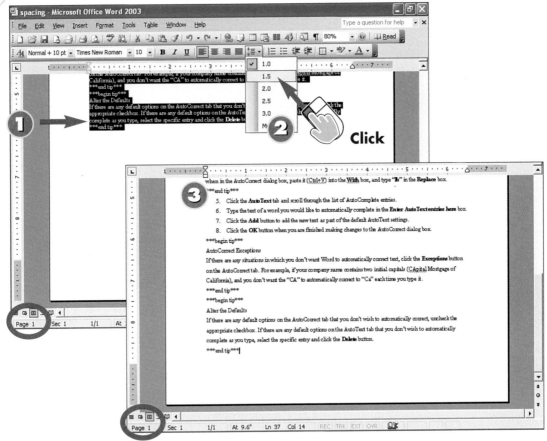

Click

---

1 Select the text whose line spacing you want to alter or press **Ctrl+A** to select the entire document. (Notice the text on this page fills only two thirds of the page.)

2 Click the down arrow next to the **Line Spacing** button on the Formatting toolbar and select a line-spacing option (in this case, 1.5). For more spacing options, select **More**.

3 The line spacing is altered such that the text in the document fills the entire page.

End

INTRODUCTION

Have you ever found yourself in a situation where you needed to fill up a page with text but just couldn't think of any more text to write? Line spacing can be a handy tool that can increase (or decrease, if needed) the amount of vertical space between lines of text—so you can stretch two-thirds of a page to fill one whole page.

TIP

Spacing Above and Below
Word uses single-line spacing by default. You can also alter the amount of space above or below a line of text. To do so, open the **Format** menu and select **Paragraph** to open the Paragraph dialog box (click the **Indents and Spacing** tab if you aren't already there). Click the spacing you desire in the **Line Spacing** drop-down list and alter the numbers in the **Before** and **After** spin boxes.

Changing Character Spacing

Start

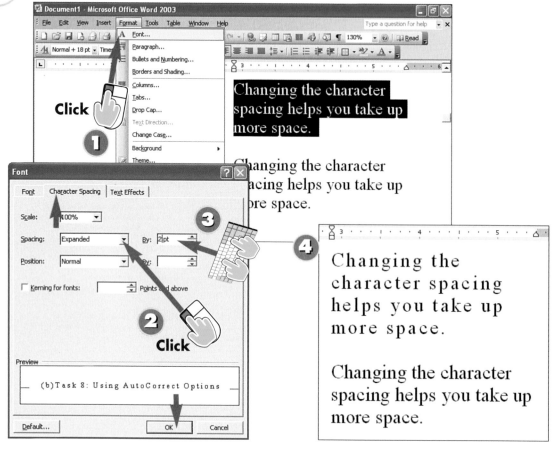

Click

1

Click

2

3

4

(b)Task 8: Using AutoCorrect Options

Changing the character spacing helps you take up more space.

① After you select the text for which you want to change the spacing between characters, open the **Format** menu and select **Font** to open the Font dialog box.

② In the **Character Spacing** tab, click the down arrow next to the **Spacing** field and select either **Expanded** (to fill the page) or **Condensed** (to shorten the page).

③ In the **By** spin box next to the **Spacing** field, type **2pt**. The Preview area shows how the character spacing will look; click **OK**.

④ The character-spacing setting is applied to the text on the page.

End

Changing Capitalization

Start

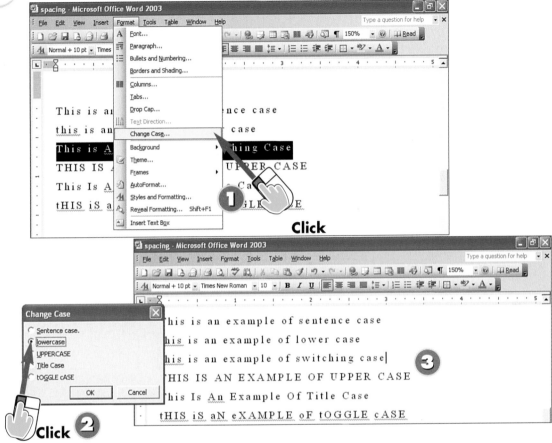

Click

Click ②

③

① After you select the text for which you want to change the capitalization, open the **Format** menu and select **Change Case** to open the Change Case dialog box.

② Select the desired case option (for example, lowercase) and click **OK**.

③ The selected text uses the case option you chose. (This figure shows an example of each case option.)

End

Have you ever received a document you needed to work on, and the person who created the document PUT EVERYTHING IN ALL CAPITALS or typed header text in sentence format (only capitalizing the first word)? Instead of retyping all the text again or initial capping all the words in a sentence, you can have Word automatically change it for you. The case change options are Sentence case, lower case, UPPER CASE, Title Case, or tOGGLE cASE.

Using UPPERCASE

Be careful when using the Uppercase option in text. It can mean different things to different people. Some interpret it as screaming in the text, while others can find it distracting.

Inserting a Drop Cap

Start

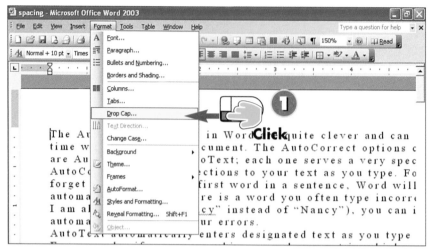

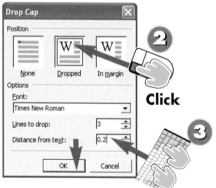
Click

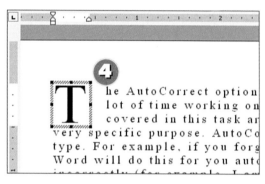

1. Place the cursor in the paragraph in which you want the initial character to have a drop cap, and then open the **Format** menu and select **Drop Cap**.

2. In the **Position** area of the Drop Cap dialog box, click **Dropped** or **In Margin** to specify where the drop cap should appear.

3. Select settings in the **Options** area—for example the **Font**, the number of **Lines to Drop** (defaults to 3 lines), and the **Distance from Text** (in inches). Then click **OK**.

4. The drop cap is applied to the paragraph. Click anywhere outside the drop cap to deselect it.

End

Setting Tab Stops with the Ruler

Start

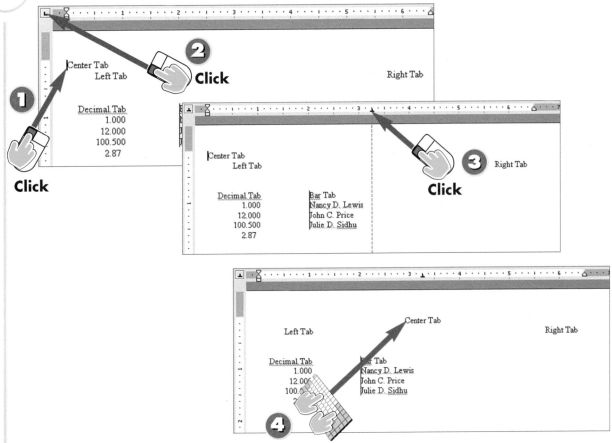

Click

Click

Click

1. Click in the paragraph or line where you want to set a tab.

2. Click the **Tab Alignment** button to toggle through the type of tab stop you want (Left, Center, Right, Decimal Tab, Bar Tab, First Line Indent, or Hanging Indent).

3. Move the mouse pointer to the place on the ruler where you want to place the tab stop, and click.

4. Press the **Tab** key on your keyboard to align the text with the tab stop.

End

INTRODUCTION

You can set different types of tab stops: left (default), right, decimal, or center. Setting tabs is useful for indenting paragraphs at one or more tab stops. Word displays the exact tab measurements in the ruler when you press the Alt key while you click to add the tab stop.

TIP

Tab Options

The tab options look like an *L* for a left tab, an upside-down *T* for a center tab, a backward *L* for a right tab, an upside-down *T* with a dot for a decimal tab, and a bar for a bar tab. Cycle through the tab options using the Tab Alignment button.

TIP

Removing a Tab Stop

If you want to remove a tab stop, select the text for which you set the tab, point to the tab marker, left-click and drag it off the ruler, and then release the mouse button. The tab stop disappears.

Copying Formatting

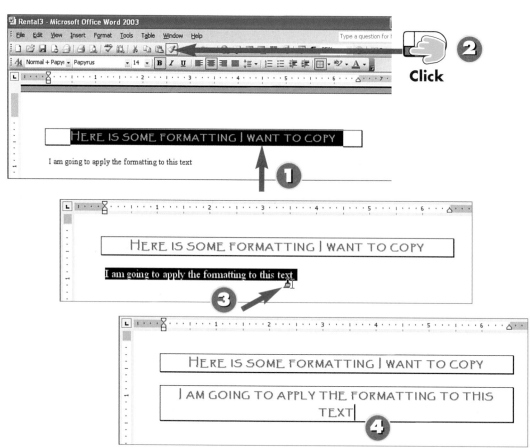

1. Select the text with the formatting that you want to copy and apply to other text.

2. Click the **Format Painter** button on the Standard toolbar; the mouse pointer changes to a Format Painter pointer (paint brush symbol).

3. Select the text to which you want to apply the copied formatting.

4. Release the mouse button. The formatting is applied to the text.

If you have taken the time to format your text just so, you might want to apply those same formatting options to other text. Instead of repeating each step in the format process on the new text, use the Format Painter button.

Removing Text Formatting

To quickly remove any text formatting, select the text you want to return to its default settings; then open the **Edit** menu and select **Clear**, **Formats**.

Clearing Formatting

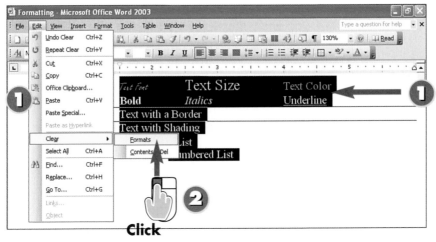

Click

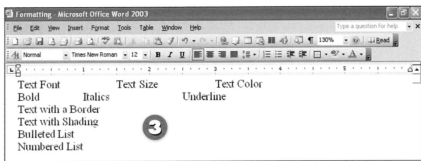

1 Select the text with the formatting that you want to clear.

2 Open the **Edit** menu and select **Clear**, **Formats**.

3 Notice that all the formatting is cleared (except for highlighted text).

INTRODUCTION

Suppose you've formatted your text but decide you don't want it to be formatted after all. Instead of unchecking options in dialog boxes or deselecting toolbar buttons, you can simply indicate that you want to clear the formatting of the text you select. This can be particularly convenient if you have tabbed between formatting and don't want the empty tab space to display any formatting.

TIP

Clearing Contents
To quickly remove document contents—for example, to clear all the cells in a Word table—select the text you want to clear and then open the **Edit** menu and select **Clear, Contents**. This is the same as pressing the Delete key.

Formatting Documents

There are all types of ways you can format your documents in Microsoft Word. For example, you can insert a page break and start text on a new page, insert a section break and have double columns in a portion of your document, or add triple columns to your entire document and create a pamphlet.

In addition to these formatting techniques, you can change your page margins or simply center text on a page so you don't have to change the document margins. If you want to print a draft copy of a report to your colleagues but let them know it is not finished, you can add a watermark that says "Draft" across each printed page. You can even add comments in the document (and print them) for your colleagues to review.

You can also use some nice finishing touches, such as page borders, page numbers, headers and footers, and symbols and special characters.

Formatting Document Options

Footnote indicator

Column separator bar

Text selected that the comment pertains to

Footnote descriptive text

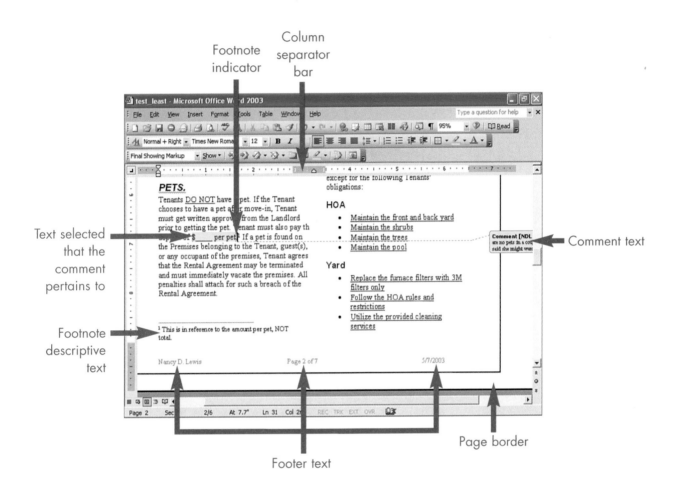

Comment text

Page border

Footer text

Inserting a Page Break

Start

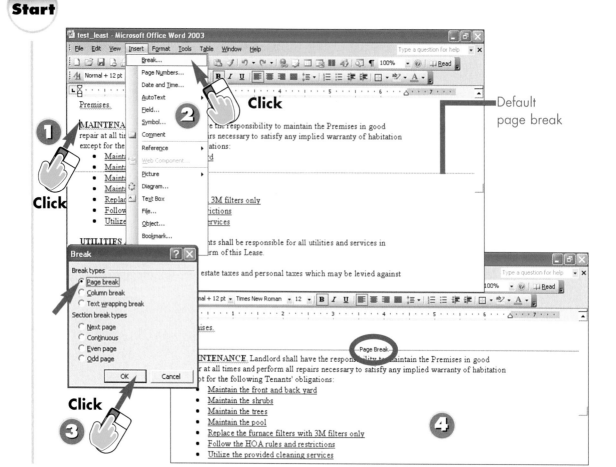

Default page break

Click

Click

Click

1. In Normal view, click in the document where you want to insert a break.

2. Open the **Insert** menu and select **Break** to open the Break dialog box.

3. Click the type of page break you want to insert—for example, **Page Break** (or Column Break or Text Wrapping Break)—and click **OK**.

4. The page break appears in the document (in Normal view). In Print Layout view, the text appears on the next page.

End

TIP

Types of Page Breaks
Breaks can be either automatic—when the break naturally places text on the next page (Page break), column (Column break), or line (Text wrapping break)—or manual (if you force text to the next page, column, or line). You can press the **Ctrl+Enter** shortcut key to insert the page break in your document. To delete a manual page break, click the dotted line that represents the page break in Normal view and press the **Delete** key on your keyboard.

Inserting a Section Break

Start

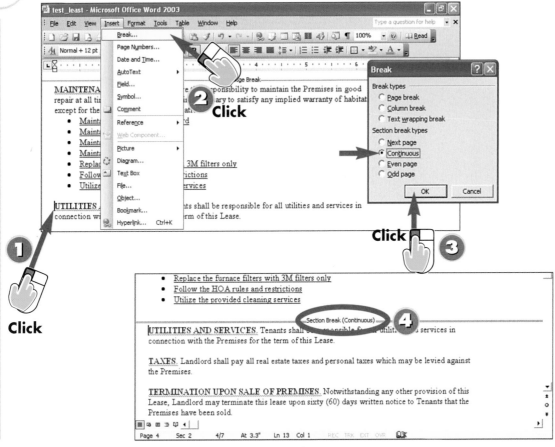

Click ①

Click ②

Click ③

- Replace the furnace filters with 3M filters only
- Follow the HOA rules and restrictions
- Utilize the provided cleaning services

············Section Break (Continuous)············ ④

UTILITIES AND SERVICES. Tenants shall be responsible for all utilities and services in connection with the Premises for the term of this Lease.

TAXES. Landlord shall pay all real estate taxes and personal taxes which may be levied against the Premises.

TERMINATION UPON SALE OF PREMISES. Notwithstanding any other provision of this Lease, Landlord may terminate this lease upon sixty (60) days written notice to Tenants that the Premises have been sold.

Page 4   Sec 2   4/7   At 3.3"   Ln 13 Col 1   REC TRK EXT OVR

① In Normal view, click in the document where you want to insert a section break.

② Open the **Insert** menu and select **Break** to open the Break dialog box.

③ Click the type of section break you want to insert—for example, **Continuous** (or Next Page, Even Page, or Odd Page)—and click **OK**.

④ The section break appears in the document. You cannot see a section break if you're in Print Layout view.

End

INTRODUCTION

In addition to adding page breaks to your document (covered in the preceding task), you can add a section break. Section breaks enable you to format each section of a document separately; for example, different portions of your document can have different margins or be formatted into two columns.

TIP

Types of Section Breaks
A next page section break starts a new section on the next page. A continuous section break starts a new section on the same page. An even page break starts a new section on the next even-numbered page, and an odd page break starts a new section on the next odd-numbered page. To delete a section break, click the double dotted line in Normal view and press the **Delete** key on your keyboard.

Adding Columns

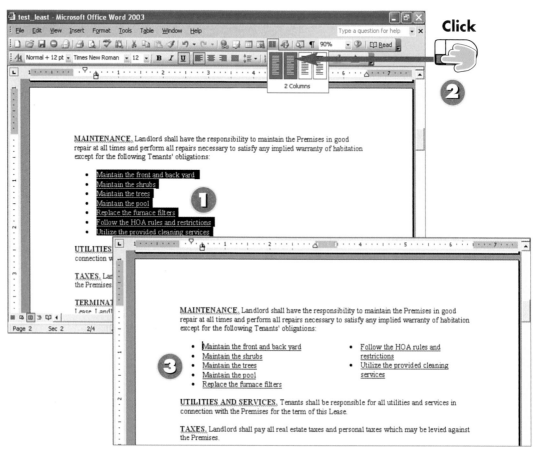

Click

1. In Print Layout view, select the text you want to format as columns. For specific paragraphs, you must insert section breaks before and after the paragraphs.

2. Click the **Columns** button on the Standard toolbar and select the number of columns you want.

3. The selected text is placed in columns.

End

TIP

Beginning Columns
A good place to begin adding a section of columns is where you have entered a section break. This adds columns from the point of the cursor down to the end of the document (or to another section break) instead of to the entire document.

TIP

Columns in the Ruler
You can tell that the columns have been added to a document by looking at the top ruler. Column separators appear between the columns.

Setting Page Margins

Start

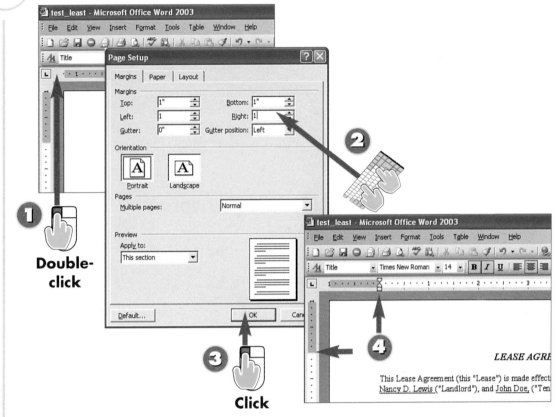

Double-click

Click

1. Double-click the gray area—where the ruler does not extend—to open the Page Setup dialog box to the Margins tab.

2. Type the new margin settings (for example, **1** inch in the **Left** spin box and **1** inch in the **Right** spin box).

3. Click the **OK** button.

4. View the new page margins applied in the document by looking at the new locations of the indent markers on the ruler.

End

INTRODUCTION

You can adjust the top, bottom, left, and right margins for a single page or for your entire document. For example, you might need to fit a large amount of text on one page and therefore need to increase the margins for the document's printable area.

TIP

Portrait and Landscape
If you need to alter your page's orientation from portrait to landscape or increase the size of your document (for example, to legal size—8.5"×14"), modify the settings in the Paper Size tab on the Page Setup dialog box.

TIP

Page Setup
You can also open the File menu, select Page Setup, and select the Margins tab to change the margins. Word's default margins are 1" for the top and bottom and 1.25" for the left and right.

Centering Text on a Page

Start

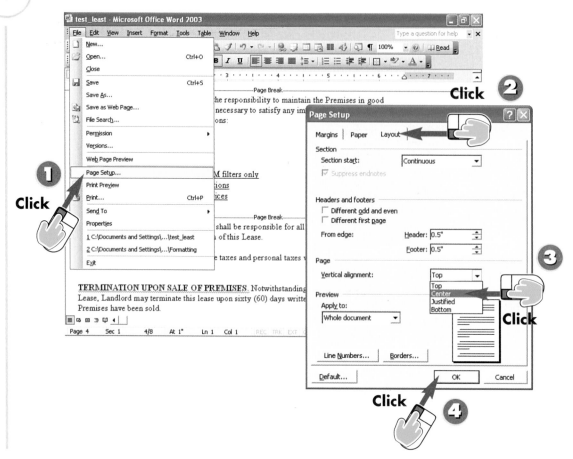

Click ①

Click ②

③

Click

Click ④

① Open the **File** menu and select **Page Setup** to open the Page Setup dialog box. (Be sure the cursor is in the page you want to center.)

② Select the **Layout** tab.

③ In the **Page** area, click the down arrow next to the **Vertical Alignment** field and select **Center** from the list.

④ Click **OK** and your document will be centered on the page. (You cannot see this in Normal view.)

INTRODUCTION

Have you ever wanted to quickly center information on a page, but it took you forever? Well, Word has a page-settings option that allows you to center your text or graphics on the page immediately. Keep in mind that this option affects all the pages in your document, unless you insert a "next page" section break (refer to the task "Inserting a Section Break" earlier in this part) and return the document-centering option back to the default setting (top).

TIP

Centering One Page
If you want to have only one page centered and the pages before and/or after it to be regular (default to top), make sure you insert a next page section break before and after the section of text you want to center on the page.

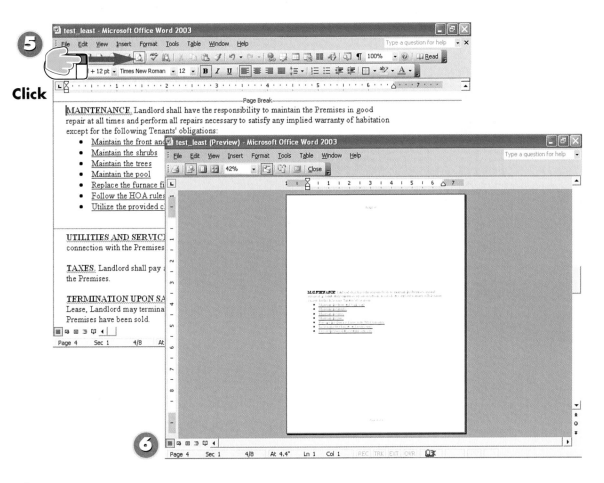

Click

5 Click the **Print Preview** button on the Standard toolbar.

6 In Print Preview, you can see what your centered page will look like.

End

Inserting Page Numbers

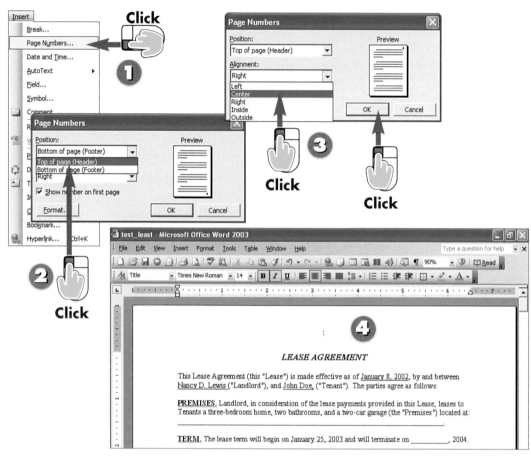

1. Open the **Insert** menu and select **Page Numbers** to open the Page Numbers dialog box.

2. Click the down arrow next to the **Position** field and select whether you want the page number at the top or bottom of the page.

3. Click the down arrow next to the **Alignment** field and specify where you want the page number—left, right, centered, or on the inside/outside of the page. Click **OK**.

4. You can see the page number (grayed out) in Print Layout view.

INTRODUCTION Word can automatically insert page numbers in your documents and print the page numbers in the position you specify. That way, you don't have to manually enter and manage the page numbers yourself.

TIP First Page Numbers If you don't want a page number on the first page of a document, for example, a cover page, click to remove the checkmark from the **Show Number on First Page** check box on the Page Numbers dialog box.

TIP Page-number Formats Alter the page number format to be letters or Roman numerc by clicking the Format button on the Page Numbers dialog box. Or, include a chapter an page number (for example, 2- for page 1 of chapter 2).

86 PART 5

Inserting a Header and Footer

Start

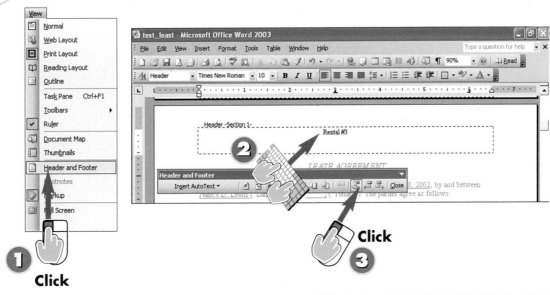

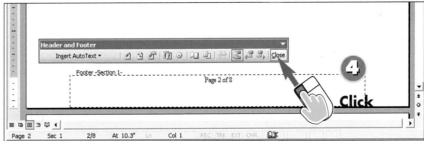

Click

Click

Click

Click

End

1. Open the **View** menu and select **Header and Footer** to open the Header and Footer toolbar. The cursor then moves to the header area in Print Layout view.

2. Type any text you want to print at the top of each page, pressing the **Tab** key to move between a left-aligned, centered, or right-aligned entry.

3. Click the **Switch Between Header and Footer** button to move from the header to the footer.

4. Move the mouse pointer over each button on the Header and Footer toolbar to review the available options. Click the toolbar's **Close** button when you're finished.

INTRODUCTION

Headers and *footers* are text that prints at the top and/or bottom of pages in Word documents—headers at the top, footers at the bottom. For example, you might want to place your name and the date as a header at the top of the document and the document's filename as a footer at the bottom.

TIP

Header and Footer Toolbar Options
You can include any type of text, page numbers, or the current date and time, and you can even apply formatting to the information in a header or footer. Click a button on the Header and Footer toolbar for each standard entry you want in your header or footer—for example, Insert Page Number, Insert Number of Pages, Format Page Number, Insert Date, and Insert Time. You can also open the Insert AutoText drop-down list to select from the various AutoText entries (Created by, Created on, Filename, and so on).

Inserting Footnotes

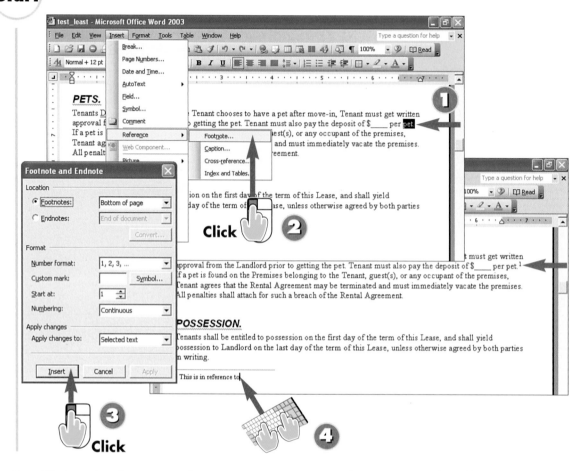

1. Click in the document where you want to insert a footnote (or select the text you want it to follow).

2. Open the **Insert** menu and select **Reference**, **Footnote** to open the Footnote and Endnote dialog box.

3. Click the **Insert** button to accept the default options of inserting a footnote with AutoNumber. Word places the cursor at the end of the page and numbers the footnote.

4. Type the text you want to appear in the footnote; when you're finished, click anywhere in the document.

End

TIP

Viewing Footnotes

If you want to view footnotes (which are visible by default in Print Layout view), place the mouse pointer on the note reference mark in the document. The text you typed appears in a pop-up above the reference mark.

TIP

Endnotes

If you want to insert an endnote instead of a footnote, click the **Endnotes** option on the Footnote and Endnote dialog box. Endnotes are always displayed at the end of the document, never throughout, like you can with footnotes.

Inserting Symbols

Start

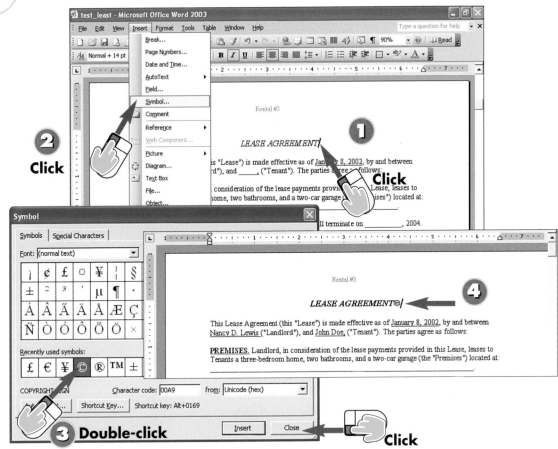

2 **Click**

3 **Double-click**

Click

① Click in the text where you want to add the symbol.

② Open the **Insert** menu and select **Symbol** to open the Symbol dialog box.

③ Double-click the symbol you want to insert into your document—for example, the **Copyright Sign** (©). Then, click **Close**.

④ The symbol is inserted in your document.

End

INTRODUCTION

The Symbol command enables you to insert special characters, international characters, and symbols such as the registered trademark (®) and trademark (™) symbols. You can easily add these and other special characters to your Word documents.

TIP

Finding Symbols
You can locate different symbols and different types of symbols by clicking the down arrow next to the Font field in the Symbol dialog box and selecting a different font. Each font provides different symbols from which to choose.

TIP

Foreign Letters
If you are using a foreign word, you can use a symbol for punctuation. To include those, click the down arrow next to the **Font** field in the Symbol dialog box and select **normal text**. You can then choose from letters with different punctuation.

Inserting and Viewing Comments

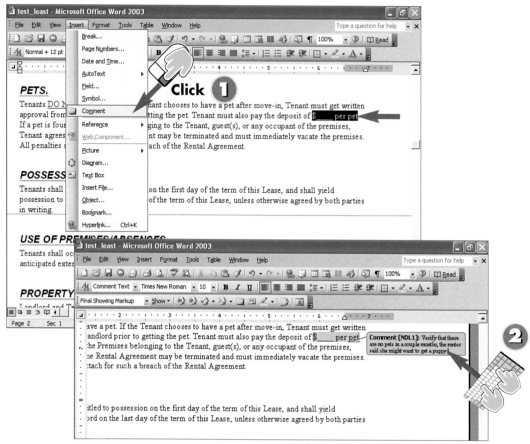

Click 1

2

1 After you select the text (or anything else in the document) where you want to insert a comment, open the **Insert** menu and select **Comment**.

2 Type your comments in the bubble (in Print Layout view; in Normal view you must type into the Reviewing pane). Click anywhere in the document when finished.

When working in a document, you might find that you need to add a note in your document to remind yourself to check on something or to verify some information when you work on the document later. Instead of adding the note directly into the text, you can add a *comment*.

TIP

Editing a Comment
You can edit your comments by selecting the highlighted area of the comment or the comment bubble with the mouse, right-clicking, and selecting **Edit Comment** from the shortcut menu that appears. Then, make any changes you want.

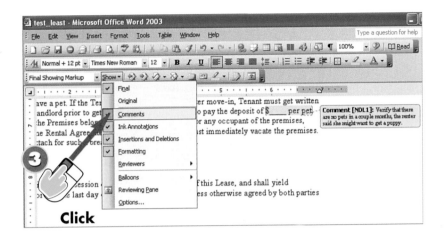

Click

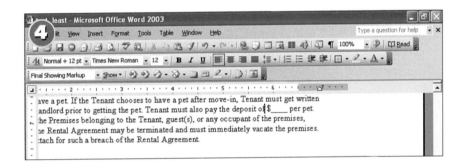

3 Deselect the **Comments** option from the **Show** menu on the Reviewing toolbar to hide your comments (open the **View** menu and select **Reviewing** if it's not displayed).

4 The comment is hidden. (Only the checked items on the Show menu appear in the document.)

Deleting a Comment
You can delete a comment by selecting the highlighted area of a comment or the comment bubble with the mouse, right-clicking, and selecting **Delete Comment** from the shortcut menu that appears.

Advanced Document Formatting

Now that you know how to edit documents, format text, and format your documents, it is time to do a little advanced work in Microsoft Word. For example, Word has a mail-merge wizard that takes you through each step to creating a form document by merging a letter (or whatever document you like) and a data source list (more on that in Part 9, "Working with Data and Charts").

This part also teaches you how to assign Word's default styles (Normal, Header 1, Header 2, and so on) to your document text as well as how to create and apply your own styles. You can use this styled text to create a table of contents to organize the information in your document.

And last, but not least, this part teaches you how to work with tables. You can create tables in your Word documents and format them in many ways. The Tables and Borders toolbar, which allows you to quickly access some of the features in this part, is very helpful. Simply open the View menu and select Toolbars, Tables and Borders.

Working with Tables

Column with increased width

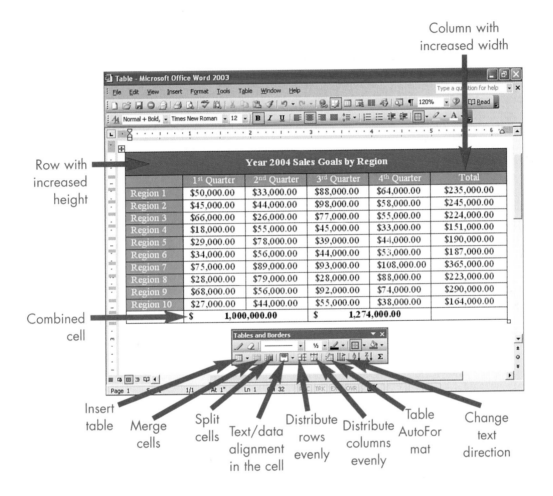

Row with increased height

Combined cell

Insert table

Merge cells

Split cells

Text/data alignment in the cell

Distribute rows evenly

Distribute columns evenly

Table AutoFormat

Change text direction

Performing a Simple Mail Merge

Start

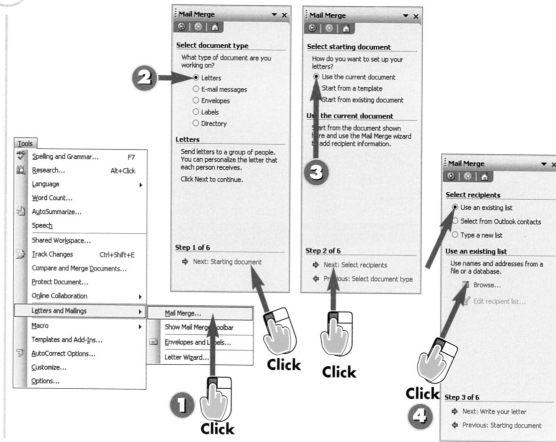

Click

Click

Click

Click

Click

1 Open the **Tools** menu and select **Letters and Mailings**, **Mail Merge** to open the Mail Merge task pane.

2 Select the type of document you want to create (in this case, **Letters**); then click the **Next: Starting Document** link.

3 Select how you want to set up your letters (for example, **Use the Current Document**), and then click the **Next: Select Recipients** link.

4 Select from where the recipient information should come (for example, **Use an Existing List**) and click **Browse**.

When you perform a mail merge, you use a data source, such as your Outlook Address Book, and a main document, such as a form letter, to create a resulting merged document. Instead of creating the letter multiple times, you can create it once and merge it with the information in your address book. The objective of this task isn't to give you every possible scenario for the different types of mail merges you can perform in Word—that could be a whole book on its own. Instead, you'll follow along the steps of merging a very simple letter—which you'll create in Word—with a data file from another application so you can begin to understand what you are being asked to provide to perform a mail merge in Word.

Mail Merge Options

TIP

You have numerous options when performing a mail merge. This task shows you the procedure for creating a form letter to send to people in your electronic address book.

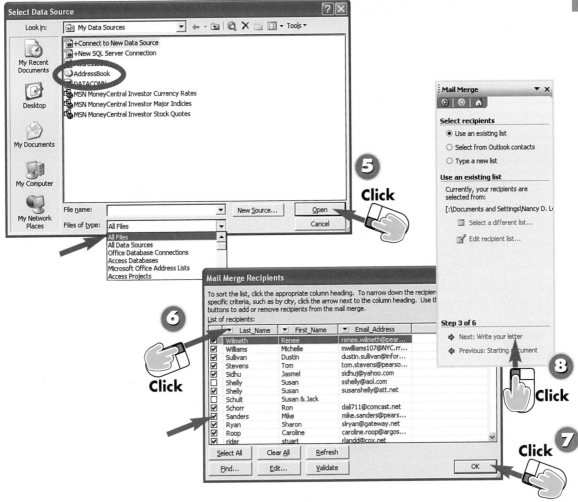

Select **All Files** from the **Files of Type** drop-down list and select your data source (for example, **AddressBook**); then click **Open**.

Click the data field headers (in this example, **Last_Name**, **First_Name**, and **Email_Address**) to sort the data in the Mail Merge Recipients dialog box.

Click the check boxes to select the mail merge recipients (click the **Clear All** button to begin; this also deselects the addresses without names). Click **OK**.

In the Mail Merge task pane, click the **Next: Write Your Letter** link to begin creating the letter you want to use in your mail merge.

Selecting Outlook Recipients
In the wizard screen shown in step 4, you can choose Select from Outlook Contacts and use the contacts you have listed in your Outlook Address Book. You can also select Type a New List and then click the Create button to begin entering information about individuals you want included in the mail-merge document.

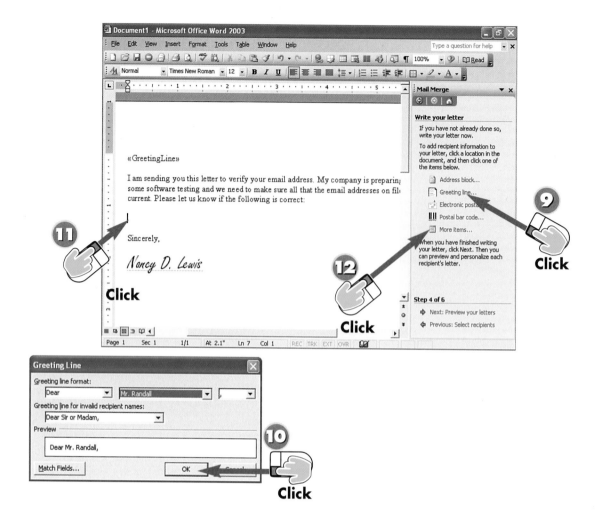

⑨ To insert a greeting in the letter, click the **Greeting Line** link in the Mail Merge task pane to open the Greeting Line dialog box.

⑩ Select options from the various drop-down lists to specify how you want the greeting to appear; then click **OK**. (In this case, simply accept the default settings.)

⑪ Type the rest of the letter, leaving blank areas for additional fields. Then, click in the document where you want to insert another merge field.

⑫ To select additional fields that correspond to your data file, click the **More Items** link in the Mail Merge task pane to open the Insert Merge Field dialog box.

Inserting an Address Block

TIP

The Address Block link in the Mail Merge task pane allows you to select formatting options for an address—for example, to place it at the top of a business letter document. You can add the recipient's name, company name, and postal address and even format it according to the destination country and region.

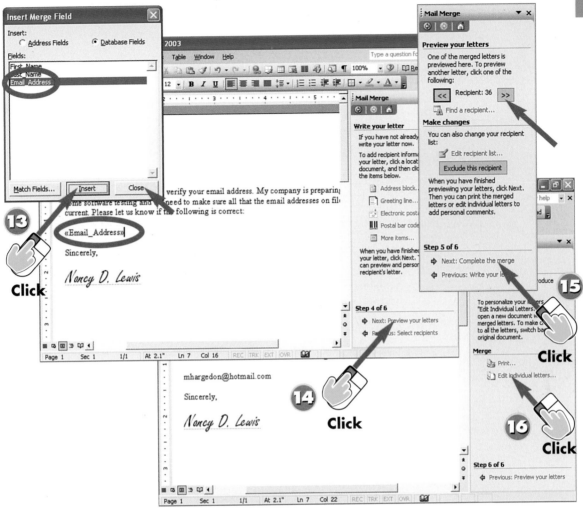

13 Select the field you want to add and click the **Insert** button to place the field in the letter. When you've finished inserting fields, click the **Close** button.

14 Click the **Next: Preview Your Letters** link to print or edit your individual letters.

15 Click the **<<** or **>>** button on the Mail Merge task pane to view the letter for each recipient. Then, click the **Next: Complete the Merge** link.

16 Click the **Print** link in the Mail Merge toolbar to send the files to the printer, or click the **Edit Individual Letters** link to review and edit each letter.

End

Previous Steps

TIP

If you need to review any steps you've already performed, click the **Previous** link at the bottom of the Mail Merge task pane to return to previous steps.

Assigning a Style to Text

Start

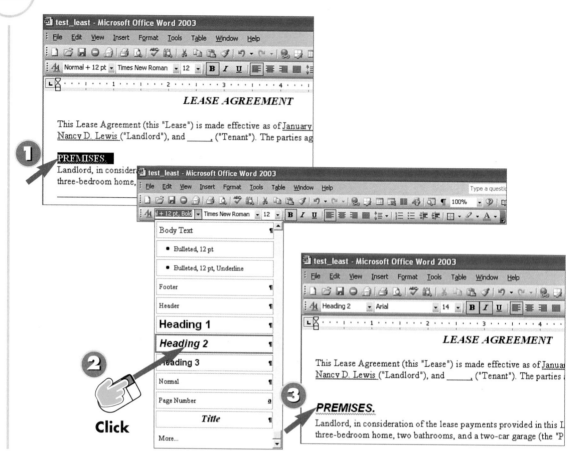

Click

End

1. Select the text to which you want to apply a style.

2. Click the down arrow next to the **Style** field on the Formatting toolbar to select a style (for example, **Heading 2**).

3. Word formats the text using the style you chose.

TIP

Creating a New Style
You can create your own styles in Word and apply them to text as you do a default Word style. Apply your desired formatting to some text, select the text, click in the **Style** drop-down list box, type a new name for the style, and press **Enter**. Then you can assign it to other text as in this task.

Inserting a Table of Contents

Start

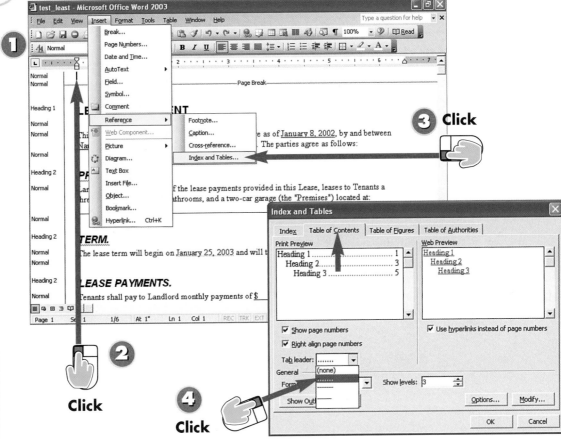

1

2 Click

3 Click

4 Click

1. Open the document for which you want to create a TOC. Be sure the text has styles assigned (see the "Display Styles" tip on this page).

2. Click the location in the document where you want the TOC to be placed (typically at the beginning or end of a document).

3. Open the **Insert** menu and select **Reference**, **Index and Tables** to open the Index and Tables dialog box; then select the **Table of Contents** tab.

4. Click the down arrow next to the **Tab Leader** field to select a different leader. Other common choices are Show Page Numbers and Right Align Page Numbers.

INTRODUCTION

You've probably referred to a table of contents (TOC) at the beginning of a book. Word lets you create your own TOCs for reports, projects, and even stories you write. A TOC simply uses Word's styles (see the preceding task) to create a list of headers that refer to page numbers in your document.

TIP

Updating the TOC
The Update Page Numbers Only option in the Update Table of Contents dialog box can be used if you only moved text around; otherwise, it is a good idea to update the entire table.

TIP

Display Styles
To display the styles on the right side of your document in Normal view, open the **Tools** menu and select Options to open the **Options** dialog box. Increase the Style Area Width to .7" and click **OK**.

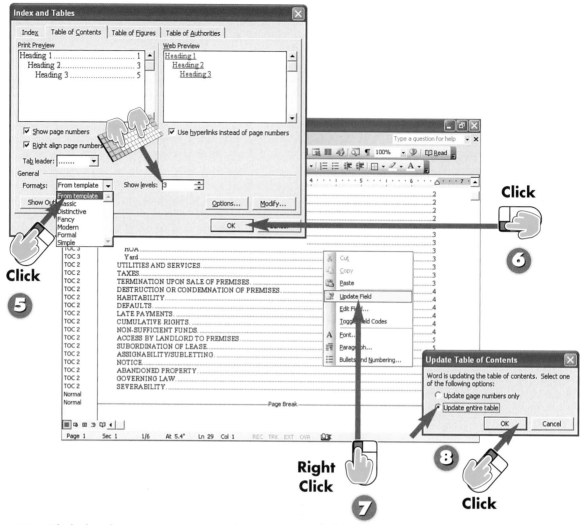

Click

Click

Right Click

Click

5 Click the down arrow next to the **Formats** field and select a text-appearance option. Then type the number of levels deep the TOC should be in the **Show Levels** spin box.

6 Click the **OK** button to accept Word's default styles as the headers list in the TOC.

7 If you make a change to the header text or move text around, have Word update the TOC by right-clicking the TOC and selecting **Update Field**.

8 The Update Table of Contents dialog box opens; click the **Update Entire Table** option and click **OK**. The TOC is automatically updated in your document.

End

Creating a New Table

Start

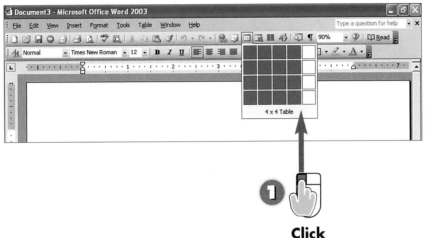

Click

①

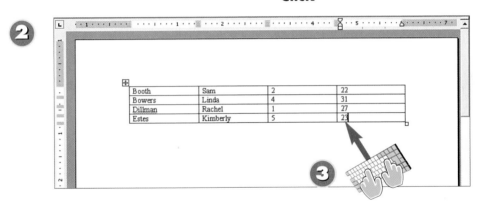

②

③

PART 6

① Click the **Insert Table** button on the Standard toolbar and select the number of rows and columns you want the table to have (for example, 4×4).

② The table is inserted at the location of your cursor.

③ Click in the first cell of the table and type the text you want placed there; press the **Tab** and **up-** and **down-arrow** keys to move through the table to add more text.

End

AutoFormatting a Table

Start

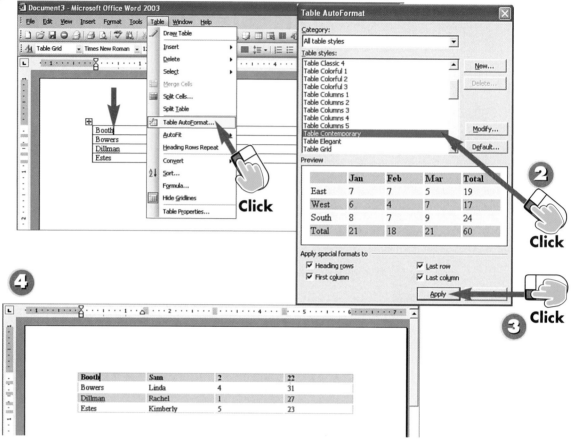

Click

2

Click

3 **Click**

4

End

1 Click anywhere in the table you want to format, and then open the **Table** menu and select **Table AutoFormat** to open the Table AutoFormat dialog box.

2 Click an option in the **Table Styles** list and view it in the **Preview** area.

3 When you find a table style you like, click the **Apply** button.

4 The style you chose is applied to your table.

INTRODUCTION

Tables present information in a way that can be quite effective to understand and review. To make a table look even better, you can format it in many ways. If you don't want to take the time to format the table on your own, Word can quickly format it for you thanks to its AutoFormat feature.

TIP

Removing Table Formatting
To quickly remove all formatting from a table, return to the Table AutoFormat dialog box, select **Table Normal** from the **Table Styles** section, and then click the **Apply** button.

TIP

Combine or Split Cells
Select multiple cells to merge, open the **Table** menu, and select **Merge Cells**. Any cell data combines. Select the cell to split, open the **Table** menu, select **Split Cells**, specify the number of rows and columns in the Split Cells dialog box, and click **OK**.

PART 6

Start

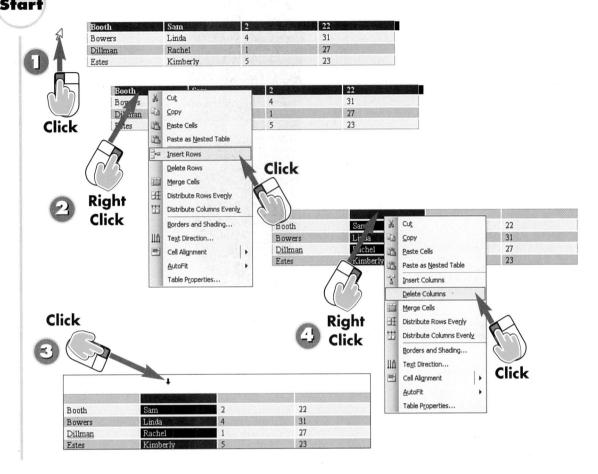

Click

2 **Right Click**

Click

Click

3

4 **Right Click**

Click

1 Click in the margin to the left of the row above which you want to insert another row; the row becomes highlighted, and the mouse pointer rotates to point up and to the right.

2 Right-click the row and select **Insert Rows**; the new row appears above it (to delete the row, select **Delete Rows**).

3 Click above the column you want to delete; the column becomes highlighted. (Notice that the mouse pointer rotates to point downward.)

4 Right-click the column and select **Delete Columns** to delete the column (to insert a column to the left, select **Insert Column**).

End

INTRODUCTION

When working with Word tables, you might find that you need another row or column after you have already created a table. Word lets you easily insert and delete rows and columns while working in a table.

Deleting Text Only
Selecting a row and then pressing the Delete key removes the text within the cells, leaving the row empty but intact.

Adding a Row at the End
To add a row to the bottom of the table, place the cursor at the end of any text in the bottom-right cell in the table and press the **Tab** key.

Altering Row Height and Column Width

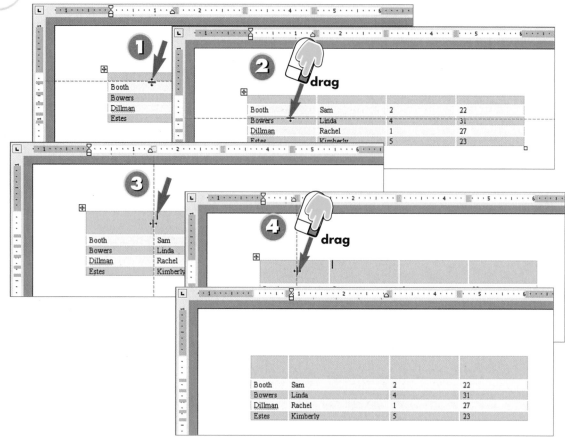

1. Move the mouse pointer over the bottom edge of the row you want to alter. The mouse pointer changes to an up-and-down arrow with parallel lines.

2. Press and hold down the left mouse button and drag the row edge to the new size; when you release the mouse button, the line drops in the new location.

3. Move the mouse pointer over the right edge of the column you want to alter. The mouse pointer changes to a left-and-right arrow with parallel lines.

4. Press and hold down the left mouse button and drag the column to the new size; when you release the mouse button, the line drops in the new location.

End

INTRODUCTION

When adding text to your table, you might notice either too much or too little space between the table's lines and the text. Word enables you to easily change the row height and column width to minimize or maximize space.

TIP

Distributing Evenly
If you want to distribute the columns (or rows) evenly, select the entire table, right-click, and select **Distribute Columns Evenly** (or **Distribute Rows Evenly**).

TIP

Altering Multiple Items
In addition to changing the height and width of a single row or column, you can select multiple items; the formatting you then apply is used for all the items.

Deleting a Table

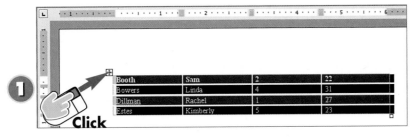

Booth	Sam	2	22
Bowers	Linda	4	31
Dillman	Rachel	1	27
Estes	Kimberly	5	23

Click

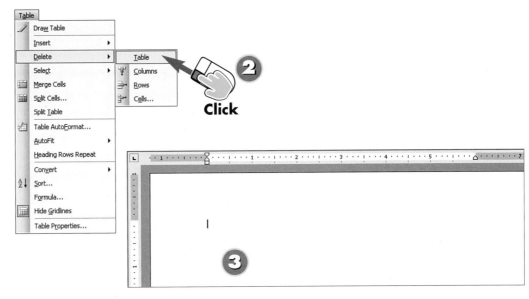

Click

1. Click the four-headed arrow at the upper-left corner of the table to select the entire table. (Move the mouse pointer over the table to make the four-headed arrow appear.)

2. Open the **Table** menu and select **Delete**, **Table**.

3. The table disappears.

INTRODUCTION

Suppose you decide not to use a table in your document after all. In that case, you can delete the entire table from your document.

Deleting with Cut
Another way to delete the entire table is to select all the rows in the table and click the **Cut** button on the Standard toolbar.

Table to Text
You can convert a table to text instead of deleting it. Select the table; open the **Table** menu; and select **Convert**, **Table to Text.** Click **OK** on the Convert Table to Text dialog box, and Word converts the selected table into tabbed columns.

Getting Started with Excel

When you start the application, Excel displays a blank workbook. A *workbook* is a file in which you store your data, similar to a three-ring binder. Within a workbook are worksheets, chart sheets, and macro sheets. A new workbook contains three sheets, named Sheet1 through Sheet3. You can add sheets, up to 255 per workbook, depending on your computer's available memory.

Multiple sheets help you organize, manage, and consolidate your data. For example, you might want to create a sales forecast for the first quarter of the year. Sheet1, Sheet2, and Sheet3 could contain worksheet data for January, February, and March; Sheet4 could be a summary for the three months of sales data; and Sheet5 could be a chart showing sales over the three-month period.

A *worksheet* is a grid of columns and rows. The intersection of any column and row is called a *cell*. Each cell in a worksheet has a unique cell reference—the designation formed by combining the row and column headings. For example, A8 refers to the cell at the intersection of column A and row 8.

The *cell pointer* is a cross-shaped pointer that appears over cells in the worksheet. You use the cell pointer to select any cell in the worksheet. The selected cell is called the *active cell*, and you always have at least one cell selected.

A *range* is a specified group of cells. A range can be a single cell; a column; a row; or any combination of cells, columns, and rows. *Range coordinates* identify a range. The first element in the range coordinates is the location of the upper-left cell in the range; the second element is the location of the lower-right cell. A colon (:) separates these two elements. The range A1:C3, for example, includes the cells A1, A2, A3, B1, B2, B3, C1, C2, and C3.

Opening Excel Workbooks

Displays the current folder

Goes back to the previously viewed folder

Goes up one folder level

Displays recently saved files

Displays files on the desktop

Displays files in the My Documents folder

Displays folders and drives on your computer

Displays shared network folder and drives

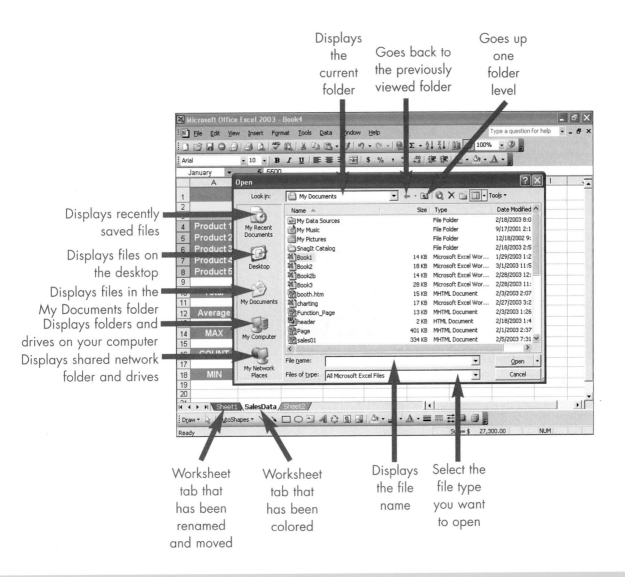

Worksheet tab that has been renamed and moved

Worksheet tab that has been colored

Displays the file name

Select the file type you want to open

Entering Data

Start

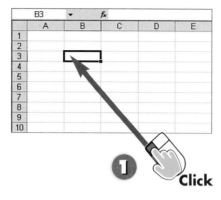

1 Click

2

3

4

End

1 Click the cell to which you want to add data (for example, **B3**), making it the active cell.

2 Type some data (in this example, **January**) in the cell. As you type, the data also appears in the Edit bar.

3 When you finish typing, press **Enter**. Excel makes the cell immediately below it the active cell.

4 Type some data into a few different cells and press the arrow keys to move to the next cell (for example, enter some row headers and column headers).

INTRODUCTION

Data is the technical term for the text and numbers you enter into an Excel worksheet. Data in a specific cell can contain text, numbers, or any combination of both; it can even be a graphic or some other type of object you insert into the worksheet. You can enter data into a blank worksheet or add data to an existing worksheet.

TIP

Correcting As You Type
If you make a mistake when typing data, press the **Backspace** key to delete your entry and type the correct data. You can also click the red **X** to the left of the Edit bar to cancel your current data entry or press the **Esc** key.

TIP

Editing Data
If you pressed Enter to accept a data entry but that entry is incorrect, click the cell with the incorrect data to make it active. Then, type the correct data over the old data.

Entering Repeat Cell Text

Start

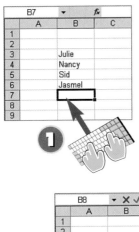
①

②

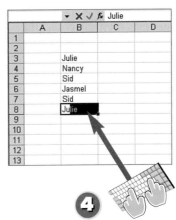
③

④

End

① Type some names into cells B3, B4, B5, and B6 (for example, **Julie**, **Nancy**, **Sid**, and **Jasmel**) and press **Enter**.

② In cell B7, type the first letter of one of the original four names—for example, **S.** The name Sid automatically fills the cell. Press **Enter** to accept the entry.

③ In cell B8, type the first letter of another name—for example, **J.** No name automatically fills the cell because the inferred name could be either Julie or Jasmel.

④ Type the second letter of the name—for example, **u**. The name Julie appears. Press either the **Enter** or the **down-arrow** key to enter the name into the cell.

INTRODUCTION

Sometimes you'll find that you are entering the same text-based data in multiple cells in the same row or column. To save time, Excel tries to infer the data you want to enter (only for text entries, not numbers).

TIP

Overriding Excel's Entry

Suppose cell B3 contains the text **paper clips**, cell B4 contains **pencils**, and you want to type **paper** in cell B5. When you do, Excel automatically enters **Paper clips** in the cell. To ensure the cell holds only the data you want, simply continue to type the word **paper** and press the **Delete** key on the keyboard when you finish. The rest of the text disappears; press **Enter** and move on to your next cell entry.

Selecting Cells

Start

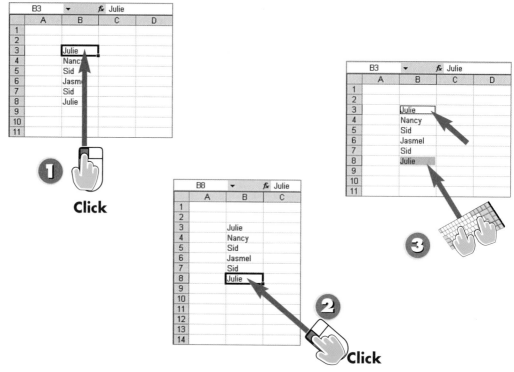

Click

Click

1 Click the cell you want to make active (for example, **B3**). A thick, black border around the cell indicates it is the active cell.

2 Click another cell (for example, **B8**) to select it as the active cell. Notice that a border no longer appears around cell B3.

3 Press the **Ctrl** key on the keyboard and click cell **B3**. The active cell is B3, but cell B8 now has a light blue background, indicating that both cells are selected.

End

Excel displays numerous rows and columns that make up thousands of cells. Most likely you won't use them all, but you do need a way to select specific cells and frequently select more than one cell at a time. When you want to select an individual cell, you just click it.

Unselecting Cells
If you click a cell that you didn't want in the selection, your only option is to release the Ctrl key and click somewhere in the worksheet to clear the noncontiguous range. Then, start selecting the cells again more carefully.

Selecting the Whole Worksheet
You can select an entire worksheet by pressing Ctrl+A. This is convenient when you want to format all the cells in a worksheet the same way—for example, making everything bold, blue, and 16-point font.

Selecting a Range of Cells

Start

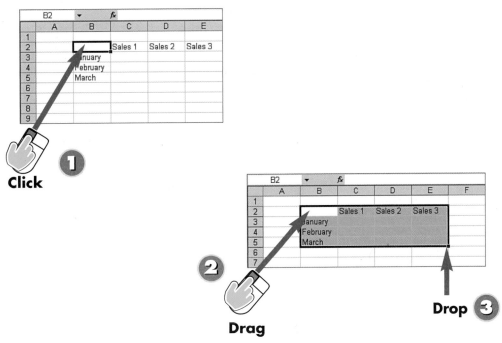

Click 1

2 **Drag**

Drop 3

1 Click the cell you want to be the first cell in a range of cells (for example, **B2**).

2 Press and hold down the left mouse button while you drag the pointer to the last cell you want to include in the range (for example, **E5**).

3 When the desired range is selected, release the mouse button.

End

INTRODUCTION

Sometimes you'll want to select multiple cells that are adjacent to each other (known as a *range*). You will use this feature frequently when you are formatting your data and want to format multiple cells in the same manner.

TIP

Range References
A range of cells is indicated with a *range reference*. This includes the upper-leftmost cell in the selection, a colon, and the lower-rightmost cell in the selection. For example, the range reference for cells G2 through F9 would be G2:F9.

TIP

Using Shift
Another way to select a range of cells is to click a cell, press the Shift key, and then click the cell at the other end of the desired range. All the cells between the two clicked cells will be selected.

Automatically Filling a Series of Data

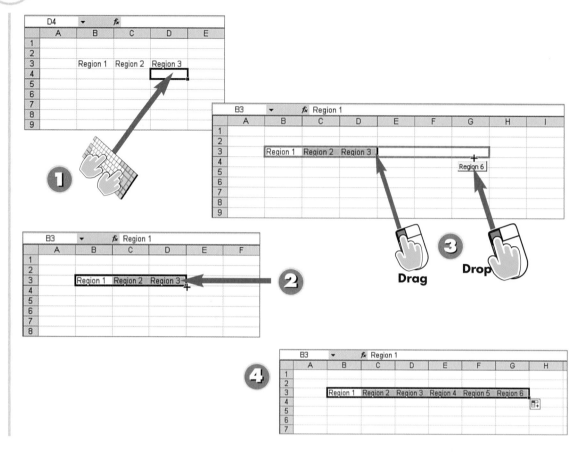

Drag

Drop

① Type the data for the first few cells in the series you want to fill. For example, type **Region 1**, **Region 2**, and **Region 3** into cells B3, C3, and D3, respectively.

② Select cells **B3**, **C3**, and **D3** and move the mouse pointer over the lower-right corner of the range until the pointer turns into a thin, black plus.

③ Pressing and holding down the mouse button, drag horizontally or vertically until all the cells you want to fill are selected.

④ Release the mouse button when you have filled the correct number of series data.

End

If you have ever typed each and every cell of a series of data into a worksheet (for example, Monday, Tuesday, Wednesday, and so on), the information in this task will save you a lot of time. In a couple quick steps, Excel completes all the time-consuming, repetitive data entry work for you. Be sure to check Excel's work.

Using Auto Fill Options
Use the Auto Fill Options drop-down list to copy the series cells (Copy Cells); fill the series as is, with formatting (Fill Series); fill only the series formatting (Fill Formatting Only); or fill the series without the formatting (Fill Without Formatting).

Using Intuitive Series
Excel automatically fills and repeats common series, such as days of the week, month names, and so on. To experiment, type **January** into a cell, and then click and drag to select the number of cells you want to fill.

Renaming and Coloring Worksheet Tabs

Start

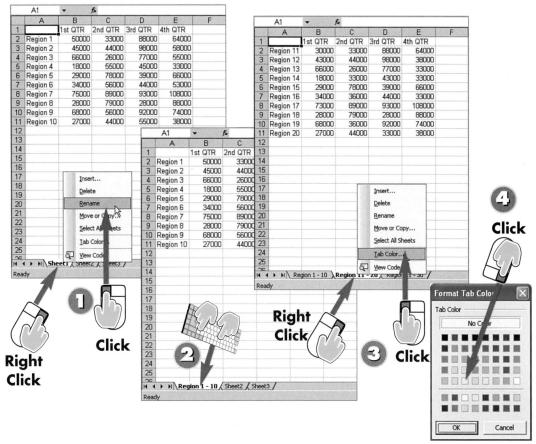

Right Click

Click

Right Click

Click

Click

1 Right-click the tab of the worksheet you want to rename (for example, **Sheet1**), and select **Rename** from the shortcut menu.

2 Type a new name for the worksheet and press the **Enter** key. Repeat this for each tab you want to rename.

3 Right-click the tab of the worksheet you want to colorize and select **Tab Color** from the shortcut menu.

4 The Format Tab Color dialog box opens; click the desired color and click **OK**. The worksheet tab displays the selected color.

End

The more you work in Excel, the more you will need to organize and keep track of your worksheets and the data they contain. A quick way to maintain the worksheets within a workbook is to assign them individual names, such as Region1Sales, Region2Sales, and so on. In addition, if you want to indicate something specific about a worksheet (for example, if a worksheet contains information about a particular sales region that is not doing well), you can assign it a tab color.

Double-Clicking a Tab to Rename It

If you prefer, you can double-click a worksheet tab to rename it. Simply type in the new name and continue working.

Inserting and Deleting Worksheets

Start

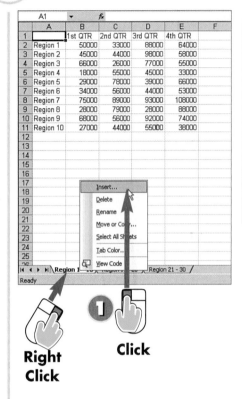

Right Click

Click

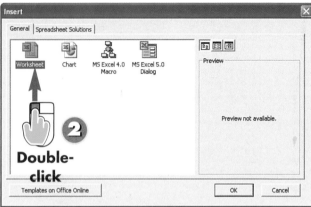

Double-click

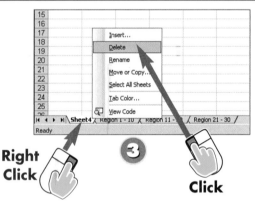

Right Click

Click

1. Right-click the tab of the worksheet that you want a new worksheet placed in front of, and select **Insert** from the shortcut menu.

2. The Insert dialog box opens. Double-click the type of worksheet you want to insert (select **Worksheet**). A new worksheet (the next sheet number in the sequence) appears.

3. To delete a worksheet, right-click the worksheet tab and select **Delete** from the shortcut menu. The worksheet is removed from the workbook.

End

INTRODUCTION

When the default three worksheets per workbook just aren't enough, you will need to insert additional worksheets. Other times, you'll discover you no longer need a worksheet included in a workbook and need to delete it. (Just be sure when you delete worksheets that you definitely no longer need the information.)

TIP

Inserting Worksheets
You can also open the Insert menu and select Worksheet to automatically insert a worksheet into your workbook in front of the currently selected worksheet. If you need to rearrange the worksheets, see the next task.

TIP

Workbook Buttons
If the worksheet tabs aren't visible with a large number of worksheets, you can use the workbook buttons to the left of the worksheet tabs. Click the following buttons: > (next right) or < (next left); |< (first worksheet) or >| (last worksheet).

Moving or Copying Worksheets

Start

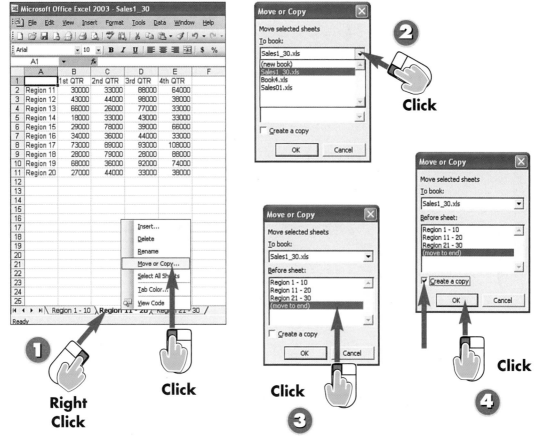

Right Click

Click

Click

Click

Click

1 Right-click the worksheet tab you want to move or copy and select **Move or Copy** from the shortcut menu.

2 In the Move or Copy dialog box, click the **To Book** drop-down list and select the workbook to which you want to move or copy the worksheet.

3 In the **Before Sheet** list, click the name of the worksheet in front of which you want the moved or copied worksheet to be placed or choose **(Move to End)**.

4 Click the **Create a Copy** check box to copy the worksheet instead of moving it. If you want to move the worksheet, leave it unchecked. Then, click **OK**.

End

INTRODUCTION

When Excel inserts a new worksheet, it always places it *in front of* the currently selected worksheet. If you aren't in the correct worksheet tab before you insert the worksheet, however, you can simply move the worksheet to the desired location. In addition, Excel understands that many times data in one worksheet can be used as a starting point in new worksheets and even other workbooks (or perhaps you need multiple sets of data); for this reason, it enables you to copy a worksheet.

TIP

Moving a Worksheet by Dragging
You can click a worksheet tab and drag it in front of or behind another worksheet tab to change its location. This is a lot faster if you need to rearrange your worksheets.

Saving a Workbook

Start

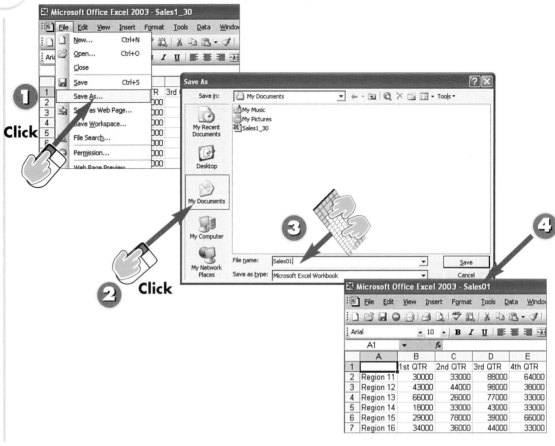

Click

Click

End

1 With the worksheet you want to save open in the Excel window, open the **File** menu and select **Save As** to open the Save dialog box.

2 Click the **My Documents** icon or, if necessary, move through the folder structure to save the file where you want (My Documents is the default on most computers).

3 In the **File Name** field, type a descriptive name for the file. Then, click the **Save** button.

4 The Excel title bar now contains your workbook's name.

INTRODUCTION

Until you save the workbook in which you are working, the data in the file is not stored on disk. You should regularly save your workbooks as you work in them so you don't lose your work. Also, after you save a workbook, you can retrieve it later to work on.

Using Save In Options

If you don't want to save your file in the My Documents directory, you can select the **Save in** drop-down list box and maneuver through your folders to save the file in a different location.

Using the Save Button

If you have already saved and named your file, you can resave it after making additional changes by clicking the **Save** button on the Standard toolbar.

Closing a Workbook

Start

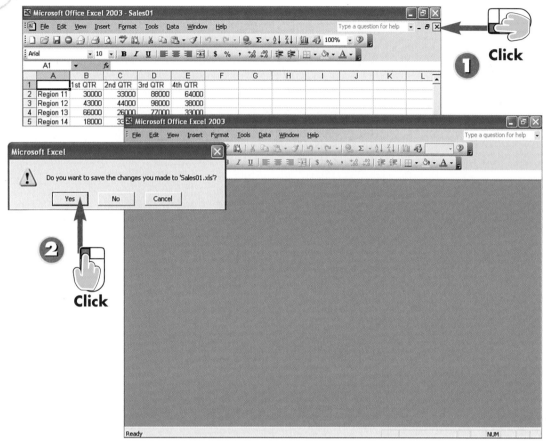

Click

Click

---

1 Click the **Close (x)** button in the document window. If you have edited the workbook since saving it last, Excel asks whether you want to save it.

2 Click the **Yes** button to save your changes; click **Cancel** to continue working in the document; or click **No** to close Excel without saving changes.

3 Excel closes the workbook.

End

When you finish working on a workbook, you can close it—with or without saving changes—and continue to work in the application. If you have been working in a workbook and try to close it, Excel asks you whether you want to save the workbook before it closes.

Program Window
Make sure you click the Close button in the document window, not the program window. Otherwise, you'll close all the open workbooks in Excel.

Available Buttons
When Excel has no workbooks open, only a few buttons are available on the Standard toolbar. As soon as you create a new workbook or open a workbook, the buttons become available again.

Creating a New Workbook

Start

Click

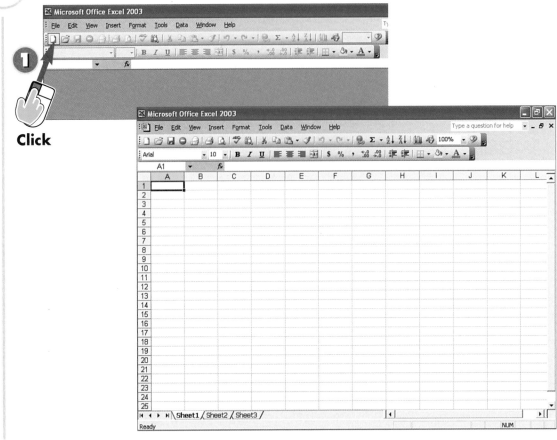

1 Click the **New** button on the Standard toolbar.

2 Excel opens a new blank workbook.

End

INTRODUCTION

Excel presents a new blank workbook each time you start the application. You can create another new workbook at any time, however. For example, when you save and close one workbook, you might want to begin a new one.

Sample Workbooks
For more options, open the **File** menu and select **New**. Then, peruse the options in the New Workbook Task pane. Click the link of the type of new workbook or template you want to create.

Understanding Default Filenames
The default filename for each new workbook (Book1, Book2, Book3, and so on) increases sequentially as you open new books. If you exit and restart Excel, the numbers begin at 1 again.

Opening a Workbook

Start

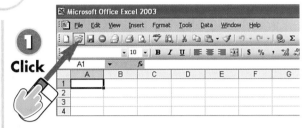

Click

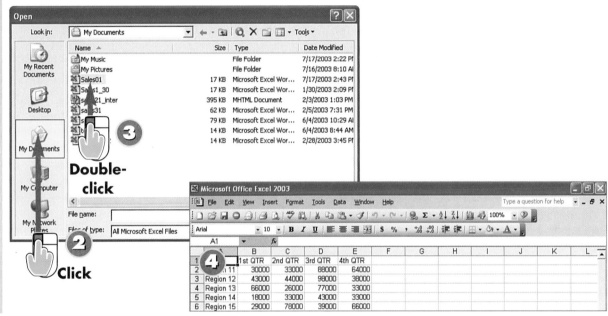

Double-click

Click

(1) Click the **Open** button on the Standard toolbar. The Open dialog box appears.

(2) Click the **My Documents** icon on the Places bar, or use the **Look in** drop-down list to move through the folders to find the file you want.

(3) Double-click the file you want to open.

(4) Excel opens the workbook.

End

INTRODUCTION

You have many options from which to choose in the Open dialog box. If necessary, click the **Look in** drop-down arrow and select a folder from the list. To move up a folder level, click the **Up One Level** button on the Open dialog box's toolbar.

TIP

Viewing Multiple Workbooks

Instead of constantly switching between workbooks, you can simultaneously view multiple workbooks onscreen in Excel. Select **Window**, **Arrange** to open the Arrange Windows dialog box. Then, select how you want the windows arranged (for example, **Horizontal**) and click **OK**. Click the title bar or in the body of the workbook in which you want to work to make it the active one (the active workbook is the one that displays a darker title bar); the active cell is then visible in the active workbook. To return to viewing only one workbook, double-click its title bar.

Editing Worksheets

The old paper-and-pencil method of calculating was time consuming because if you made a mistake or forgot something, you had to do a lot of erasing—maybe even redo the whole thing. With an electronic worksheet, however, you can easily make changes.

If you forget something, you can insert a cell, row, or column. You also can delete entries. You can change a value, find and replace data, and even check for spelling errors. Besides editing the data in your worksheets, you can add comments to remind yourself of information and track when changes are made and by whom.

Inserting Comments and Changes

Click to accept the currently reviewed tracked change

Click to reject the currently reviewed tracked change

Click to accept all tracked changes

Click to reject all tracked changes

Click to close stop reviewing tracked changes

Tracked change indicator

Current tracked change

Comment indicator

Visible comment

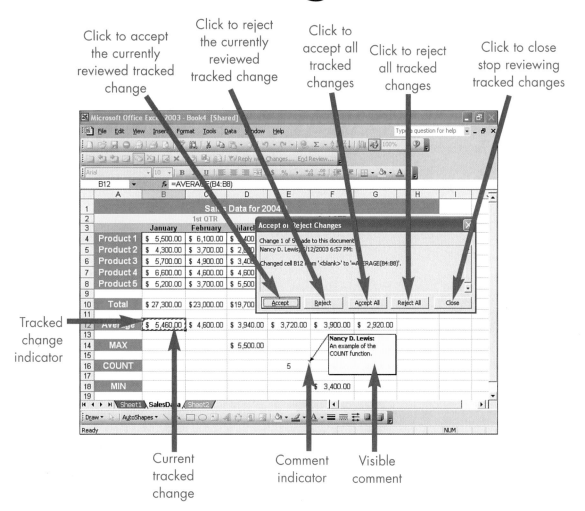

Inserting and Deleting Rows and Columns

Start

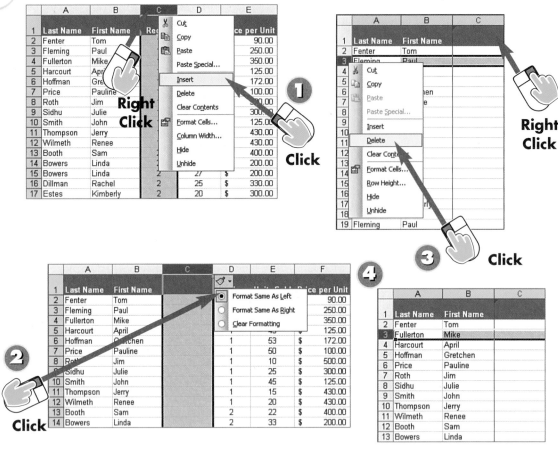

Right Click

Click

Right Click

Click

Click

Click

① Right-click a column header that you want to insert a column to the left of (or row header above, if inserting a row), and select **Insert** from the shortcut menu.

② The **Insert Options Format Painter** smart tag appears with the new column. Click it to format the new column like the one on the left or right, or with no formatting.

③ Right-click the row header (or column header) that you want to remove and select **Delete** from the shortcut menu.

④ The selected row (or column) is deleted.

End

Inserting Cells

Start

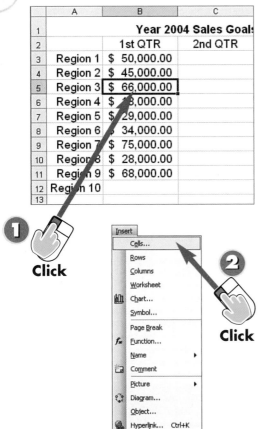

Click

Click

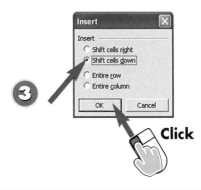

Click

Click

1. Click the spot in your worksheet where you want to insert a new cell (in this example, cell **B5** is selected).

2. Open the **Insert** menu and select **Cells** to open the Insert dialog box.

3. Choose how you want the surrounding cells shifted when the new cell is inserted—for example, **Shift Cells Down**—and click **OK**.

4. The existing cells shift down, and a new cell is inserted.

End

INTRODUCTION

There might be times when you are entering data into your worksheet and notice that you've typed the wrong information, so that you are off by one cell in a column or row. To avoid retyping all the data, or copying and pasting, you can insert new cells and shift the current cells to their correct locations.

Using the Shortcut Menu
Another way to insert a cell is to right-click the spot in your worksheet where you want the new cell to appear and select Insert from the shortcut menu that appears. The Insert dialog box opens, and you can proceed as normal.

Using the Insert Options Format Painter Smart Tag
When the new cell is inserted, the Insert Options Format Painter smart tag appears; click it to apply formatting to the inserted cell. Format the new cell like the cell above or below, or with no formatting.

Deleting Cells

Start

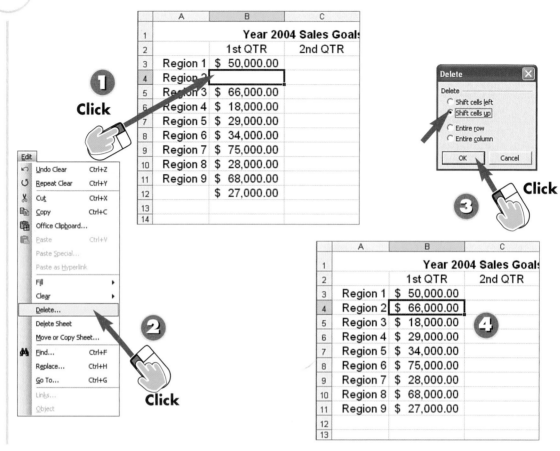

Click

Click

Click

1 Click the cell you want to delete (in this example, cell **B4**).

2 Open the **Edit** menu and select **Delete** to open the Delete dialog box.

3 Choose how you want the surrounding cells shifted when the selected cell is deleted—for example, **Shift Cells Up**—and click **OK**.

4 The selected cell is deleted, and other existing cells are shifted up.

End

As you work with worksheets, you might find that data needs to be eliminated to keep the worksheet up-to-date. Or you might accidentally add an extraneous cell of data in a row or column. To avoid typing all your data again, you can delete extraneous cells and shift other cells to their correct locations.

TIP

#REF! Error
If the **#REF!** error appears after you delete a cell, it means you deleted a cell or cells that contained data your worksheet needs to calculate a formula. To resolve the problem, undo the change; the task "Undoing and Redoing Changes" later in this part tells you how.

Using Merge and Center on Cells

Start

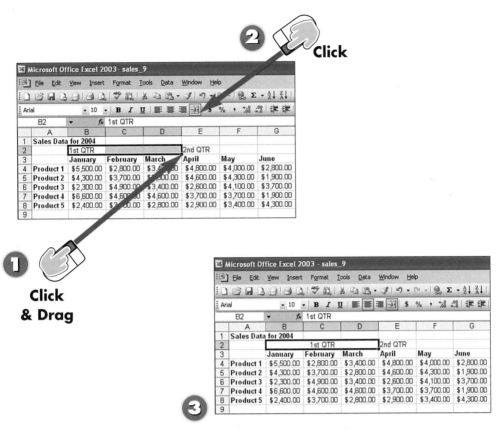

Click

Click & Drag

1. Select the cells you want to merge, including the cells that don't contain any data.

2. Click the **Merge and Center** button on the Formatting toolbar.

3. The cells in the group header are merged, and the data is centered. Repeat the steps in this task as needed to group additional columns in your worksheet.

End

INTRODUCTION

Using Excel's Merge and Center feature, you can group similar data under one heading. Columns of data usually have column headers, but they can also have group header information representing multiple columns.

Inserting a Row

If no blank row exists above the row of cells you want to merge and center, from step 1, click the row above which you want the new row to be placed, open the **Insert** menu, and select **Row**.

Undoing Merged and Centered Cells

Select the cells to separate. Next, open the **Format** menu, select **Cells**, click the **Alignment** tab, deselect the **Merge Cells** check box, and click **OK**.

Cutting, Copying, and Pasting Data

Start

Click 1

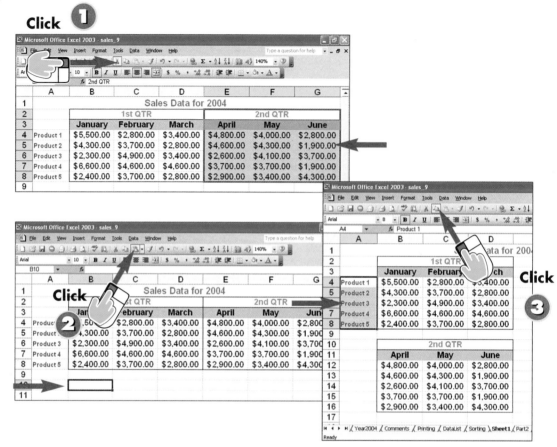

Click 2

Click 3

1. Select the cells you want to cut, and click the **Cut** button. These cells now display an active selection border.

2. Click in the worksheet where you want to paste the cut data, and click the **Paste** button.

3. The cut cells appear in the new location. Select the cells you want to copy and click the **Copy** button. The cells display an active selection border.

You can save the time and trouble of retyping duplicate information in a worksheet by cutting or copying cell text and data and pasting it. In addition to the cut, copy, and paste commands, use the Office Clipboard task pane to work with multiple items known as *scraps*. For example, if you need to copy two different selections of data from the beginning of a worksheet to two different locations toward the end of a worksheet, you can use the Clipboard to perform the procedure in fewer steps than if you were to copy and paste each separately.

Cutting Versus Copying

When you want to move (rather than copy) data from its current location to a new location, click the **Cut** button on the Standard toolbar. The Cut option removes the selected value from the old location.

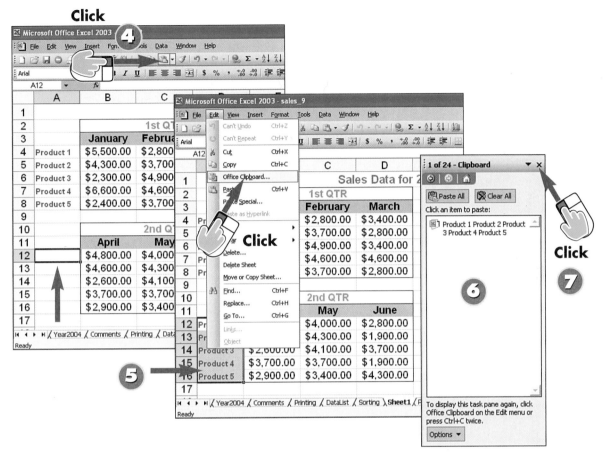

Click

4. Click in the worksheet where you want to paste the copied data, and click the **Paste** button.

5. The copied text is pasted in the new location. Unless it's displayed, open the **Edit** menu and select **Office Clipboard**.

6. The copied data displays on the Clipboard. Additional cut or copied items will display on the Clipboard; click each "scrap" to paste them.

7. Click the **Close (x)** button on the Clipboard task pane when finished.

End

Using the Paste Button
Use the Copy or Cut and Paste buttons on the Standard toolbar to perform a single cut/paste or copy/paste. The Clipboard task pane appears only when you click the Copy or Cut button multiple times before clicking the Paste button.

Using the Clipboard
If you want to clear all the items copied to the Clipboard, click the **Clear All** button in the Clipboard task pane. To paste all the items saved to the Clipboard in one location, click the **Paste All** button in the task pane.

Pasting Formulas
If you paste cells using the Ctrl+V keyboard shortcut, you can paste cell formulas. If you paste cells with formulas from the multielement Clipboard, you paste the values, not the formulas.

Moving Data

Start

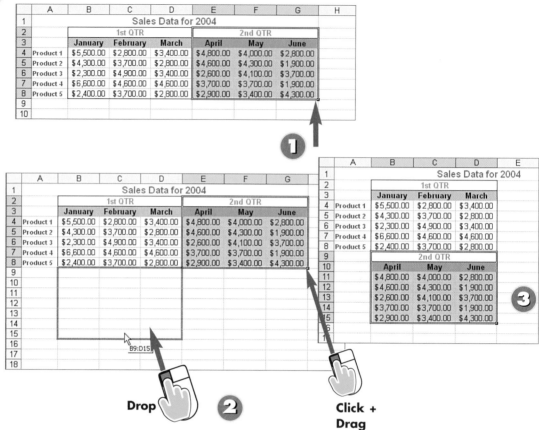

Drop (2) **Click + Drag**

(1) Select the cells that contain the data you want to move.

(2) Click the border of the selected cells, drag the cells to their new location, and release the mouse button to drop the data in the desired spot.

(3) The data is moved to the new location.

End

There are numerous reasons you might want to move data in a worksheet. For example, if the layout of your worksheet changes, you might need to move data accordingly. Excel lets you move information from one cell to another cell instead of retyping data in the new cell and then erasing the old data.

TIP

Undoing a Move
If you move the wrong data or move the data to the wrong location, click the **Undo** button on the Standard toolbar to undo the most recent move. Then start over.

Overwriting and Deleting Data

Start

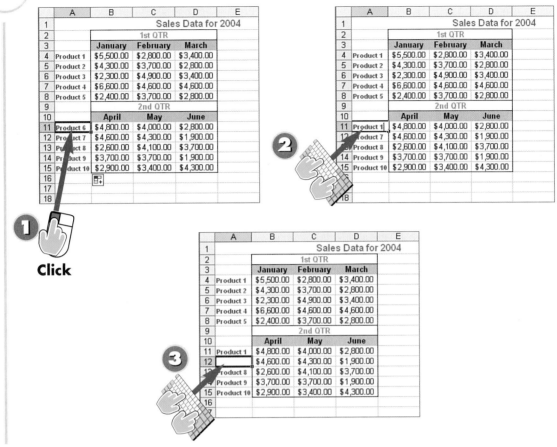

Click

End

1. Click the cell whose contents you want to overwrite.

2. Type the correct data into the cell and press the **Enter** key.

3. To delete the data in the selected cell, press the **Delete** key on your keyboard.

INTRODUCTION

When you *overwrite* a cell, you replace the cell's contents with new data. Overwriting is handy when you want to correct typing errors or when a cell contains the wrong data. You can also easily erase the contents of a cell by using the Delete key on your keyboard.

TIP

Overwriting Formulas
Be sure you don't overwrite a formula in a cell (unless that is your intention); otherwise, Excel will no longer update the formula. If you accidentally overwrite a formula but you've saved your spreadsheet recently, you can reopen a version of the spreadsheet that was saved before the overwrite operation occurred. Another option is to click the **Undo** button to undo the overwrite (see the task "Undoing and Redoing Changes" later in this chapter for more information).

PART 8

Inserting a Picture from a File

Start

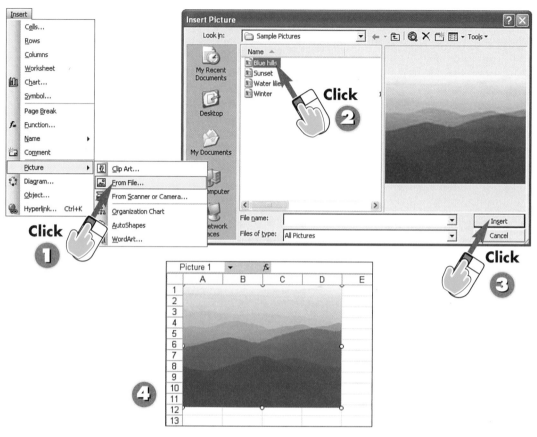

Click ❶

Click ❷

Click ❸

❹

❶ Open the **Insert** menu and select **Picture**, **From File** to open the Insert Picture dialog box.

❷ Locate the file you want to use, and click it to see a preview (you might need to select **Preview** from the dialog box **Views** button).

❸ Click **Insert**.

❹ The image is inserted into your worksheet.

End

Thanks to the proliferation of digital cameras, sharing pictures online has become more popular; likewise, you might want to insert a digital picture of your own into an Excel spreadsheet. You can insert many types of graphics files: Windows Metafiles, JPEG files, PNGs, Macintosh PICT files, Kodak Photo CD files, and many more.

Inserting Other Clip Art
Excel includes clip art you can add to your workbooks. Open the **Insert** menu and select **Picture, Clip Art**. The Clip Art task pane opens; scroll through the available images until you find one you like.

Resizing and Moving Graphics
The task "Resizing or Moving Objects" in Part 13 provides information about resizing and moving graphic objects in PowerPoint; the information in that task applies to Excel as well.

Undoing and Redoing Changes

Start

Click 1

Click 2

Click 3

Click 4

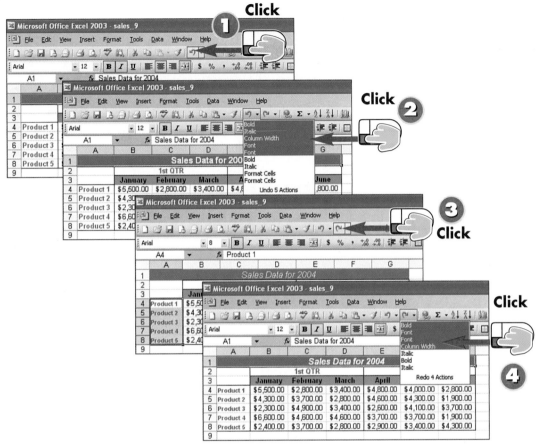

1. To undo your most recent action, click the **Undo** button on the Standard toolbar. Continue clicking the **Undo** button to undo more of your recent actions.

2. To undo multiple actions, click the down arrow next to the **Undo** button and select the number of actions to undo.

3. If you undo an action in error, click the **Redo** button on the Standard toolbar to redo the action. Continue clicking the **Redo** button to redo more actions.

4. To redo multiple actions, click the down arrow next to the **Redo** button and select the number of actions to redo.

End

If you make a mistake while working on your spreadsheet and you detect your error immediately, you can undo your action. In addition, if you undo an action by mistake, you can use Excel to quickly redo it.

Keyboard Undo
A quick and easy way to undo an action is to press the Ctrl+Z keyboard shortcut; you can redo an action by pressing Ctrl+Y.

Undo Not Available?
When you save your worksheet, the available actions in the Undo/Redo lists are erased, so be sure you are happy with any changes before you perform a save operation.

Finding Data

Start

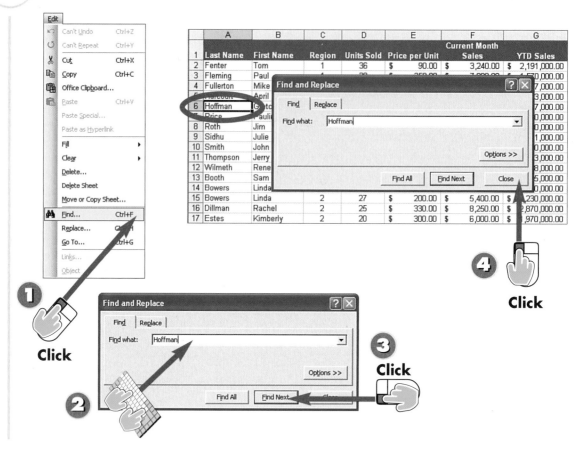

Click

Click

Click

1. Open the **Edit** menu and select **Find**. The Find and Replace dialog box opens with the Find tab displayed.

2. In the **Find What** text box, type the data you want to find (in this example, **Hoffman**).

3. Click the **Find Next** button.

4. Excel finds the first instance of the data and makes it the active cell. Click **Find Next** to search for the next instance, or click **Close** to end the search.

End

INTRODUCTION

Sometimes, you'll need to find specific information in a large spreadsheet. For example, suppose you want to quickly find the row that deals with sales data in Region 5 of your company. Instead of scanning each row for the data you need, which can be time-consuming, you can use Excel's Find feature.

TIP

Finding All Instances of Data
Click the **Find All** button in the Find and Replace dialog box to view a list, complete with cell locations and worksheet tab names, of all the instances of the data you entered in the Find What text box.

Replacing Data

Start

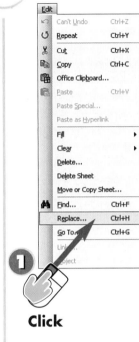

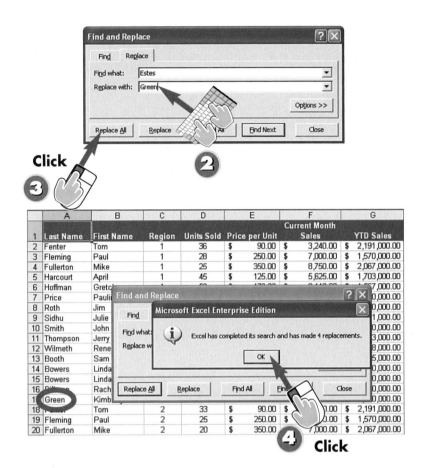

Click

Click

Click

Click

1. Open the **Edit** menu and select **Replace**. The Find and Replace dialog box opens with the Replace tab displayed.

2. In the **Find What** text box, type the data you want to find. Press the **Tab** key to move the cursor to the **Replace with** text box, and type the replacement data.

3. Click **Replace All** to replace all instances. (Or, click **Find Next** to find the first instance of the data, and then click **Replace** to replace it; repeat as necessary.)

4. Excel notifies you of the number of replacements it made; click **OK**. When you're finished using the Find and Replace dialog box, click its **Close** button to close it.

End

Perhaps you've misspelled a company's name in your worksheet or that a person you reference in several cells has gotten married and changed her name. Fortunately, Excel enables you to search for instances of incorrect or outdated data and replace it with new data using the Find and Replace feature.

TIP

Narrowing Search Criteria

Click the **Options** button on the Find and Replace dialog box to make your search criteria more specific. To conduct a case-sensitive search (for example, finding all instances of **Green** but not **green**), select the **Match Case** option. Select **Match Entire Cell Contents** to limit your search to cells that contain no more and no less than the data you type (for example, to find all instances of **Green** but not **Greenwood**).

Adding and Viewing Cell Comments

Start

	A	B	C	D	E	F	G
1	Last Name	First Name	Region	Units Sold	Price per Unit	Current Month Sales	YTD Sales
2	Fenter	Tom	1	36	$ 90.00	$ 3,240.00	$ 2,191,000.00
3	Fleming	Paul	1	28	$ 250.00	$ 7,000.00	
4	Fullerton	Mike	1	25	$ 350.00	$ 8,750.00	
5	Harcourt	April	1	45	$ 125.00	$ 5,625.00	
6	Hoffman	Gretchen	1	53	$ 172.00	$ 9,116.00	
7	Price	Pauline	1	50		$ 5,000.00	
8	Roth	Jim	1	10		$ 5,000.00	
9	Sidhu	Julie	1	25		$ 7,500.00	
10	Smith	John		45		$ 5,625.00	
11	Thompson	Jerry	1	15		$ 6,450.00	
12	Wilmeth	Renee	1	20		$ 8,600.00	
13	Booth	Sam	2	22		$ 8,800.00	
14	Bowers	Linda	2	33		$ 6,600.00	
15	Bowers	Linda	2	27		$ 5,400.00	
16	Dillman	Rachel	2	25		$ 8,250.00	
17	Green	Kimberly	2	20		$ 6,000.00	
18	Fenter	Tom	2	33		$ 2,970.00	
19	Fleming	Paul	2	25		$ 6,250.00	
20	Fullerton	Mike	2	20		$ 7,000.00	$ 2,067,000.00
21	Harcourt	April	2	37		$ 4,625.00	$ 1,703,000.00
22	Harmdon	Mendy	2	10		$ 5,000.00	$ 2,500,000.00
23	Hoffman	Gretchen	2	47		$ 8,084.00	$ 1,567,000.00
24	Lewis	Ella Mae	2	30		$ 10,500.00	$ 3,454,000.00

Shortcut menu:
- Cut
- Copy
- Paste
- Paste Special...
- Insert...
- Delete...
- Clear Contents
- Insert Comment
- Format Cells...
- Pick From List...
- Add Watch
- Create List...
- Hyperlink...

Right Click

1

2

Region	Units Sold	Price per Unit	Current Month Sales	
1	36	$ 90.00	$	3,240.00
1	28	$ 250.00	$	7,000.00
1	25	$ 350.00	$	8,750.00
1	45			5,625.00
1	53			9,116.00
1	50			5,000.00
1	10			5,000.00
1	25	$ 125.00	$	5,625.00

Nancy D. Lewis:
This is the highest number of units sold.

3

Region	Units Sold	Price per Unit	Current Month Sales
1	36	$ 90.00	$ 3,240.00
1	28	$ 250.00	$ 7,000.00
1	25	$ 350.00	$ 8,750.00
1	45	$ 125.00	$ 5,625.00
1	53	$ 172.00	$ 9,116.00
1	50	$ 100.00	$ 5,000.00
1	10	$ 500.00	$ 5,000.00
1	25	$ 300.00	$ 7,500.00
1	45	$ 125.00	$ 5,625.00
1	15	$ 430.00	$ 6,450.00
1	20	$ 430.00	$ 8,600.00
2	22	$ 400.00	$ 8,800.00
2	33	$ 200.00	$ 6,600.00

Click

4

Region	Units Sold	Price per Unit	Current Month Sales	
1	36	$ 90.00	$ 3,240.00	$
1	28	$ 250.00	$ 7,000.00	$
1	25	$ 350.00	$ 8,750.00	$
1	45			$
1	53			
1	50			
1	10			
1	25	$ 125.00	$ 5,625.00	$
1	45	$ 125.00	$ 5,625.00	$
1	15	$ 430.00	$ 6,450.00	$
1	20	$ 430.00	$ 8,600.00	$
2	22	$ 400.00	$ 8,800.00	$

Nancy D. Lewis:
This is the highest number of units sold.

End

1 Right-click the cell to which you want to add a comment, and select **Insert Comment** from the shortcut menu that appears.

2 Type the desired text into the comment area. When you're finished, click anywhere in the worksheet to accept the comment.

3 The cell's upper-right corner now contains a red triangle, indicating the presence of a comment.

4 To view the comment as a ScreenTip, move the mouse pointer over the triangle.

INTRODUCTION

Some cells contain data or formulas that require an explanation or special attention. *Comments* provide a way to attach this type of information to individual cells without cluttering the cells with extraneous information. A red triangle indicates that a cell contains a comment, which you can view in several ways.

TIP

Working with Comments
To quickly edit or delete a comment, right-click the cell that contains the comment marker and select the desired command (Edit Comment or Delete Comment) from the shortcut menu that appears.

TIP

Displaying Comments
You can make it so that Excel automatically displays the full text of a cell's comments while you work in the worksheet. To do so, right-click the commented cell and select **Show/Hide Comment** from the shortcut menu that appears.

Protecting and Sharing Workbooks

Start

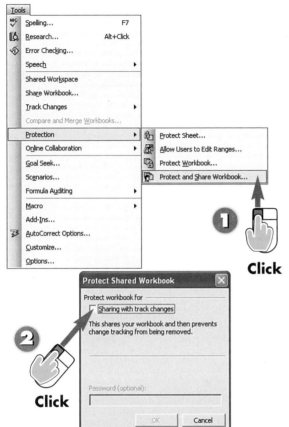

Click

Click

1. Open the **Tools** menu and select **Protection**, **Protect and Share Workbook**. The Protect Shared Workbook dialog box opens.

2. Click the **Sharing with Track Changes** check box to select it; this activates Excel's Track Changes feature and prevents others from turning off the feature.

3. To require people to enter a password to access your worksheet, type the password you want to use in the **Password (Optional)** text box and click **OK**.

4. The Confirm Password dialog box opens. Type the password you typed in step 3 and click **OK**. Excel notifies you that the workbook will be saved; click **OK**.

End

INTRODUCTION

If you share your workbooks with other users, you might want to protect your workbooks by restricting access to them and tracking changes made to them. Don't forget the passwords you assign to your workbooks; otherwise, you won't be able to access them!

TIP

File-sharing Options
Excel offers two other file-sharing options. Protect Sheet allows you to protect the contents and objects in a worksheet. Protect Workbook allows you to protect the structure and windows in a workbook.

TIP

Unprotecting a Workbook
To remove the protection from a workbook, open the **Tools** menu and select **Protection**, **Unprotect Shared Workbook** to open the Unprotect Sharing dialog box. Enter the correct password and click the **OK** button.

Tracking Changes

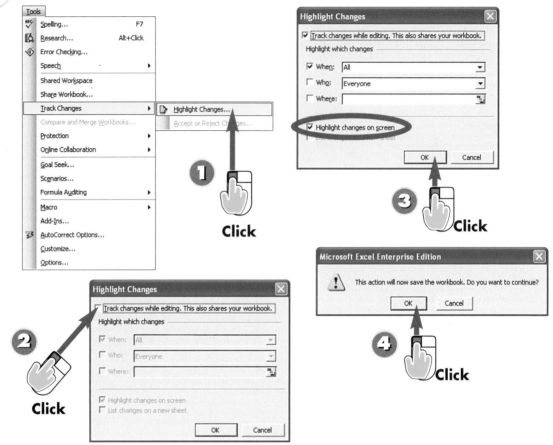

Click

Click

Click

Click

1. Open the **Tools** menu and select **Track Changes**, **Highlight Changes**. The Highlight Changes dialog box opens.

2. Click the **Track Changes While Editing** check box to select it.

3. The **Highlight Which Changes** options become available; click **OK** to accept the default options.

4. Excel notifies you that the workbook will be saved; click **OK**. The workbook is now shared with Track Changes enabled.

Suppose you're working on a team project and each member has access to the same workbook. To keep track of who makes what changes to the workbook, use Excel's Track Changes feature; each person's edits appear in a different color. An edit can be changing the current information or adding new information to the workbook.

No Track Changes While Editing Check Box?

If you already performed the steps in the task "Protecting and Sharing Workbooks" to protect your worksheet, the Track Changes While Editing check box featured in step 2 of this task will not be available because Excel's Track Changes feature has already been enabled.

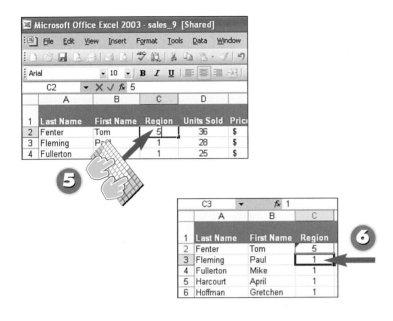

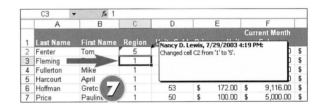

5 Notice that **[Shared]** is displayed next to the workbook filename. Type a change in a cell and press **Enter**.

6 The upper-left corner of the cell in which you typed now contains a comment marker (the blue triangle), and the cell is surrounded by a colored border.

7 Move the mouse pointer over the revised cell. A ScreenTip appears, showing the change that was made, who made the change, and when.

End

Rejecting Changes
If a member of your team has changed the value in a cell in error, you can reject the change; see the next task to learn how.

Stop Sharing/Tracking
Notice the word **[Shared]** in the title bar of your workbook, which indicates that other people can use it. This is useful in a network setting, in which others can access your worksheet via the network. When you turn on Excel's Track Changes feature, you share the workbook. To disable sharing and tracking, open the **Tools** menu and select **Track Changes**, **Highlight Changes**. In the Highlight Changes dialog box, deselect the **Track Changes While Editing** check box.

Accepting or Rejecting Tracked Changes

Start

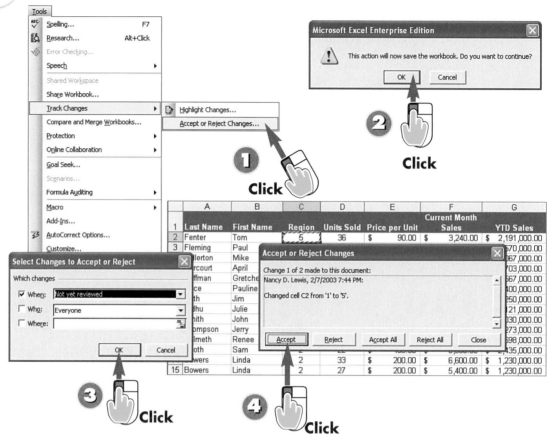

1 Open the **Tools** menu and select **Track Changes**, **Accept or Reject Changes**.

2 Excel notifies you that the workbook will be saved; click **OK**. (If you have already saved your changes to the workbook, you won't get this message.)

3 The Select Changes to Accept or Reject dialog box opens. Click **OK** to accept the default options.

4 Excel locates the first changed cell in your worksheet. To accept the change, click **Accept**; to reject it, click **Reject**. When you're finished, click **Close**.

End

INTRODUCTION

When you are ready to finalize a worksheet containing tracked changes, you must determine which changes you want to keep, or *accept*, and which you want to reject. When you reject a change, Excel restores the cell to its previous value.

TIP

Accepting or Rejecting All Changes
To accept all the changes made to your workbook in one fell swoop, click the **Accept All** button in the Accept or Reject Changes dialog box. To reject all the changes, click the **Reject All** button.

Checking Spelling

Start

Click

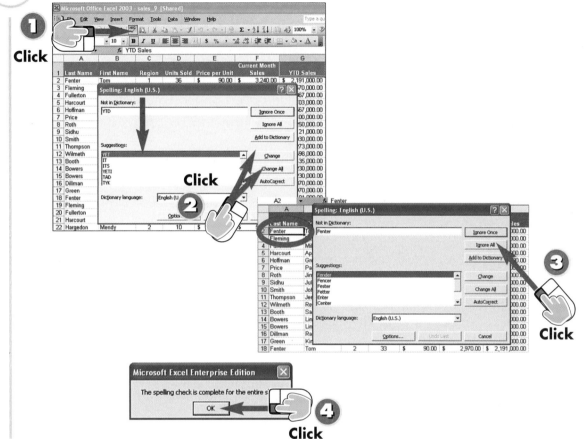

Click

Click

Click

Microsoft Excel Enterprise Edition

The spelling check is complete for the entire s

OK

Click

1. Click the **Spelling** button on the Standard toolbar. The Spelling dialog box opens, displaying the first spelling error it finds and suggested replacements.

2. If the correct spelling of the word appears in the **Suggestions** list, click the word and click **Change**. (Click **Change All** to correct all instances of the word.)

3. Excel finds the next spelling error. If a word is spelled correctly (for example, a proper name), click **Ignore Once**. (Click **Ignore All** to ignore all instances.)

4. As Excel continues locating spelling errors, change or ignore them as necessary. Excel notifies you when all inaccuracies have been reviewed; click **OK**.

End

INTRODUCTION

If your worksheet is for your eyes only, you might not think that misspellings are a big deal. But if you plan to turn your worksheet over to your manager, she might not think the mistakes are so minor. Fortunately, you can use Excel to check your spelling quickly and easily.

TIP

Checking from Beginning
You don't have to start at the beginning of a workbook to check for spelling errors. If you start in the middle of a workbook, Excel checks until it reaches the end and then asks whether you want to continue checking from the beginning.

HINT

Adding Dictionary Words
If you notice that Excel incorrectly flags a certain word as a misspelling, you can add that word to the Office dictionary Excel uses to check your spelling. To do so, click the **Add to Dictionary** button in the Spelling dialog box.

Working with Data and Charts

In Excel, a *formula* calculates a value based on the values in other cells of the workbook. Excel displays the result of a formula in a cell as a numeric value.

A *function* is an abbreviated formula that performs a specific operation on a group of values. Excel provides more than 250 functions that can help you with tasks ranging from determining loan payments to calculating investment returns.

You've already learned the fundamentals of creating a worksheet, so now you can concentrate on some of the other features that add to the data presentation. For example, you can create a chart based on data in a worksheet. Charts are very useful for interpreting data; however, different people look at data in different ways. To account for this, you can quickly change the appearance of charts in Excel by clicking directly on the chart. You can change titles, legend information, axis points, category names, and more.

The *axes* are the grid on which the data is plotted. On a 2D chart, the y-axis is the vertical axis on a chart (the *value axis*) and the x-axis is the horizontal axis (the *category axis*). A 3D chart has these two axes, plus a z-axis. You can control all the aspects of the axes—the appearance of the line, the tick marks, the number format used, and more.

Formatting Numbers and Charts

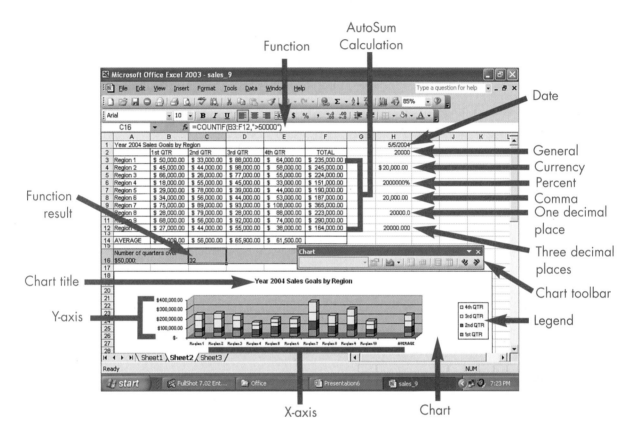

Formatting the Display of Numeric Data

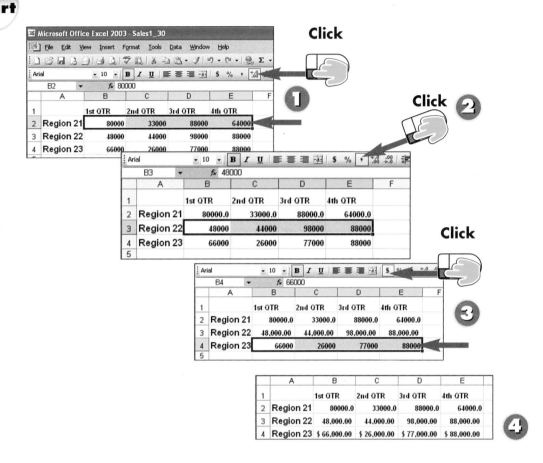

1. Select the cells in which you want to increase the number of decimals displayed, and click the **Increase Decimal** button once for each additional decimal place.

2. Select the cells in which you want to apply commas to your numeric data, and click the **Comma Style** button.

3. Select the cells in which you want to apply currency formatting (commas, two decimal places, and a dollar sign $), and click the **Currency Style** button.

4. The numeric data formatting options are applied to the selected cells.

End

INTRODUCTION

You can alter the display of different numbers depending on the type of data the cells contain. This can also make it easier to read. For example, sales numbers can be displayed in a currency format, and scientific data can be displayed with commas and decimal points.

TIP

Percent Style
If you click the Percent Style button on the Formatting toolbar, your numbers are converted to a percentage and displayed with a % symbol.

TIP

Choosing Other Styles
You can choose from numerous other styles to apply to data. To see the other styles, select **Format**, **Cells** and click through the many Category options.

Performing Calculations with AutoSum

Start

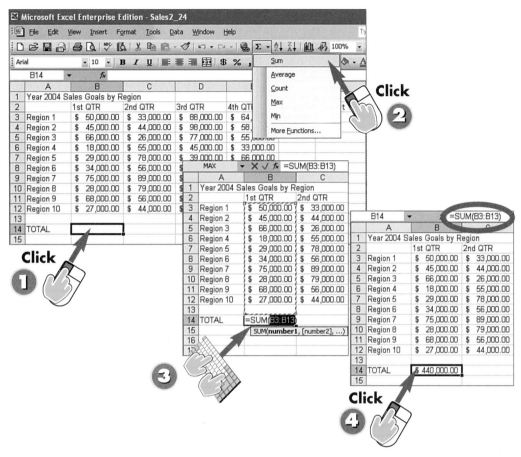

Click **2**

Click **1**

3

Click **4**

1 Click the cell in which you want the AutoSum function to appear.

2 Click the **AutoSum** button on the Standard toolbar and select the preferred function from the drop-down list (in this example, **Sum**).

3 If Excel automatically selected the correct range (the selected range is surrounded with a flashing dotted line), press the **Enter** key. If not, see the tip at the bottom of the page.

4 Click the cell containing the function. Notice that the formula is displayed in the Formula bar.

End

INTRODUCTION

Excel can use formulas and functions to perform calculations for you. Because a formula refers to the cells themselves rather than to the values they contain, Excel updates the sum whenever you change the values in the cells. You'll probably use the AutoSum formula frequently—it adds numbers in a range of cells.

TIP

Selecting Specific AutoSum Cells
If you don't want to use the range of cells AutoSum selects for you, click the first cell you want, hold down the **Ctrl** key, and click each additional cell you want to include in the calculation. When you finish selecting the cells you want to calculate, press **Enter**. For more information on selecting cells, see "Selecting Cells" and "Selecting a Range of Cells" in Part 7, "Getting Started with Excel."

Entering a Formula

Start

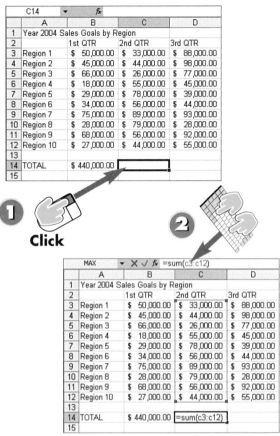

Click

1. Click the cell in which you want the formula to appear.

2. In the Formula bar, type **=sum(C3:C12)** (which translates to "add the values in cells C3 through C12") and press **Enter**.

3. The values in the specified cells are added together.

End

INTRODUCTION

There might be times when you don't want to use AutoSum because you want to perform calculations on specific cell references. In these instances, you can simply type the desired formula directly into the cell. You can include any cells in your formula; they do not have to be next to each other. Also, you can combine mathematic operations—for example, C3+C4–D5. After you enter a formula, if you change the values in the referenced cells, Excel automatically recalculates the value of the formula based on your changes.

TIP

Canceling a Formula
If you start to enter a formula and then decide you don't want to use it, you can cancel it by pressing the Esc key.

Copying a Formula

Start

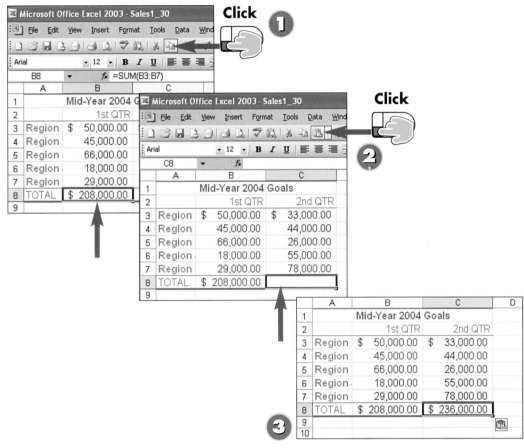

Click **1**

Click **2**

3

1 Select the cell that contains the formula you want to copy, and click the **Copy** button on the Standard toolbar.

2 Select the cell (or multiple cells) into which you want to paste the formula, and click the **Paste** button.

3 The formula automatically performs the calculation on similarly located data, placing the results into the selected cell(s).

End

INTRODUCTION

When you build your worksheet, you might want to use the same data and formulas in more than one cell. With Excel's Copy command, you can create the initial data or formula once and then place copies of this information in the appropriate cells.

TIP

Order of Operation
Excel first performs any calculations within parentheses. Then, it performs multiplication or division calculations, from left to right. Finally, it performs any addition or subtraction, from left to right.

Entering a Function

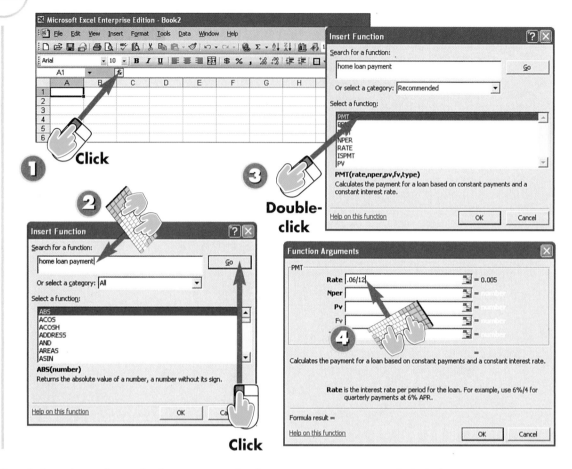

1 Select the cell in which you want the function to appear, and click the **Insert Function** button to open the Insert Function dialog box.

2 If you don't know the name of the function you want to use, type a brief description of it in the **Search for a Function** box and click **Go**.

3 The recommended function (in this case, PMT) is highlighted in the Select a Function list. Read the function's description to ensure that it's the one you want. If so, double-click it.

4 The Function Arguments dialog box opens. Click in the **Rate** field and type, for example, **.06/12** for a 6% interest loan with monthly payments.

A function is one of Excel's many built-in formulas for performing a specialized calculation on the data in your worksheet. For example, instead of totaling your sales data, suppose you want to determine the average of each quarter per region (the Average function), the highest sales numbers for the year (the Max function), or the lowest sales numbers for the year (the Min function). Or perhaps, as in this task, you want to find how much your payment would be on a home loan given a specific interest rate (Rate), number of periods (Nper), and price (Present Value). (Note that this calculates only the principal and interest portion for your home loan payment [PMT]).

TIP

Opening the Insert Function Dialog Box
You can also select AutoSum, More Functions on the Standard toolbar to open the Insert Function dialog box, or you can select Insert, Function.

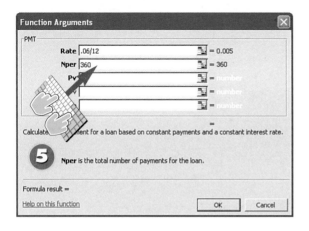

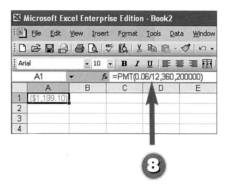

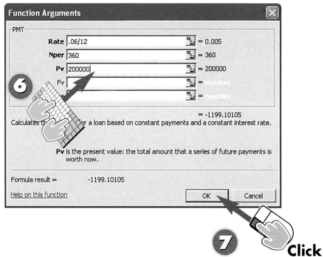

Click

5 Assuming the loan is a 30-year loan, click in the **Nper** field and type, for example, **360** (12 months times 30 years on the loan).

6 Click in the **Pv** field and type **200000** for a $200,000 loan. You can leave any fields blank that are not bolded.

7 Click **OK**.

8 The calculation of the payment function is displayed in the cell and in the Formula bar.

End

Correcting Formula and Function Errors

Start

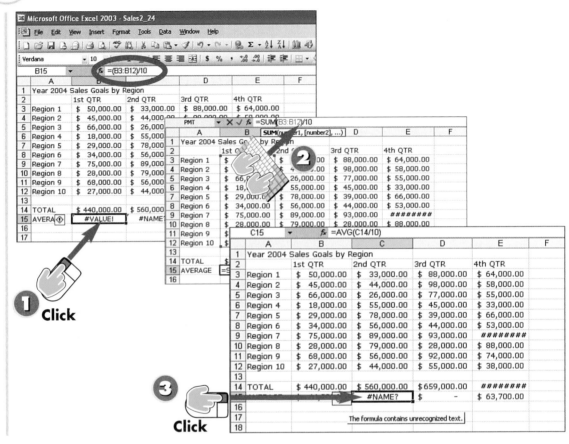

1 Click

2

3 Click

1 Click a cell with a **#VALUE!** message and review the cell's formula in the Formula bar. Can you find the error?

2 To add the values C2 through C12 and divide by 10, the formula must include "SUM" in the function. Type **SUM** in the Formula Bar and press **Enter**.

3 Click a cell with a **#NAME?** message. Move the mouse pointer over the cell to review a ScreenTip about the error.

INTRODUCTION

Excel notifies you when there are errors in your data by displaying different error descriptions. **#VALUE?** means the formula in the cell contains either nonnumeric data or cell/function names that cannot be used in the calculation. **#NAME?** means the formula contains incorrectly spelled cell/function names. **#REF!** indicates that the formula contains a reference to a cell that isn't valid. **####** means the column is not wide enough to display the data. **#DIV/0!** means that the formula is trying to divide a number by 0 or that the formula is referencing an empty cell.

TIP

Tracing Errors
Check formulas by tracing precedents (all cells that are referenced [in order] in the formula). You can also trace dependents (start with a cell that is referenced in a formula, and then trace all the cells that reference that cell).

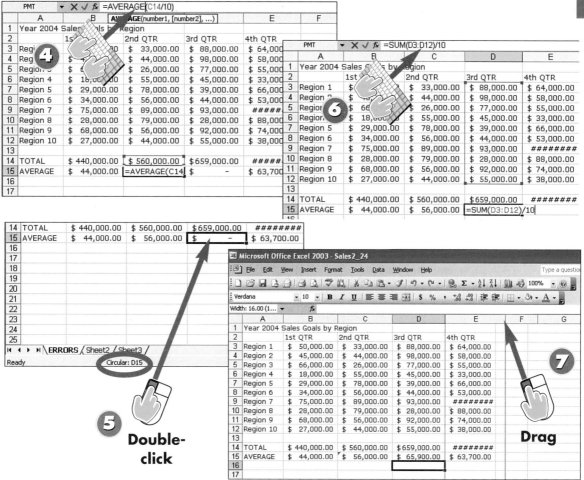

Double-click

Drag

4️⃣ In this example, **avg** is not the correct name of the desired function; the correct name is **average**. In the Formula bar, replace **avg** with **average** and press **Enter**.

5️⃣ If the status bar displays a Circular reference error (for example, Circular: D15), double-click the cell it references.

6️⃣ In this case, the formula is referencing its own cell. Type the correct formula in the Formula bar (in this example, **=SUM(D3:D12)/10**) and press **Enter**.

7️⃣ If a cell displays **#####**, the column isn't wide enough to display all the cell's data. Click and drag the column border to make it wider, and the error is gone.

End

Performing a Trace
Click the cell with the error, select **Tools**, **Formula Auditing**, and select either **Trace Precedents** or **Trace Dependents**.

Circular References
The formula for cell E15 in this task is the average for fourth-quarter sales for the 10 regions, displayed as follows: =E14/10. If you instead wrote this formula as =E3:E12/10, it would still be correct (E14 just happens to be the total for the regions). But, if you accidentally wrote =E3:E15/10, including the cell in which you want the answer, there would be a circular reference. You cannot produce an answer for cell E15 while including it in the calculation; the answer would go round and round, continuously changing—hence the name *circular reference*.

Inserting Charts

Start

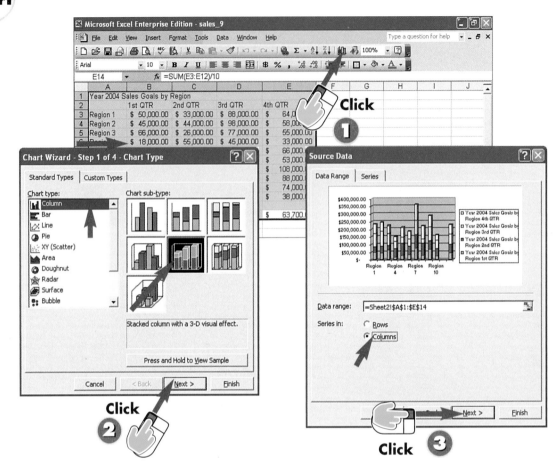

Click 1

Click 2

Click 3

1 Select the cells you want to include in your chart, and click the **Chart Wizard** button on the Standard toolbar.

2 The first page of the Chart Wizard opens. Select a type from the **Chart Type** list and the **Chart Sub-type** list; then click **Next**.

3 Depending on how you want your information to display in the chart, select either **Rows** or **Columns** in the **Series in** area; then click **Next**.

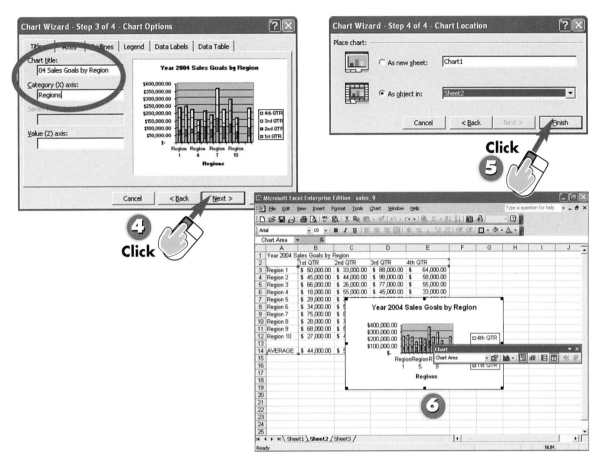

Click 5

Click 4

Click 6

4 Type a **Chart title**, a value for the **Category (X) axis**, and any other values you want; then click **Next**.

5 Click the **As New Sheet** option button to enter the chart as a new sheet, or click the **As Object in** option button to enter the chart in the sheet you select. Click **Finish**.

6 Excel creates the chart, displaying it along with a Chart toolbar.

End

Moving a Chart
Regardless of your selection in step 8, you can always move your chart to another (perhaps new) worksheet. To move your chart to a new worksheet, simply right-click a blank area in the chart and select **Location** from the shortcut menu that appears. Click the **As New Sheet** option in the Chart Location dialog box, and type in a new worksheet name. If you want to move it to a different worksheet, click the **As Object in** option and select the worksheet name from the drop-down list. Click **OK**, and Excel places the chart on a new worksheet.

Using the Back and Cancel Buttons
At any time while using the Chart Wizard, you can click the Back button to return to previous screens or the Cancel button to start over. Click the Finish button at any time and add information to your chart afterward.

Editing Charts with the Chart Toolbar

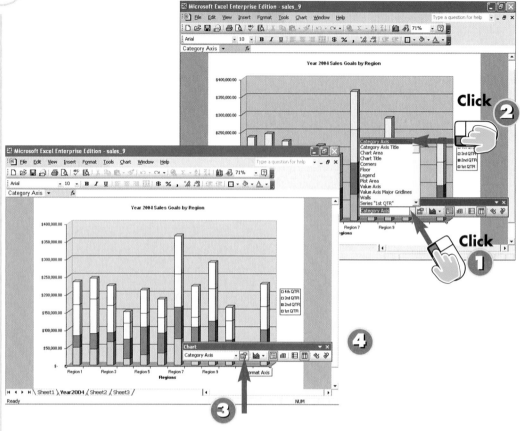

1 Click the **Chart Objects** down arrow and select the object in the chart you want to edit (scroll through the list if necessary).

2 After you select the object, for example, the **Category Axis**, you can use the other buttons on the Chart toolbar to make changes to it.

3 Move the mouse pointer over the rest of the buttons on the Chart toolbar to see ScreenTips of the other types of edits you can make to your chart.

4 Format the object, alter the chart type, add a legend and/or data table, swap the series data by row or by column, and change text objects' direction angle.

INTRODUCTION

Charts are useful for interpreting data, but different people look at data in different ways. To accommodate different users, you can change titles, legend information, axis points, category names, and more. The Chart toolbar—which you can activate by opening the View menu and selecting Toolbars, Chart—lists all the items in your chart that you can alter. Simply indicate which chart object you want to alter, and then click the appropriate button. If you don't know the name of the item you want to format on your chart, simply click the object on the chart and the name will appear in the Chart Objects list box on the Chart toolbar.

TIP

Double-Clicking the Chart
One of the fastest ways to edit a chart's options is to double-click the element in the chart you want to alter. The appropriate dialog box opens, enabling you to make the changes you need.

Using AutoCalculate

Start

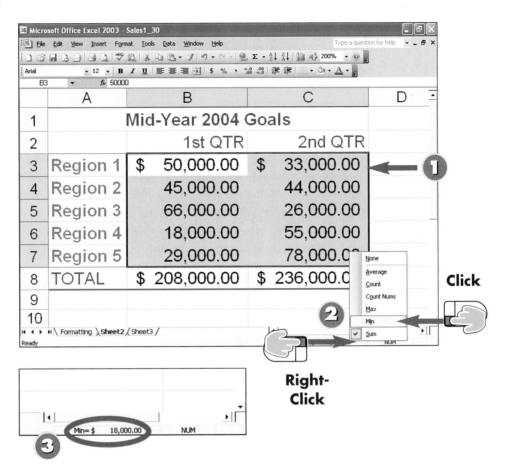

Click

Right-Click

① Select the cells you want to AutoCalculate.

② Right-click the status bar and select the **AutoCalculate** option from the shortcut menu. (The default AutoCalculate operation is to sum the numbers.)

③ The status bar displays the selected calculation, for example, the lowest number in the selection **(Min = $18,000.00)**.

End

INTRODUCTION

Suppose you want to see a function performed on some of your data—in this example, to determine the lowest quarterly sales goal of any region in 2004—but you don't want to add the function directly into the worksheet. Excel's AutoCalculate feature can help.

TIP

Turning Off AutoCalculate
AutoCalculate continues to work until you turn it off. You can turn off the AutoCalculate feature by selecting None from the AutoCalculate shortcut menu.

Sorting Data Lists

Start

Click ②

Click ③

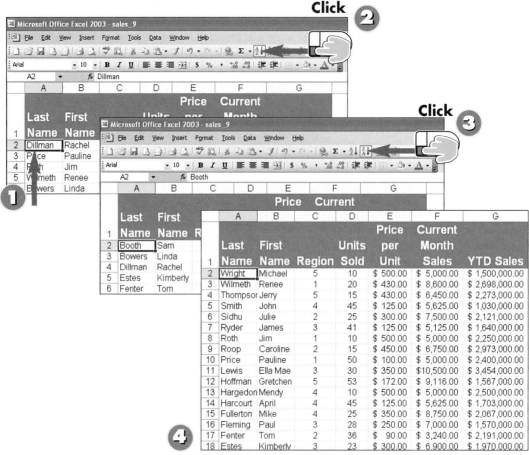

④

① Select a cell in the column you want sorted alphabetically or numerically (depending on whether the sort column contains text data or numeric data).

② Click the **Sort Ascending** button on the Standard toolbar.

③ The data is sorted alphabetically from A to Z or numerically from the lowest amount to the highest. Click the **Sort Descending** button.

④ This sorts the data alphabetically from Z to A, or numerically from the highest amount to the lowest.

End

INTRODUCTION

You can easily change the order of the data in your worksheet. If, for example, you want to alphabetically arrange the names in a data list of sales representatives, you can sort on Last Name. Alternatively, you might want to sort your sales representatives by the region in which they work or by YTD sales.

TIP

Sorting on Multiple Columns
To sort on multiple columns of data, select **Data, Sort** to open the Sort dialog box. Select the first **Sort by** column name (for example, **Region**) from the drop-down list box; then choose up to two more options from the **Then by** drop-down list box (for example, **YTD Sales**). Make sure you indicate whether you have a header row (if not, the columns will list as Column1, Column2, and so on), and click the **OK** button to perform the sort on your data.

Freezing Rows and Columns

Start

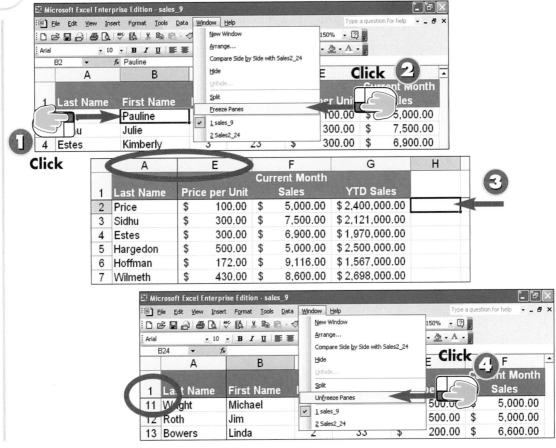

1 Click the cell to the right of and below the area you want to freeze. (Typically, this is cell B2 if your main header row is Row 1 and your main column is Column A.)

2 Open the **Window** menu and select **Freeze Panes**.

3 Move through the worksheet using the arrow keys on your keyboard. Frozen Row 1 and Column A enables you to view your data without losing sight of the titles.

4 Open the **Window** menu and select **Unfreeze Panes** to unfreeze the columns and rows.

End

INTRODUCTION

Many of your worksheets might be large enough that you cannot view all the data onscreen at the same time. In addition, if the worksheet contains row or column titles and you scroll down or to the right, some of the titles are too far to the top or left of the worksheet for you to see.

TIP

Splitting a Worksheet

By splitting a worksheet, you can scroll independently into different horizontal and vertical parts of a worksheet. This is useful if you want to view different parts of a worksheet or copy and paste between different areas of a large worksheet. Simply unfreeze the panes, and then open the **Window** menu and select **Split**. You can move the split bars by clicking and dragging them as necessary.

Preparing for Printing Worksheets

Excel's Print Preview mode is a convenient way to prepare your workbooks and worksheets for printing, without having to print numerous copies to get it right. Using Print Preview mode, you can access all the printing options and even make changes that will be saved with your worksheet in case it's printed again in the future.

In Excel, you can print your worksheets by using a basic printing procedure, or you can enhance the printout with several print options. Options for setting up the printed page include orientation (portrait or landscape), scaling, paper size, and page numbering. You can use these options to change how the worksheet is printed on the page or even so that your multipage worksheet prints on a single page.

There are also sheet options that control which elements of your worksheet are printed—gridlines, notes, row headings, and so on. You might want to make some changes to these options depending on how you want your printout to look. Another common change is to repeat column or row headings on a multipage worksheet. On worksheets that span two pages, the information on the second page might not make sense without proper headings.

Using Print Preview Mode

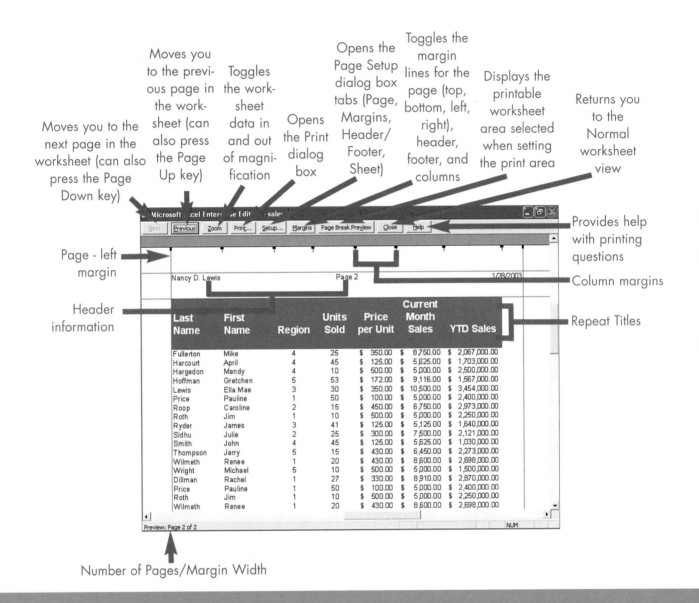

Moves you to the next page in the worksheet (can also press the Page Down key)

Moves you to the previous page in the worksheet (can also press the Page Up key)

Toggles the worksheet data in and out of magnification

Opens the Print dialog box

Opens the Page Setup dialog box tabs (Page, Margins, Header/Footer, Sheet)

Toggles the margin lines for the page (top, bottom, left, right), header, footer, and columns

Displays the printable worksheet area selected when setting the print area

Returns you to the Normal worksheet view

Provides help with printing questions

Page - left margin

Header information

Number of Pages/Margin Width

Column margins

Repeat Titles

Microsoft Excel Enterprise Edition - sales

| Next | Previous | Zoom | Print... | Setup... | Margins | Page Break Preview | Close | Help |

Nancy D. Lewis   Page 2   1/28/2003

Last Name	First Name	Region	Units Sold	Price per Unit	Current Month Sales	YTD Sales
Fullerton	Mike	4	25	$ 350.00	$ 8,750.00	$ 2,067,000.00
Harcourt	April	4	45	$ 125.00	$ 5,625.00	$ 1,703,000.00
Hargedon	Mendy	4	10	$ 500.00	$ 5,000.00	$ 2,500,000.00
Hoffman	Gretchen	5	53	$ 172.00	$ 9,116.00	$ 1,567,000.00
Lewis	Ella Mae	3	30	$ 350.00	$ 10,500.00	$ 3,454,000.00
Price	Pauline	1	50	$ 100.00	$ 5,000.00	$ 2,400,000.00
Roop	Caroline	2	15	$ 450.00	$ 6,750.00	$ 2,973,000.00
Roth	Jim	1	10	$ 500.00	$ 5,000.00	$ 2,250,000.00
Ryder	James	3	41	$ 125.00	$ 5,125.00	$ 1,640,000.00
Sidhu	Julie	2	25	$ 300.00	$ 7,500.00	$ 2,121,000.00
Smith	John	4	45	$ 125.00	$ 5,625.00	$ 1,030,000.00
Thompson	Jerry	5	15	$ 430.00	$ 6,450.00	$ 2,273,000.00
Wilmeth	Renee	1	20	$ 430.00	$ 8,600.00	$ 2,698,000.00
Wright	Michael	5	10	$ 500.00	$ 5,000.00	$ 1,500,000.00
Dillman	Rachel	1	27	$ 330.00	$ 8,910.00	$ 2,870,000.00
Price	Pauline	1	50	$ 100.00	$ 5,000.00	$ 2,400,000.00
Roth	Jim	1	10	$ 500.00	$ 5,000.00	$ 2,250,000.00
Wilmeth	Renee	1	20	$ 430.00	$ 8,600.00	$ 2,698,000.00

Preview: Page 2 of 2   NUM

Using Print Preview

Start

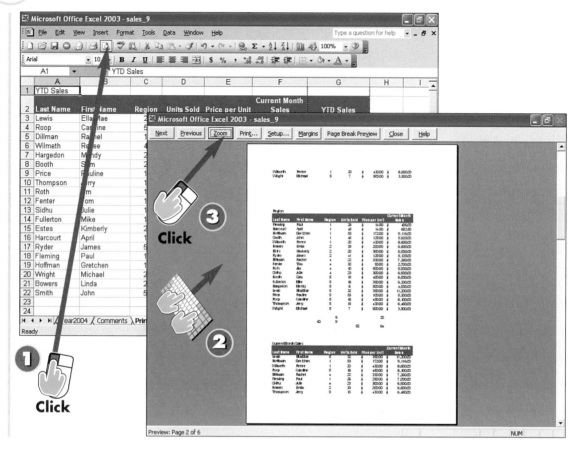
Click

Click

1 With the worksheet you want to print open on your desktop, click the **Print Preview** button on the Standard toolbar.

2 The Print Preview window opens, displaying the worksheet in Print Preview mode. Press the **Page Up** and **Page Down** keys to view the pages in your worksheet.

3 Click the **Zoom** button to toggle between increasing and decreasing the worksheet size. You can also simply click once on the worksheet to zoom in.

Workbooks or worksheets with a lot of data can generate large print jobs, possibly containing hundreds of pages. Waiting until all these pages are printed to verify that the information is printed correctly can cost a lot in both time and printing supplies. To help prevent printing mistakes, use Print Preview to ensure that all the necessary elements appear on the pages being printed.

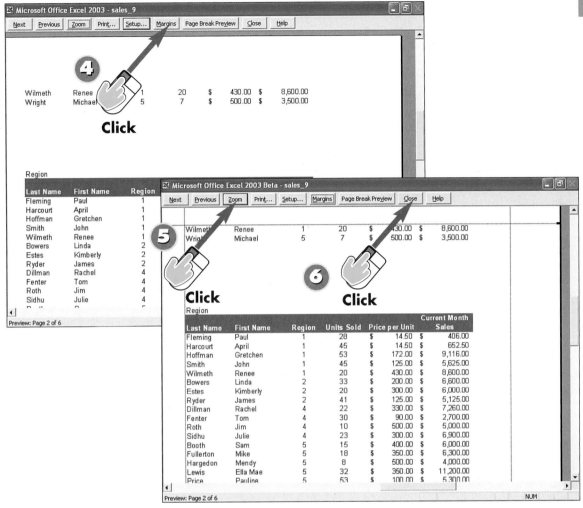

④ Click the **Margins** button to display the current worksheet margins. (For more information about working with margins, see p. 162.)

⑤ Click **Zoom** again to toggle between increasing and decreasing the size of the worksheet in Print Preview mode; here you zoom out. You can also click the worksheet once.

⑥ Click the **Close** button to exit Print Preview mode.

End

> **Using the Page Break Preview Button**
> Clicking the Page Break Preview button takes you from Normal view to Page Break Preview view, in which you can see exactly what is selected to print (in the print area). If you haven't set the print area, see the next task, "Setting the Print Area." If you are already in Page Break Preview view when you click the Print Preview button, the toolbar button will display Normal view instead, which shows your entire worksheet (regardless of whether you have set the print area).

Setting the Print Area

Start

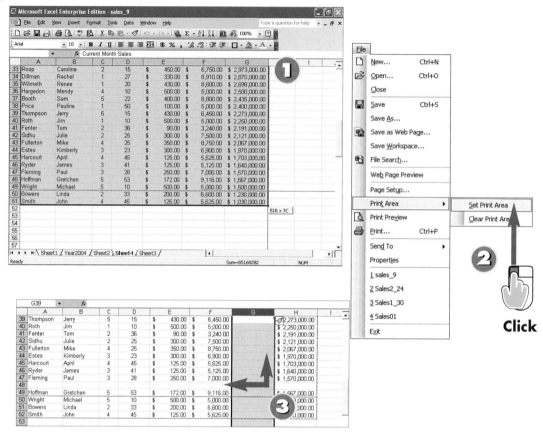

Click

1. Select the cells you want to print (in this example, all the cells in the first two tables in this worksheet).

2. Open the **File** menu and select **Print Area**, **Set Print Area** to store the print area. Every time you print this worksheet, only the cells in the print area will print.

3. Insert a row and column into your worksheet. Parts of the table now fall outside the current print area.

Worksheets can include several rows and columns, and setting the print area enables you to specify which rows and columns to print. If you don't set a print area, all cells that contain data will be printed.

TIP

Choosing the Print Area
You can also select the print area from the Page Setup dialog box (select **File**, **Page Setup** and select the **Sheet** tab) as long as you aren't in Print Preview mode.

TIP

Using Print Preview Mode
You can also set your print area by clicking the **Page Break Preview** button in Print Preview mode. Then, click and drag the page break indicators to the locations you prefer to print in your worksheet.

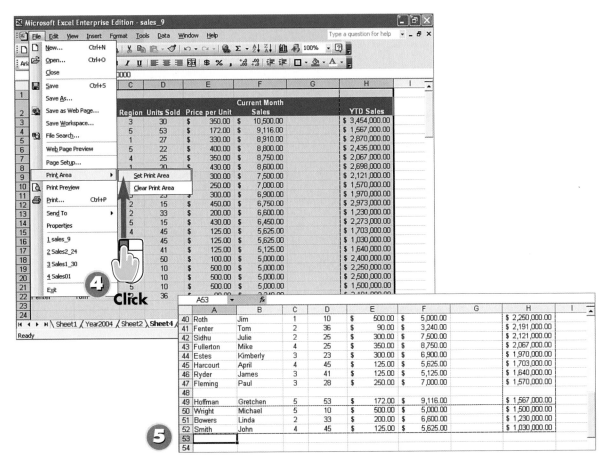

4 To reset the print area to include the new row or column, again choose the cells you want to print, and select **File**, **Print Area**, **Set Print Area**.

5 Your print area is again stored as part of this worksheet.

End

Long and Short Dashes
The long dashed lines in your worksheet indicate the print area, whereas the smaller dashed lines indicate the current page margins. If your print area data (long dashed lines) falls outside the current page margins (short dashed lines), you will need to alter the page margins (see the next task).

Clearing the Print Area
If you need to set the print area to print a portion of data in your worksheet only once, you will probably want to clear the print area after you print. Simply open the **File** menu and select **Print Area**, **Clear Print Area**.

Setting Page Margins

Start

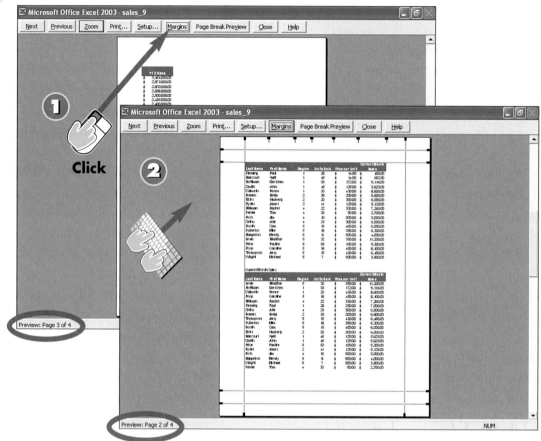

1 Click

2

Preview: Page 3 of 4

Preview: Page 2 of 4

NUM

1 In Print Preview mode, if you find a page whose print area exceeds the page margins, click the **Margins** button.

2 Excel activates Print Preview's margin lines.

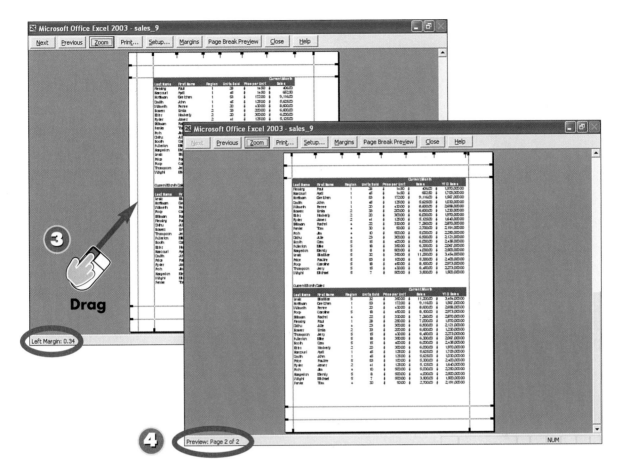

Drag

Left Margin: 0.34

Preview: Page 2 of 2

NUM

③ Drag the **Left Margin** line from the default 1" to 0.34" (you can see the exact measurement in the bottom-left corner of the screen).

④ Thanks to the margin change, the total number of pages to print is reduced from four to two. The column that exceeded the margins in the print area now fits on the page.

End

TIP
Entering Specific Margins
There might be times when you need to set your worksheet margins to a specific measurement. Perhaps your worksheet data is being placed in a binder, and you need to have a left margin of 1.25". You can either alter this in Print Preview mode or select **File**, **Page Setup**, click the **Margins** tab, and alter the margins as necessary (Left, Right, Top, Bottom, Header, or Footer). Click the **OK** button to return to your worksheet, or click the **Print** button to print immediately.

TIP
Removing Margin Lines
If you no longer want to see the margin lines in Print Preview mode, click the **Margins** button on the Print Preview toolbar to toggle the margins off.

PART 10

Printing a Worksheet on One Page

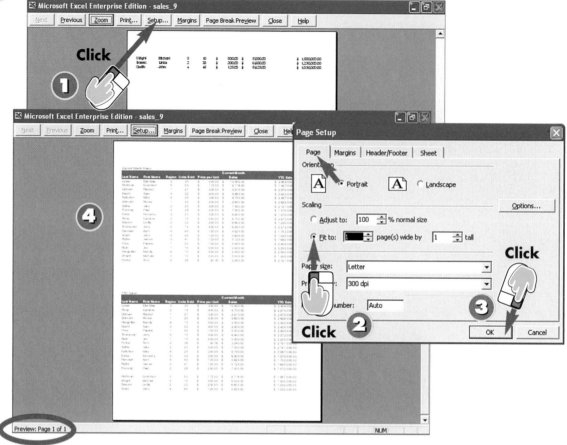

1. View your worksheet in Print Preview mode. If only a few rows of data spill onto a second page, you can alter the page scale; click the **Setup** button to begin.

2. On the **Page** tab of the Page Setup dialog box, click the **Fit to 1 Pages(s) Wide by 1 Tall** option button. (Or, type the number of pages to fit.)

3. Click **OK**.

4. Your worksheet appears in Print Preview mode, all on one page. Notice that the scaling change reduced the total number of pages to print from two to one.

End

INTRODUCTION

By default, Excel prints your worksheet at a scale of 100%. You can decrease this percentage if you want to fit more data on a page, or you can increase it to fit less. In addition, you can have Excel fit your entire worksheet on one page. (Although, if your worksheet is large, the data might become too tiny to read.)

Changing from Letter to Legal
To choose a different paper size for your printout, click the **Options** button on the Page Setup dialog box. The scaling setting automatically adjusts to the selected paper size.

Returning to the Default Scale
When you want to return the preview of your worksheet to the default scale, click the **Adjust to** option and type **100** into the **% Normal Size** field.

Printing in Portrait or Landscape Orientation

Start

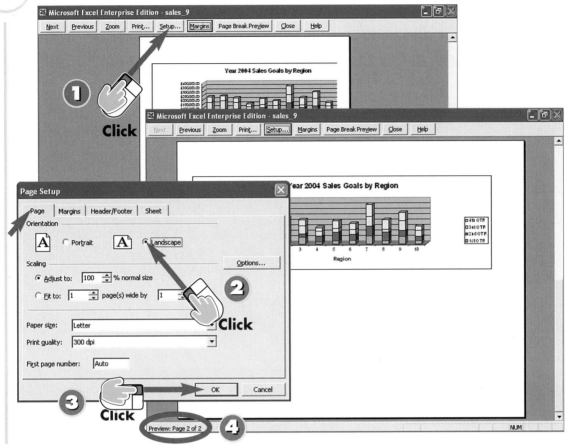

1. View your worksheet in Print Preview mode. If your worksheet is too wide to fit all its columns on a single page in portrait mode, click the **Setup** button.

2. On the **Page** tab of the Page Setup dialog box, click the **Landscape** option button.

3. Click the **OK** button.

4. Your worksheet now appears in Print Preview mode with a landscape orientation. The orientation change has reduced the total number of pages from four to two.

End

Centering a Worksheet on a Page

Start

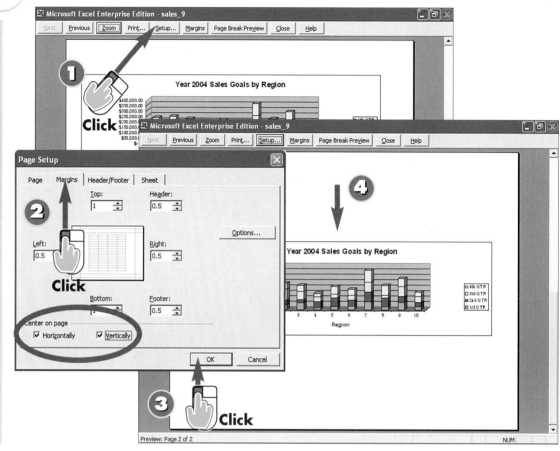

1. View your worksheet in Print Preview mode. If the data in your worksheet appears toward the top or on the far left of the page, click the **Setup** button.

2. Click the **Margins** tab in the Page Setup dialog box, and then click the **Horizontally** and/or **Vertically** check boxes in the **Center on Page** area.

3. Click **OK**.

4. Your worksheet appears in Print Preview mode, centered.

End

Printing Gridlines and Row/Column Headers

Start

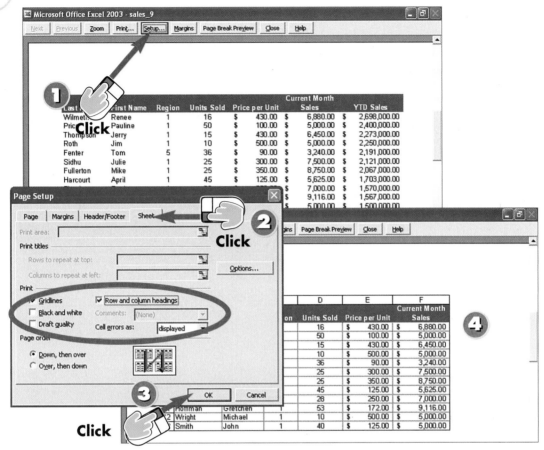

Click

Click

Click

1. View your worksheet in Print Preview mode. If no gridlines or row/column headers appear, click the **Setup** button.

2. Click the **Sheet** tab in the Page Setup dialog box, and click the **Gridlines** and **Row and Column Headings** check boxes in the **Print** area to select them.

3. Click **OK**.

4. Your worksheet now appears in Print Preview mode with gridlines and row and column headers visible.

End

Repeating Titles

TIP

Displaying row and column headers is not the same as printing repeating titles. *Repeating titles* are column headers and row headers you have assigned in your worksheet. For more information, see the task "Printing Repeating Row and Column Titles" later in this part.

Printing Headers and Footers

Start

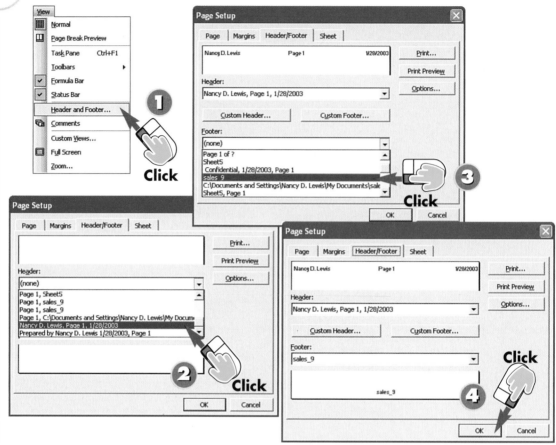

Click

Click

Click

Click

End

---

1. Open the **View** menu and select **Header and Footer** to open the Page Setup dialog box with the Header/Footer tab displayed.

2. Click the down arrow next to the **Header** field and scroll through the header options. If you see one you like, click it to see what it looks like.

3. Click the down arrow next to the **Footer** field and scroll through the footer options. If you see one you like, click it to see what it looks like.

4. Click **OK**. If you want, you can view the worksheet in Print Preview mode to get an idea of what your printed worksheet will look like with headers and footers.

Headers and footers appear at the top and bottom of printed pages of Excel worksheets. They can display the filename, the date and time the worksheet was printed, the worksheet's name, the page number, and more. Excel offers many standard headers and footers, or you can create custom headers and footers.

Creating Custom Headers and Footers

TIP

You can create your own custom header or footer by clicking **Custom Header** or **Custom Footer** in the Page Setup dialog box. A separate Header or Footer dialog box appears, allowing you to click a button to place text or the following fields in the header/footer: Page Number, Total Pages Number, Date, Time, Path & Filename, Filename Only, Tabs, and Insert Graphic Objects. You can add page numbers and the total page count to the header or footer. Clicking the appropriate button inserts the field codes so "&[Page] of &[Pages]" displays as "Page 1 of 2".

Printing Repeating Row and Column Titles

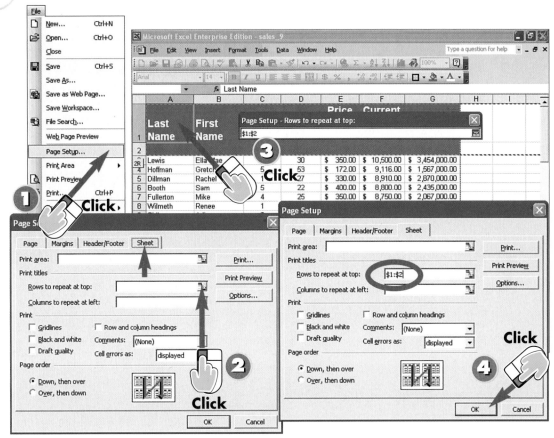

1 Open the **File** menu and select **Page Setup**; then select the **Sheet** tab on the Page Setup dialog box.

2 Click the **Rows to Repeat at Top** selection box in the **Print Titles** area. Excel shrinks the Page Setup dialog box, making your focus the worksheet on your desktop.

3 Select the row(s) containing the titles you want to repeat on each page of your worksheet; then press **Enter** to reopen the Page Setup dialog box with your selection.

4 Click **OK**. If you want, you can view the worksheet in Print Preview mode to get an idea of what your printed worksheet will look like with repeating row headings.

End

INTRODUCTION

You might have noticed that, when a worksheet spans multiple pages, keeping the column and row titles organized is difficult. A quick way to rectify this is to make particular titles repeat on each page of the printed worksheet. In this task, you'll learn how to make row headers repeat.

TIP

Repeating Titles in Print Preview Mode

You cannot assign repeating titles while you are in Print Preview mode; you must be in the worksheet view and select **File, Page Setup**.

TIP

Repeating Column Headings

To repeat column headings across several pages, follow the steps in this task, but click the **Columns to Repeat at Left** selection box in step 2. Then, click the columns you want to repeat and proceed as normal.

Printing Worksheets

Start

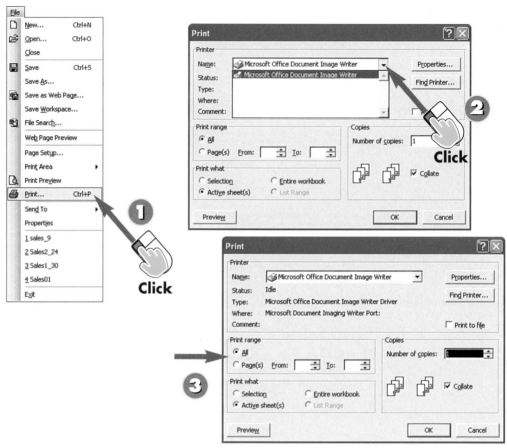

Click ①

Click ②

Click ③

① Open the **File** menu and select **Print** to open the Print dialog box.

② Click the down arrow next to the **Printer Name** field to select the printer or fax you want to use (unless you have only one printer, like here).

③ In the **Print Range** area, select **All** to print all the pages in your worksheet, or select **Page(s) From** and **To** to specify the pages (for example, From **2** To **5**).

INTRODUCTION

Printing a worksheet, workbook, or chart sheet can be quite simple, but setting the *options* for printing can be complex. The number of options that must be set before printing depends on the amount of data stored in the workbook, how it is arranged, how much of it needs to be printed, and how you want the printout to look.

Quickly Printing
If you simply click the **Print** button on the Standard toolbar, your entire worksheet will print using the default printing options unless you recently selected a different printer.

Setting Additional Print Options
To set additional print options, such as the paper size, graphic options, font options, and printer details, click the **Properties** button in the Print dialog box.

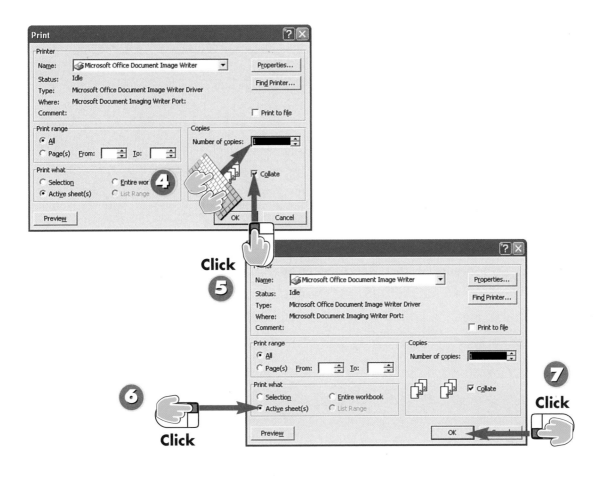

Click
5

6
Click

Click

7
Click

4. Type the number of copies you want to print in the **Number of Copies** field, which defaults to **1**.

5. If you want the printed pages to be collated, click the **Collate** check box to select it.

6. In the **Print What** area, select **Selection** (specific cells), **Active Sheet(s)** (the current sheet), or **Entire Workbook** (all worksheets and chart sheets).

7. Click **OK** to send your printout to the printer. Alternatively, click **Preview** to preview your printout; then click the **Print** button on the Print Preview toolbar.

End

Vertical or Horizontal Page Order
If you are working with a large worksheet, you can specify the page order by which your worksheet is printed. Select **File**, **Page Setup**, and select the **Sheet** tab. Review the options of **Down, Then Over** (default) and **Over, then Down** in the **Page Order** area of the Page Setup dialog box. This is convenient if you have numerous columns you want printed according to a specific row header.

Canceling Printing
If you've already "sent" the workbook or worksheet to the printer, double-click the **Printer** icon in the system tray (to the left of the clock on the taskbar) and click the **Cancel** button in the Printing window.

Formatting Worksheet Data

When you *format* a worksheet, you can change the appearance of the data in it. With Excel's formatting tools, you can make your worksheet more attractive and readable. For example, you can increase and decrease the width of columns and height of rows, as well as change the color of your data or the cell background.

In addition to changing the look of your cell data, you can change how it is displayed in your worksheet. For example, you can merge and center a title or add header information. You can change the placement of the data in a cell so that it is at the top, bottom, left, right, justified, centered, or even displayed vertically.

After you add all the formatting to your data, you can always clear it and return to just the regular default data format. Or, after you have applied formatting to your data, you can choose one of Excel's default formats, known as *AutoFormats*. Excel even lets you apply formatting based on a set of conditions you establish.

Adding Data Formatting

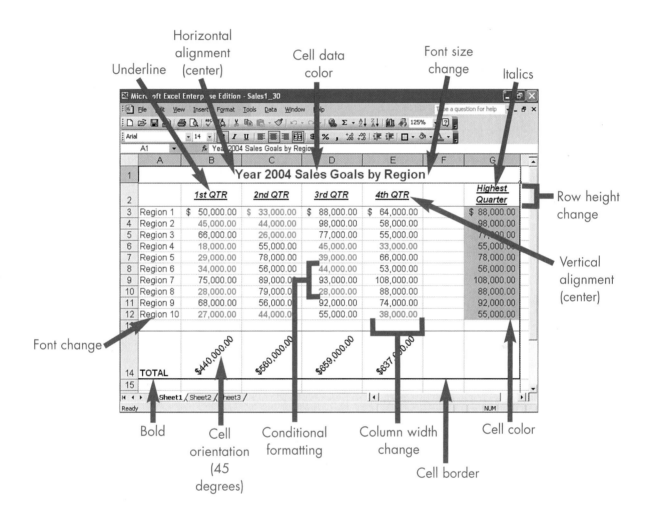

Underline

Horizontal alignment (center)

Cell data color

Font size change

Italics

Row height change

Vertical alignment (center)

Font change

Bold

Cell orientation (45 degrees)

Conditional formatting

Column width change

Cell border

Cell color

Changing the Font and Font Size

Start

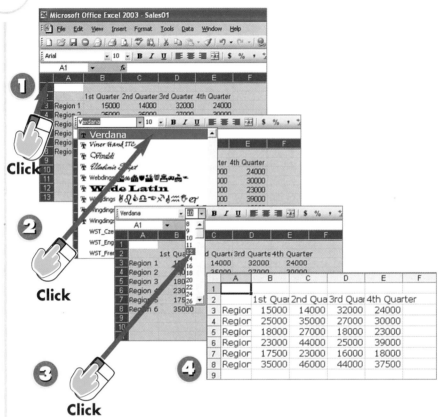

Click

Click

Click

1 Select the cells whose font and font size you want to change, or click the **All Cells** button (to the left of column A and above row 1) to format all the cells in the worksheet.

2 Click the **Font** field down arrow on the Standard toolbar, scroll through the available fonts, and select the font name.

3 Click the **Font Size** field down arrow and scroll through the available sizes. Select the size or type it into the Font Size field.

4 The font and font size you selected are applied.

End

One way to format data in your worksheet is to change the font used to display it. Changing the font gives data a different look and feel, which can help differentiate the type of data a cell contains. You can also change the font's size for added emphasis.

Viewing Font Samples
Office enables you to see a sample of each font in the Font drop-down list box, which means you know what the font looks like *before* you apply it to your cells. This helps you choose the right font more quickly.

Formatting Options
To format only a portion of a cell's data, select only that portion and then change the font. You can also select a font (or other options) *before* you begin typing. Then all the data in a cell will be that font.

Changing Column Width

Start

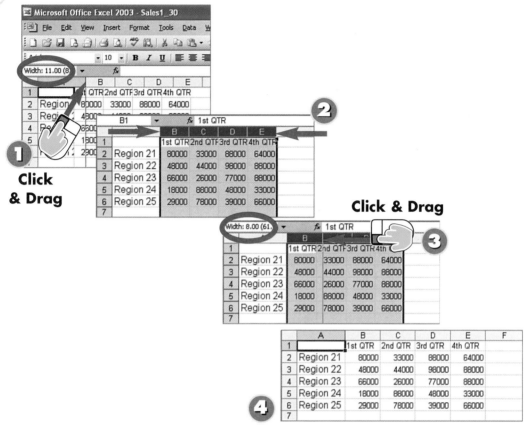

Click & Drag

Click & Drag

1. Move the mouse pointer over one side of the column header, and click and drag to the desired width. The column size displays in the Name box.

2. Release the mouse pointer and the column is resized. To resize *multiple* columns simultaneously, select the columns you want to alter.

3. Click and drag one of the selected column's header edges to the desired width and release it.

4. All the selected columns are resized to the same width.

End

Sometimes data is too wide to be displayed within a cell, particularly if you just applied formatting to it. Excel provides several ways to remedy this problem. You can select columns and specify a width, or you can force Excel to automatically adjust the width of a cell to exactly fit its contents.

TIP

Specific Widths

To resize a column to an exact width, open the **Format** menu and select **Column**, **Width**. Enter the exact width in the dialog box that appears and click **OK**; the exact column width will be set. To automatically make an entire column (or multiple columns) fit the width of the widest cell in that column (or columns), open the **Format** menu and select **Column**, **AutoFit Selection**. Or, move the cursor over the right side of the column header and double-click when the cursor changes to a two-headed arrow.

Wrapping Data in a Cell

Start

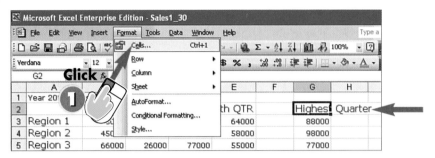

Click

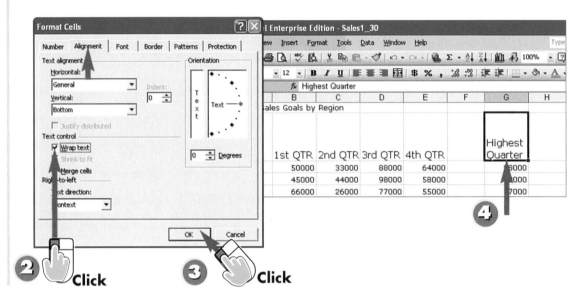

Click   **Click**

4

1. After you select the cell or cells whose text you want to wrap, open the **Format** menu and select **Cells**.

2. On the **Alignment** tab of the Format Cells dialog box, select the **Wrap Text** check box in the **Text Control** area.

3. Click **OK**.

4. The data in the selected cells is automatically wrapped. (You might need to adjust the column width, as in the previous task.)

End

Excel provides several ways to format data. One way is to allow text to wrap in a cell. For example, suppose a heading (row or column, for example) is longer than the width of the cell holding the data. If you are trying to make your worksheet organized and readable, you should wrap the text in the heading so it is completely visible in a cell.

Aligning Wrapped Text
You can align data that has been wrapped to give your text a cleaner look. See p. 180 and p. 181 later in this part to learn how to align data in cells.

See p. 180 and p. 181 later in this part to learn how to align data in cells.

Changing Row Height

Start

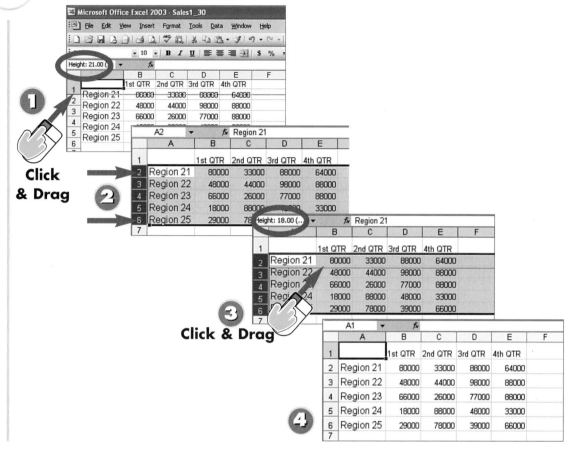

Click & Drag

1

2

Click & Drag

3

4

End

1 Move the mouse pointer over the bottom edge of the row header, and click and drag to the desired height. The row size displays in the Name box.

2 Release the mouse pointer and the row is resized. To resize *multiple* rows simultaneously, select the rows you want to alter.

3 Click and drag one of the selected row's bottom edges to the desired height, and then release it.

4 All the selected rows are resized to the same height.

INTRODUCTION

Depending on the formatting changes you make to a cell, data might not display properly. Increasing the font size or forcing data to wrap within a cell might prevent data from being entirely displayed or cause it to run over into other cells. You can frequently avoid these problems by resizing rows.

TIP

Specific Heights
To format a row to an exact height, open the **Format** menu and select **Row, Height**. Enter the exact height in the dialog box that appears and click **OK**; the exact row height will be set. To automatically make an entire row fit the height of the tallest cell, open the **Format** menu and select **Row, AutoFit Selection**. Or, move the cursor over the bottom of the row header and double-click when the cursor changes to a two-headed arrow.

Applying Bold, Italic, and Underline

Start

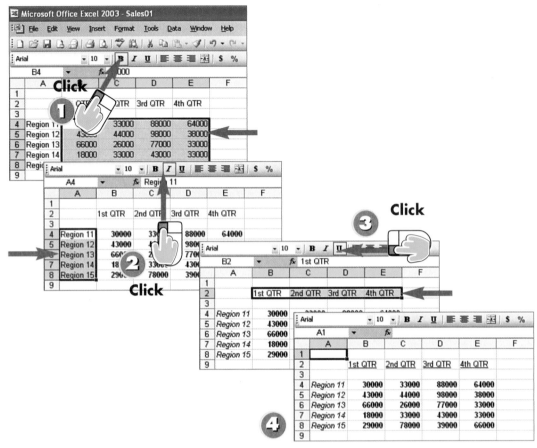

1. Select the cells in which you want to apply bold formatting, and click the **Bold** button.

2. Select the cells in which you want to apply italic formatting, and click the **Italic** button.

3. Select the cells in which you want to apply underline formatting, and click the **Underline** button.

4. The bold, italics, and underlining are applied to the selected cells.

End

You can format the data contained in one or more cells as bold, italic, or underlined (or some combination of the three) to draw attention to it or make it easier to find. Indicating summary values, questionable data, or any other cells is easy with formatting.

Combination Formatting
You can use several formatting techniques in combination, such as applying bold, italic, and underlining all at the same time. Simply select the text you want to format and click each of the buttons on the toolbar.

Formatting Blank Cells
Because you selected cells B2–G2 (B2:G2), note that cell F2 (which has no data in it) will retain the formatting. If you typed something in F2 now, it would appear bold, italic, and underlined.

Changing the Cell Background and Font Color

Start

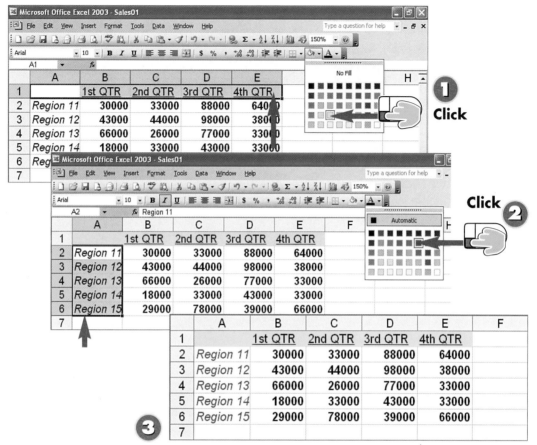

Click ①

Click ②

③

① Select the cells in which you want to apply a cell background color, click the **Fill Color** down arrow, and choose a color.

② Select the cells in which you want to apply a font color, click the **Font Color** down arrow, and choose a color.

③ The background color and font color are applied to the selected cells.

End

INTRODUCTION

Generally, cells present a white background for displaying data, but you can apply other colors or shading to the background. In addition, you can change the color of the data contained within your worksheet's cells. As with most formatting options, this can help emphasize more important data.

CAUTION

Choosing Colors

Be sure a shading or color pattern doesn't interfere with the readability of data. To improve readability, you might need to make the text bold or select a text color that goes well with your cells' background colors. Also, be aware that if you print the worksheet to a noncolor printer, the color you choose prints gray—and the darker the gray, the less readable the data. Yellows generally print as pleasing light grays that don't compete with the data.

Changing Horizontal Data Alignment

Start

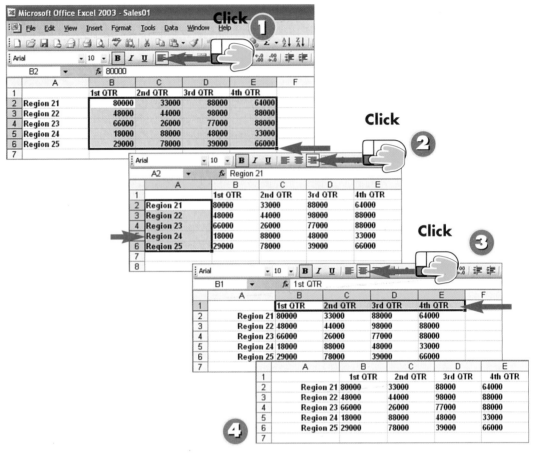

End

1. Select the cells in which you want to align the data to the left, and click the **Align Left** button on the Formatting toolbar.

2. Select the cells in which you want to align the data to the right, and click the **Align Right** button.

3. Select the cells in which you want to center the data, and click the **Center** button.

4. The alignments are applied to the selected cells.

The most common alignment changes you'll make are probably to center data in a cell, align data with a cell's right edge (right-align), or align data with a cell's left edge (left-align). The default alignment for numbers is right-aligned; the default alignment for text is left-aligned.

More Alignment Options

If you want more alignment options than are readily available on the Formatting toolbar, open the **Format** menu, select **Cells**, and click the **Alignment** tab in the dialog box that appears. In the **Horizontal** drop-down list, scroll through the additional options available to you. If, after you select data to align, you click the same alignment toolbar button a second time, the cell returns to its default alignment.

Changing Vertical Data Alignment

Start

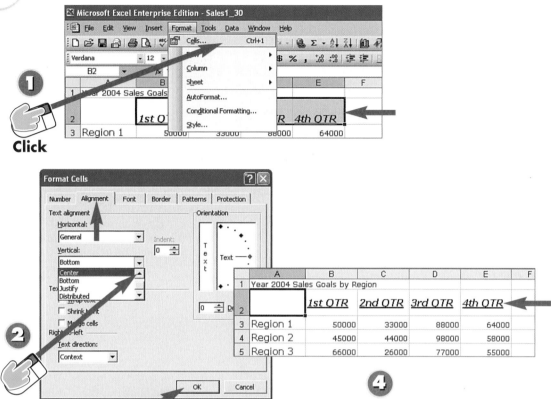

Click

Click

Click

---

1 After you select the cell or cells whose contents you want to vertically align, open the **Format** menu and select **Cells** to open the Format Cells dialog box.

2 On the Format Cells dialog box **Alignment** tab, click the **Vertical** field down arrow and scroll through the options: Top, Center, Bottom, Justify, and Distributed.

3 After you make your selection, click **OK**.

4 The data is vertically aligned within the cell.

End

INTRODUCTION

In addition to aligning the data in your cells horizontally, you can align your cell data in a vertical format. Perhaps you want the data in your cells to align to the top of the cell, bottom of the cell, or center of the cell, or maybe you want to justify it within the cell. Cell data defaults to the bottom of the cell, but you can change this according to the look you want.

TIP

Justifying Cell Text
If you selected the Justify option in step 3, you must have enough text in the cell to fill from the top to the bottom of the cell, for example, a sentence. The text will automatically wrap to fit the cell.

Changing Cell Orientation

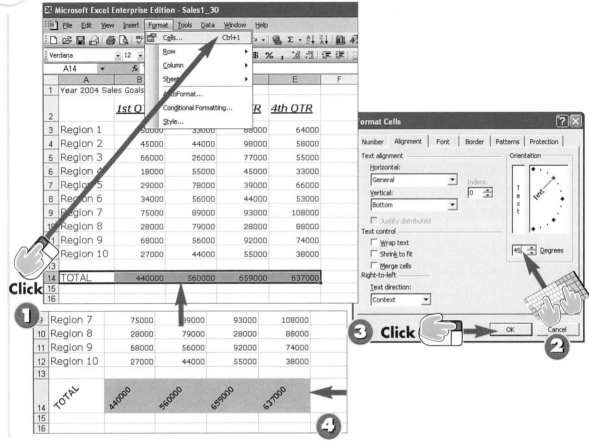

Click ❶

Click ❸

❷

❹

---

① After you select the cell or cells whose orientation you want to alter, open the **Format** menu and select **Cells** to open the Format Cells dialog box.

② On the **Alignment** tab of the Format Cells dialog box, type the desired angle in the **Degrees** field in the **Orientation** area.

③ Click **OK**.

④ The data reorients within the cell. (You might need to increase or decrease the height and width of the cells.)

End

Excel lets you alter the orientation of a cell—that is, the angle at which it displays information. The main reason for doing this is to help draw attention to important or special text. This feature can be convenient when you have a lot of columns in a worksheet and don't want your column headers to take up much horizontal space, or if you simply want the information to stand out.

Rotating Data
Click the half circle in the **Orientation** section of the **Alignment** tab to quickly change the angle at which data is rotated within the selected cell(s).

Changing Borders

Start

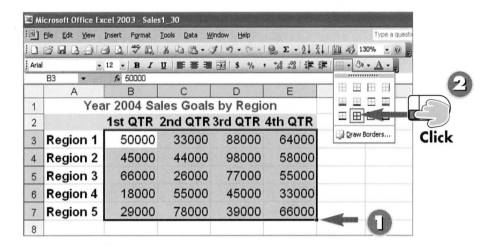

② Click

① ←

③

	A	B	C	D	E	F
1	Year 2004 Sales Goals by Region					
2		1st QTR	2nd QTR	3rd QTR	4th QTR	
3	Region 1	50000	33000	88000	64000	
4	Region 2	45000	44000	98000	58000	
5	Region 3	66000	26000	77000	55000	
6	Region 4	18000	55000	45000	33000	
7	Region 5	29000	78000	39000	66000	
8						

① Select the cells to which you want to add some type of border.

② Click the down arrow next to the **Borders** button on the Formatting toolbar and select an option from the list that appears—for example, select **All Borders**.

③ The border is applied.

End

INTRODUCTION

Each side of a cell is considered a *border*. These borders provide a visual cue as to where a cell begins and ends. You can customize borders to indicate other beginnings and endings, such as grouping similar data or separating headings from data. For example, a double line is often used to separate a summary value from the data being totaled. Changing the bottom of the border for the last number before the total accomplishes this effect.

Removing Borders

TIP

To remove a border, select the bordered cells, click the down arrow next to the **Borders** button on the Formatting toolbar, and select the **No Border** option. Be careful, though; you might eliminate an intended border in a nearby cell.

Copying Formatting

Start

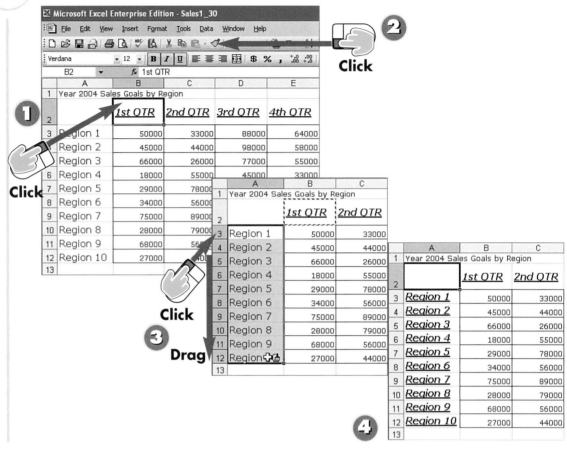

Click

1 Click the cell with the formatting that you want to copy and apply to other cells.

2 Click the **Format Painter** button on the Standard toolbar; the mouse pointer changes to a Format Painter pointer (paintbrush symbol).

3 Select the cells to which you want to apply the copied formatting.

4 Release the mouse button. The formatting is applied to the data in the selected cells.

End

If you have taken the time to format a specific cell just so, you might decide you want to apply those same formatting options to other cells. Instead of repeating each step in the format process over and over again, you can simply use Excel's Format Painter feature.

TIP

Removing Cell Formatting
To quickly remove any cell formatting, select the cells you want to return to their default settings; then open the **Edit** menu and select **Clear**, **Formats**.

Using AutoFormat

Start

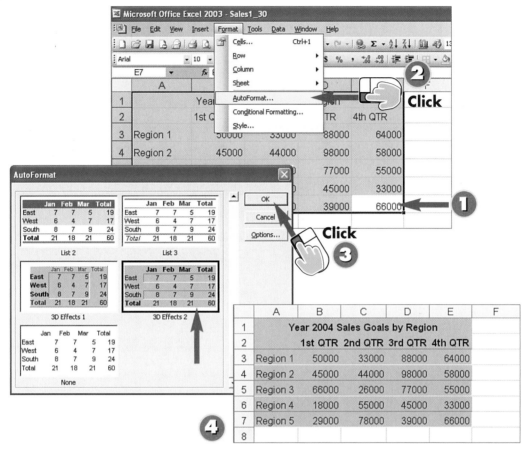

Click ②

Click ③

④

①

Select the cells to which you want to apply an AutoFormat. Open the **Format** menu and select **AutoFormat**.

② Scroll through the available formats on the AutoFormat dialog box.

③ Click the AutoFormat you want to apply to your data and click **OK**.

④ The AutoFormat is applied.

End

INTRODUCTION

Using all the formatting capabilities discussed to this point, you could format your worksheets in a very effective and professional manner—but it might take a while to get good at it. In the meantime, you can use Excel's AutoFormat feature, which can format selected cells using predefined formats. This feature is a quick way to format large amounts of data and provides ideas on how to format data manually.

TIP

Modifying AutoFormats
If you find a format in the AutoFormat dialog box that almost—but doesn't quite—meet your requirements, you can apply that format but then make any necessary changes to it directly in the worksheet.

Using Conditional Formatting

Start

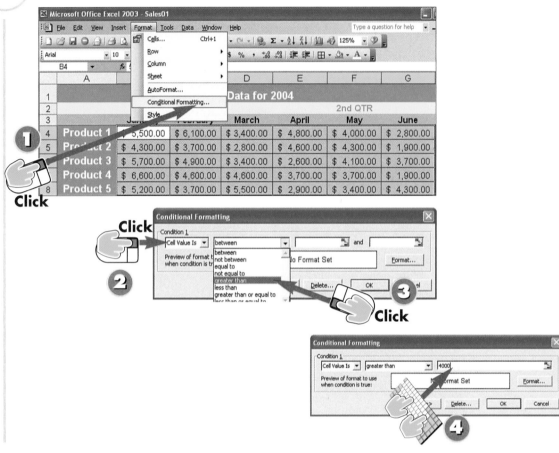

Click

Click

Click

1. Select the cells to which you want to apply conditional formatting, then open the **Format** menu and select **Conditional Formatting**.

2. In the Conditional Formatting dialog box, keep the default **Condition 1** as **Cell Value Is** (use **Formula Is** to indicate a specific formula).

3. Display the second drop-down list to select the type of condition (for example, **greater than**).

4. Type the value of the condition (the number that the cells must be "greater than").

You might want the formatting of a cell to depend on the value it contains. For this, you use *conditional formatting*, which lets you specify conditions that, when met, cause the cell to be formatted in the manner defined for that condition. If none of the conditions are met, the cell keeps its original formatting. For example, you can set a conditional format such that, if sales for a particular month were above $4,000, the data in the cell is bold and red.

Painting onto Other Cells

You can copy the conditional formatting from one cell to another. To do so, click the cell whose formatting you want to copy. Then click the **Format Painter** button. Finally, drag over the cells to which you want to copy the formatting.

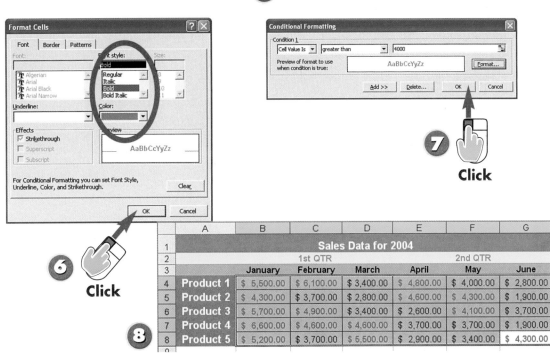

5 Click the **Format** button to set the format to use when the condition is met.

6 Click the options you want to set in the Format Cells dialog box (for example, **Purple** in the **Color** field and **Bold** in the **Font style** list), and click **OK**.

7 Click **OK** in the Conditional Formatting dialog box.

8 Excel applies the formatting to any cells that meet the condition you specified.

End

TIP

When to Use Conditional Formatting

Use conditional formatting to draw attention to values that have different meanings, depending on whether they are positive or negative, such as profit and loss values.

Getting Started with PowerPoint

You can use PowerPoint to plan every aspect of a winning presentation. PowerPoint even helps you organize the ideas in your presentation through its AutoContent Wizard, which quickly creates your presentation, including a title slide and several slides that help you come up with information.

PowerPoint lets you edit text and navigate, format, open, and close presentations at any time. You can also get creative in your slide presentations. For example, you can apply bulleted and numbered lists, change your slide layout, or even apply a design template. In addition, you can add, delete, or duplicate a slide at any time.

Office gives you the opportunity to create a new presentation each time you start PowerPoint, but you can create a new presentation at any time. Presentation documents consist of *slides* instead of pages (as in Word) or worksheets (as in Excel). You can add Word documents and Excel worksheets to your presentations, but for now, we'll stick to creating a simple new presentation.

Creating Presentations

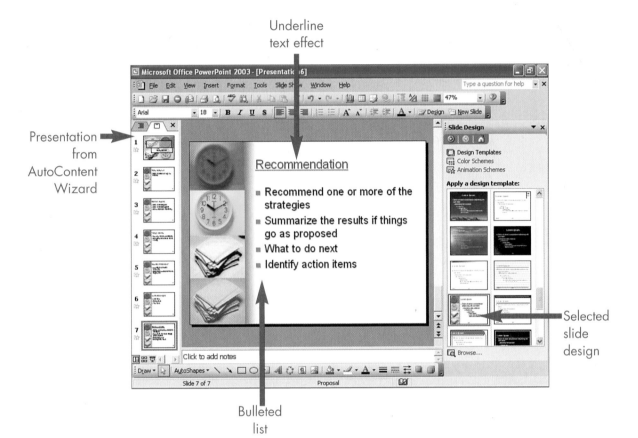

Underline
text effect

Presentation
from
AutoContent
Wizard

Selected
slide
design

Bulleted
list

Starting a Blank Presentation

Start

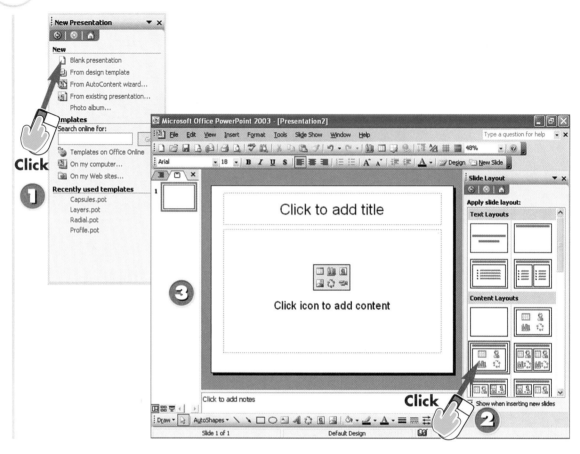

Click

Click

1. Click the **Blank Presentation** option in the New Presentation task pane. (If this task pane is not visible, open the **File** menu and select **New**.)

2. The Slide Layout task pane opens; scroll through the available layouts and click the one you want to apply to the current slide.

3. The selected layout appears on the slide, ready for you to begin working.

End

For the most control over your PowerPoint presentations, start with a blank presentation and add only the items you want. This gives you the opportunity to use your creativity. It also allows you to use PowerPoint for creating files beyond basic business presentations. Your imagination is the only limitation.

TIP

Applying the Slide Layout
If you click once directly on a slide layout in the task pane, it automatically applies the layout to only the current slide. If you first select each slide in the Slide tab (the pane on the left) by pressing Ctrl while clicking each slide, you can select the Apply to Selected Slides option. Each slide you selected will have the same slide layout.

Starting a Design Template Presentation

Start

Click

1

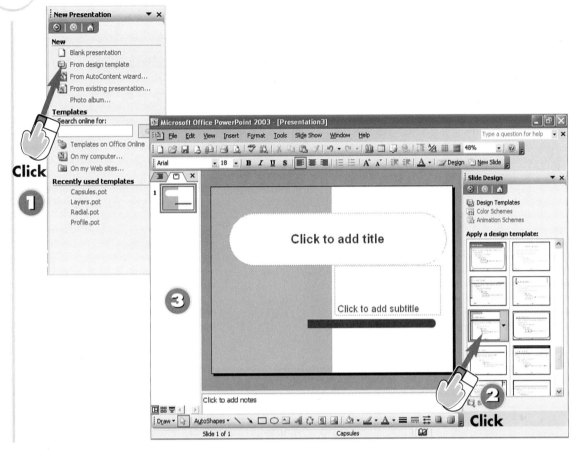

3

2

Click

1 Click the **From Design Template** option in the New Presentation task pane. (If this task pane is not visible, open the **File** menu and select **New**.)

2 The Slide Design task pane opens; scroll through the available design templates and click the one you want to apply to the current slide.

3 The selected design appears on the slide, ready for you to begin working.

End

INTRODUCTION

PowerPoint comes with several presentation templates, designed for various types of presentations and situations. These templates have basic artistic features and usually a skeleton outline you can fill in or expand on. You can take advantage of these templates to quickly create presentations.

TIP

Applying the Slide Design
If you click directly on a slide design in the task pane, it applies the design to all slides. If you select each slide in the Slide tab (the pane on the left) by pressing Ctrl while clicking each slide, you can select the Apply to Selected Slides option.

TIP

Changing the Color and Animation Schemes
You can easily change the color and animation scheme of a design template by clicking the **Color Schemes** or **Animation Schemes** link, respectively, at the top of the Slide Design task pane.

Starting a Presentation with the AutoContent Wizard

Start

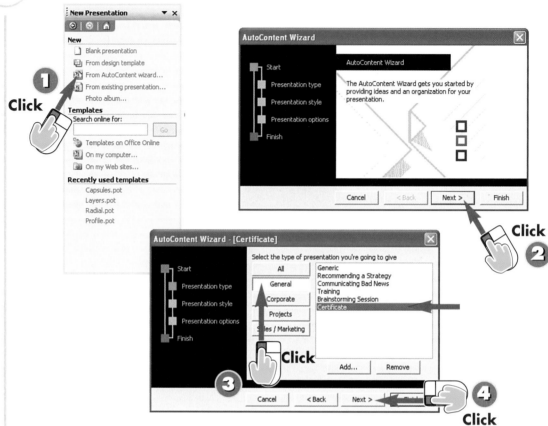

Click

Click ②

Click ③

Click ④

1. Click the **From AutoContent Wizard** option in the New Presentation task pane. (If this task pane is not visible, open the **File** menu and select **New**.)

2. Read the welcome information in the AutoContent Wizard dialog box and then click **Next**.

3. To specify which type of presentation you want to create, click one of the category buttons: **All**, **General**, **Corporate**, **Projects**, or **Sales/Marketing**.

4. The list of presentation types varies depending on your selection in step 3. Click the presentation type that best matches your needs, and click **Next**.

Displaying the New Presentation Task Pane
If the New Presentation task pane is not visible, open the **File** menu and select **New**.

Creating Presentations
The AutoContent Wizard gets a presentation off to a quick start. For more complex presentations, use the wizard to begin creating a presentation, then add to the presentation by using templates or creating new slides from scratch.

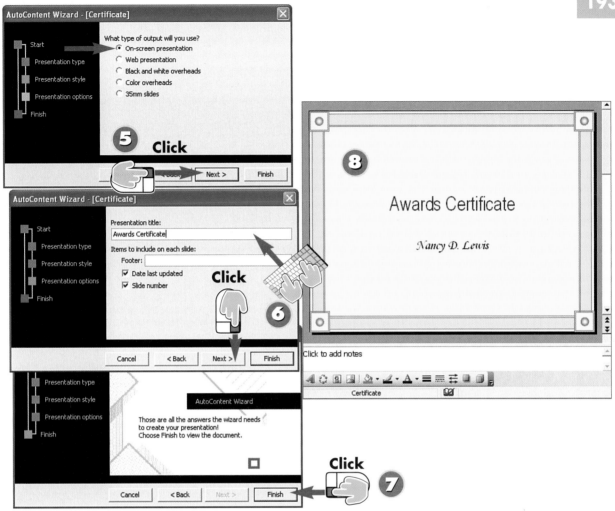

⑤ Click the desired output option, and then click **Next**.

⑥ Type a title for the presentation and any items you want included on each slide (footer information, the date, slide numbers, and so on). Click **Next**.

⑦ Click the **Finish** button.

⑧ View the presentation PowerPoint creates for you.

End

Using the Back and Cancel Buttons
You can click the **Back** button in the AutoContent Wizard dialog box at any time to return to an earlier screen to alter previously entered information. Keep in mind that you must click the particular option you want to alter before you make any changes. You can stop the AutoContent Wizard's progress at any time by clicking the **Cancel** button.

Editing AutoContent Slide Text

1 Click

2

3

4

---

1 In the Outline tab in Normal view, select the bracketed text you want to alter—for example, [name here] or [company name].

2 Type the text with which you want to replace the bracketed text; it simultaneously appears on your slide.

3 To edit bracketed slide text from within the slide itself, select the text and type over it.

4 The text is altered.

End

After you create a presentation using the AutoContent Wizard, some areas (text or graphics) in your slides between brackets will probably require input from you. This is where you personalize the information in your slides. In Normal view, you can add text in the Outline tab or directly to the slide.

Boxed Slide Instructions

If you see instructions in a slide—for example, **Click to add title**—simply click in the box and type your text. These boxes are called *text boxes*, and you can add them to your slides at any time by clicking the Text Box button (it looks like a white square with a tiny *A* in the upper-left corner) on the Drawing toolbar along the bottom of the desktop. Your mouse pointer changes to an upside-down cross. Simply click and drag the box on the slide, release the mouse button, and type the text into the box. When you click elsewhere in the slide, the text displays in the slide foreground.

Inserting Slide Text

Start

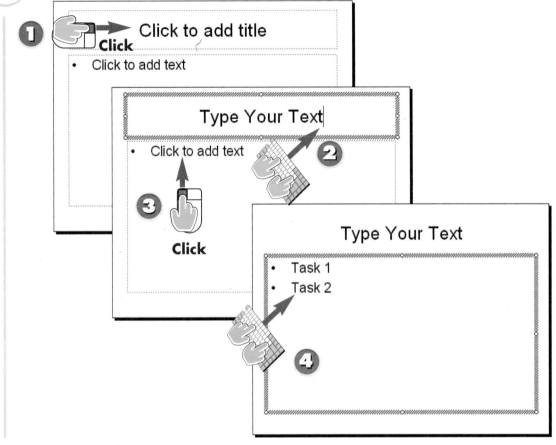

End

1 Click the **Click to Add Title** area of a slide to begin adding text.

2 Type your text into the text box. Notice that the Outline tab fills in automatically (if you are in Normal view).

3 Click the **Click to Add Text** area of a slide to begin adding text.

4 Type your text into the bulleted text box; pressing **Enter** continues the bulleted list.

After you create a presentation, whether by starting from scratch, using a design template, or using the AutoContent Wizard, you need to add the information to your slides that you want to present. You can add a table, a chart, clip art, a picture, a diagram or an organizational chart, or a media clip.

Adding Lists
If you want a slide section to contain a numbered list instead of a bulleted list, simply click the **Numbering** button on the Formatting toolbar to change your selection. If you want a slide section to contain regular text instead of a bulleted list, simply click the **Bullets** button on the Formatting toolbar to deselect it.

Saving a Presentation

Start

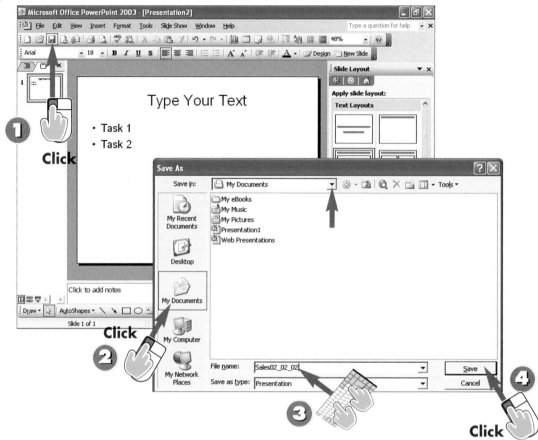

Click

Click

Click

Click the **Save** button on the Standard toolbar; the Save As dialog box appears, with a default filename for your presentation.

Click the **My Documents** icon on the Places bar, or use the **Save in** drop-down list to locate the folder in which you want to save the file.

Type a descriptive name for the presentation in the **File Name** field.

Click the **Save** button; the presentation is saved.

End

PowerPoint provides more than one method for saving presentations. You should often take advantage of at least one of these. You need to save your presentations so you can work on them later, or so you can use PowerPoint to show your slides to others. Unsaved presentations will be lost in the event anything happens to your application or computer. So, be sure you save often while you are working.

TIP

Save in Options
If you don't want to save your file in the My Documents folder, click the down arrow next to the **Save in** field and maneuver through the directories to save the file in a different location.

Closing a Presentation

Start

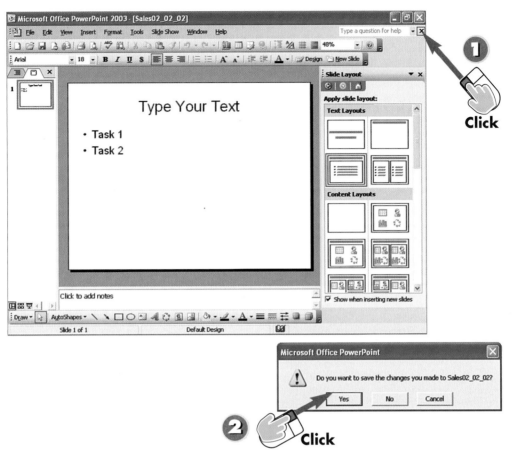

End

1. Click the **Close** (×) button on the document window's menu bar. If you have made any change to the presentation, PowerPoint asks you to save the document.

2. Click the **Yes** button if you want to save recent changes. (Click **No** if you don't want to save, or click **Cancel** to return to working on the file.)

INTRODUCTION

When you finish working on a presentation, you can close it. Closing a presentation does not close the PowerPoint application. After you close a presentation, you can continue working with other open presentations or create a new presentation.

TIP

Additional Close Options
As with most Windows applications, PowerPoint provides many ways to close a presentation. For example, you can press Ctrl+F4 to close the active presentation. You can also open the File menu and select Close.

TIP

Closing the Document Window
When you click the Close button, be sure you are clicking the one in the document window, not the application window. Otherwise, you will close the PowerPoint application.

Opening a Presentation

Start

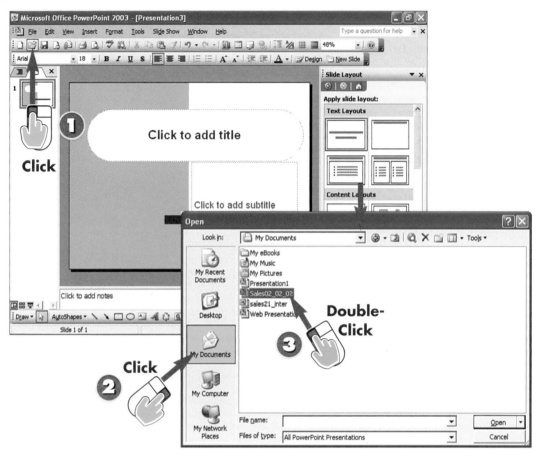

Click

Click

Double-Click

End

1. Click the **Open** button on the Standard toolbar, and the Open dialog box appears.

2. Click the **My Documents** icon on the Places bar, or use the **Look in** drop-down list to locate the folder that contains the file you want to open.

3. Double-click the file you want to open, and PowerPoint opens the presentation.

Eventually, you'll have to close PowerPoint and any presentations you have created. If you saved your work, you can continue working on your presentations at any time by opening the saved presentations.

Alternative Look in Locations
If necessary, click the down arrow next to the **Look in** field and select the folder that contains the desired file from the list. To move up a folder level, click the **Up One Level** button on the Open toolbar.

Existing Presentations
If the New Presentation task pane is open, you can always click the From Existing Presentation link to locate the file you want to open.

Changing the Slide Text's Font

Start

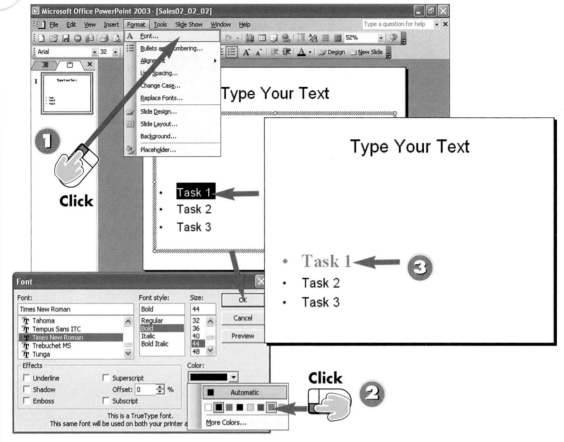

Click

End

①   After you select the text you want to alter, open the **Format** menu and select **Font** to open the Font dialog box.

②   Select the options you want to apply to your text from the various list boxes and click **OK**.

③   Your font changes are applied to the selected text.

An effective presentation gets your point across while holding the audience's attention. You can keep attention focused on your presentation by making the information on the slides stand out. One way to do this is to format the text. PowerPoint gives you many options to format your text, such as changing its font, style, size, and color.

Previewing the Font

When the Font dialog box is open and you have indicated your font changes, you can click the Preview button to review your changes before you accept them as final (in step 2). You might need to move the Font dialog box slightly out of the way to see the text.

Applying Slide Text Effects

Start

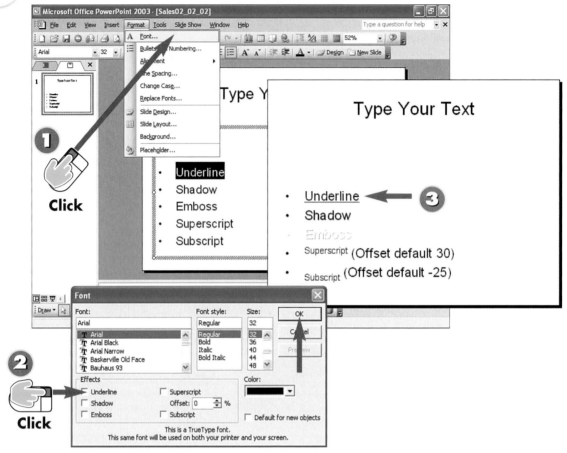

Click

Click

Type Your Text

- Underline ← 3
- Shadow
- Emboss
- Superscript (Offset default 30)
- Subscript (Offset default -25)

1. After you select the text you want to alter, open the **Format** menu and select **Font** to open the Font dialog box.

2. Click the Effects options—**Underline**, **Shadow**, **Emboss**, **Superscript**, or **Subscript**—you want to apply to your text and click **OK**.

3. Your font effects are applied to the selected text. Note in this example that each effect is applied separately to illustrate what the various effects look like.

End

You can quickly and easily apply effects to the text on your slides. Underline text or add a shadow effect to make the text look like it is in 3D. Or, apply an emboss, which looks like engraving. You can also make text superscript—for example, to indicate powers of 10—as well as subscript, for indicating bases of 10.

The Font Dialog Box
The Font dialog box gives you many ways to format your text. Instead of formatting the text and then seeing what it looks like, you can click the Preview button and make changes before you click the OK button to accept the settings.

Underline and Shadow
Notice that Underline and Shadow effect buttons are available on the default Formatting toolbar.

Altering Slide Text Alignment

 Start

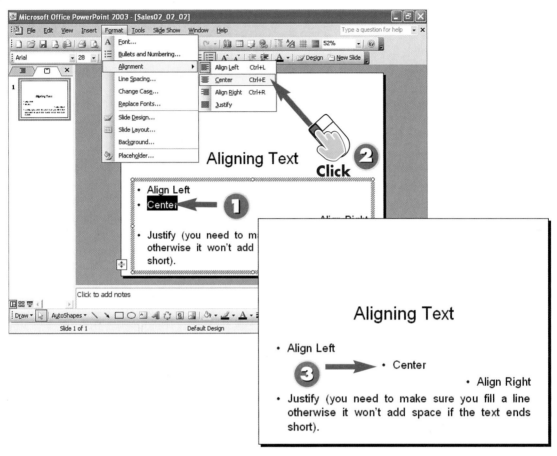

1 Select the text you want to realign.

2 Open the **Format** menu and select **Alignment**. Then click the desired alignment option from the submenu: Align Left, Center, Align Right, or Justify.

3 The selected text is aligned in the object box. Note in this example that each alignment option is applied separately to illustrate what the various alignment options look like.

 End

When you enter text into a presentation, the text automatically aligns *flush* (even) with the left margin. However, you can change the alignment of text at any time, before or after you have entered the text. You can center text, make it flush with the right margin, or justify it (make it flush with both margins).

Using the Formatting Toolbar
Notice that Left Align, Center, and Right Align buttons appear on PowerPoint's Formatting toolbar. If you prefer, you can click these buttons instead of using the options in the Format menu to align your text.

Justifying Text
If you select the Justify command in the Format menu, the text becomes flush left *and* flush right. The Justify option doesn't work on single words or sentences, only on text in a paragraph that wraps to another line.

Working with Numbered and Bulleted Lists

Start

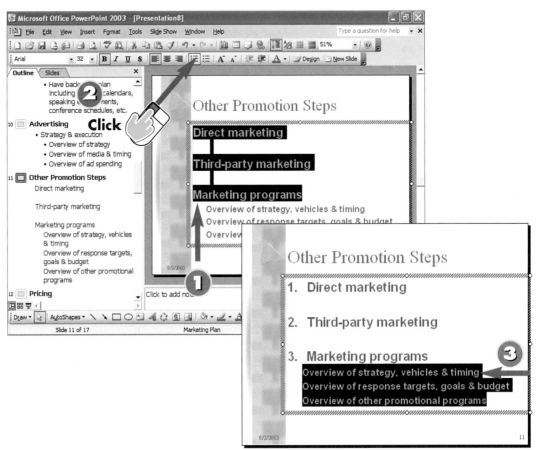

1 Select the text you want to make into a numbered list.

2 Click the **Numbering** button on the Formatting toolbar.

3 The text is formatted as a numbered list. Now select the text you want to make into a list of graphical bullets.

INTRODUCTION

Using bulleted or numbered lists is a great way to present a series of points in your slides. You can create a numbered or bulleted list by selecting existing text and clicking either the Bullets or Numbering button on the Formatting toolbar, or you can click the button first and then begin typing to create the list.

Multilevel Lists
PowerPoint enables you to create multilevel bulleted and numbered lists. When typing text into a list, simply press the Tab key to indent the list to a new level.

Bullets and Numbers
Use bullets when you are listing items that are in no particular order. Use numbers when your items are in an order, such as with a series of steps or a top-ten list.

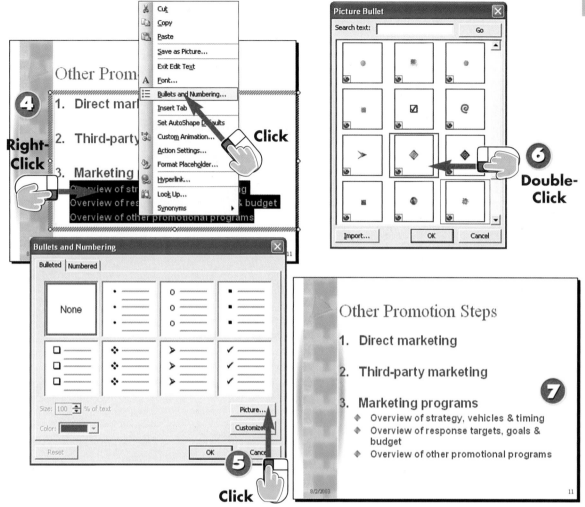

4 Right-click the selection and select **Bullets and Numbering** from the shortcut menu that appears.

5 The Bullets and Numbering dialog box opens. Click the **Picture** button. (If you want to use a standard bullet, simply double-click one in the dialog box and skip the next step.)

6 Scroll through the list of available picture bullets. When you find one you like, double-click it.

7 The text you selected in step 3 is formatted as a bulleted list using the bullet design you selected in step 6.

Changing Number Styles
To change the numbered list style—for example, from Arabic (1, 2, 3) to Roman (I, II, III)—open the **Format** menu and select **Bullets and Numbering**. Click the **Numbered** tab, select from the list of styles, and click **OK**.

Creating a New List
If you haven't yet created the list you want to number or bullet, click the **Numbering** or **Bullets** button on the Formatting toolbar, and then start typing the information. When you press Enter to start a new line, PowerPoint adds the number or bullet automatically. To stop adding bullets or numbers, press the **Enter** key more than once.

Adding and Deleting Slides

Start

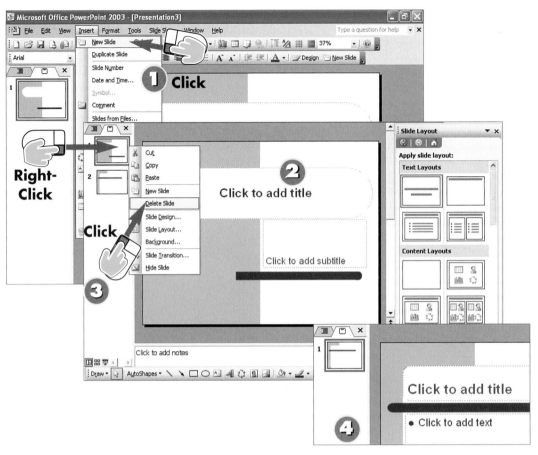

1 To insert a new slide in your presentation directly after the currently selected slide, open the **Insert** menu and select **New Slide**.

2 PowerPoint creates a new slide with the same design as the slide that was originally displayed, adds the new slide to the Outline tab, and opens the Slide Layout task pane.

3 To delete a slide, right-click the slide or slide number in the Outline tab and select **Delete Slide** from the shortcut menu that appears.

4 The slide is deleted.

End

INTRODUCTION

If you think of a new topic you want to include in your presentation, you might need to insert a new slide. On the other hand, you might determine that your presentation runs a bit long and decide to delete a slide.

TIP

Changing the Design of New Slides
Any new slides you add will have the same design of the slide that was selected before you added the new slide. To apply a different design, first scroll through the design options in the Slide Layout task pane. When you find the design you need, double-click it to apply it.

Duplicating Slides

Start

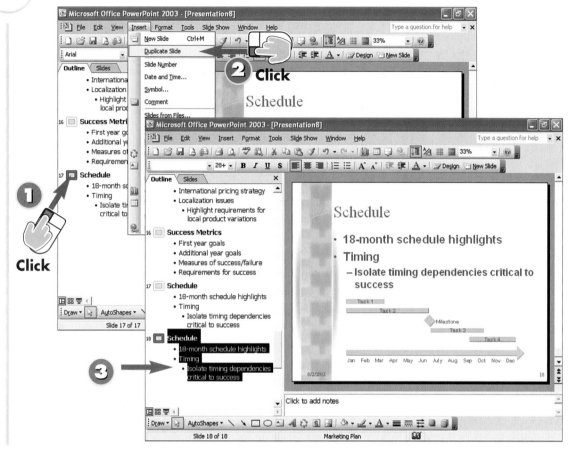

1 In Normal view, click the slide you want to duplicate in either the Outline or the Slides tab.

2 Open the **Insert** menu and select **Duplicate Slide** to duplicate the slide.

3 A duplicate of the slide is created.

End

TIP

Duplicating Layout and Design
Suppose you have applied a slide layout or slide design template to a slide and want other slides to be formatted in the same way. In that case, you could duplicate the slide repeatedly to create a base for all the slides in your presentation. For more information about applying slide layouts and design templates, see the tasks "Changing the Slide Layout" and "Changing the Slide Design" in this part.

Changing the Slide Layout

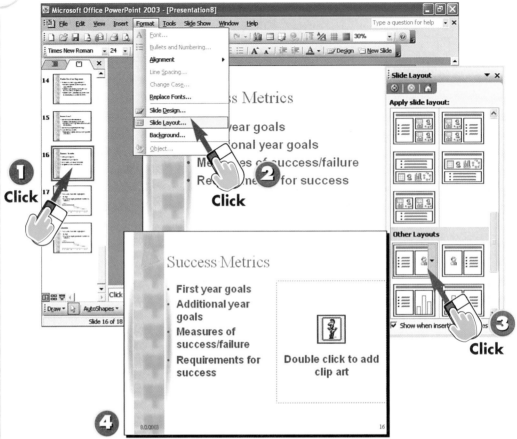

1 In Normal view, click the slide in which you want to alter the layout in either the Outline or Slides tab.

2 Open the **Format** menu and select **Slide Layout** to open the Slide Layout task pane, or select the **Slide Layout** option from the task pane drop-down list.

3 Scroll through the available slide layouts and click the one you like.

4 The selected layout is applied to the slide and the text and objects remain intact (although it might automatically resize to fit on the slide better).

INTRODUCTION
To add visual interest to your presentation, you can vary the layout of your slides. You can choose from numerous slide layouts (called *AutoLayouts*), including many that let you add features such as clip art, tables, and graphs.

TIP
Adding Clip Art and Tables
For more information on adding clip art, media clips, and tables to your slides, see Part 13.

CAUTION
Layout Overlap
If you apply a layout after you have finished a slide, some of the design formatting might overlap some of the information on your slides. If this happens, simply rearrange your information or remove the layout from the particular slide.

Changing the Slide Design

Start

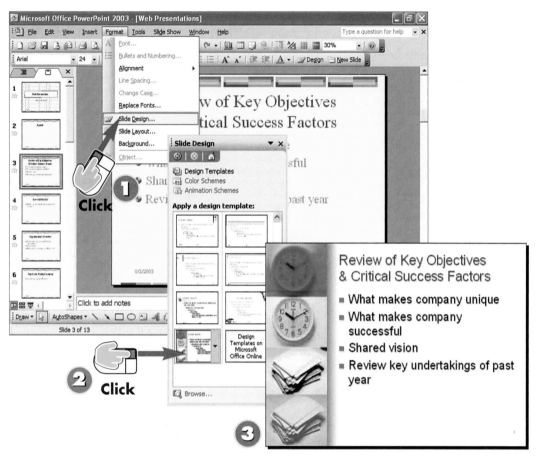

1 From any slide in the presentation, open the **Format** menu and select **Slide Design**. Or, select the **Slide Design** task page from the task pane drop-down list.

2 Scroll through the available slide designs and click the one you like.

3 The design is applied to all slides in the presentation that have not been previously assigned a specific design (and the text and objects remain intact).

End

Changing the Slide Color Scheme

Start

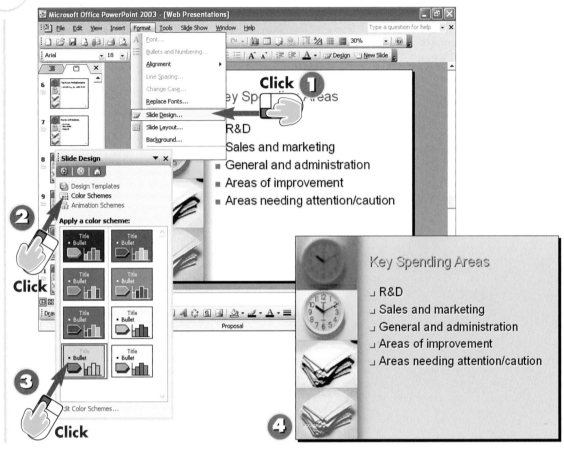

1 From any slide in the presentation, open the **Format** menu and select **Slide Design**. Or, select the **Slide Design - Color Schemes** task page.

2 Click the **Color Schemes** option on the Slide Design task pane.

3 Scroll through the available slide colors and click the one you like.

4 The color is applied to all slides in the presentation that have not been previously assigned a specific color (and the text and objects remain intact).

End

INTRODUCTION

In addition to offering numerous templates, slide layouts, and slide designs, PowerPoint lets you alter the color schemes of your slides. Some slide designs have only a few colors formats from which to choose, whereas others have several. If you are feeling adventurous, you can always edit the color schemes to your own liking.

TIP

Applying a Slide Color Scheme to Specific Slides
To apply a new slide color to specific slides in your presentation, press the **Ctrl** key while clicking each slide (in the Slides tab). When you move the mouse pointer over a slide color in the Slide Design Color Schemes Task pane, click the down arrow and choose **Apply to Selected Slides**.

Spell Checking Slide Text

Start

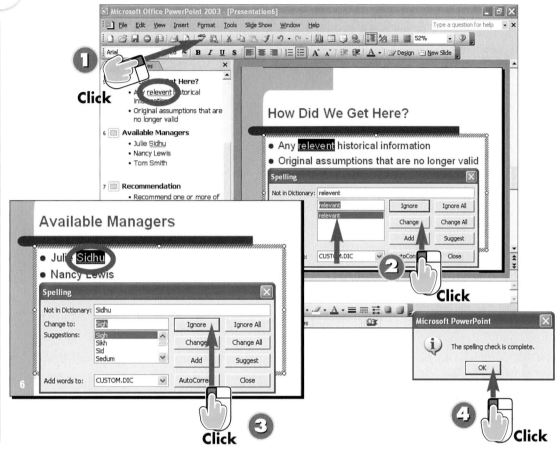

Click

Click

Click

Click

(3)

1. After you open the presentation whose spelling you want to check, click the **Spelling** button on the Standard toolbar to launch the spell check.

2. If PowerPoint finds an error, it highlights the misspelled word and opens the Spelling dialog box. Click the correct spelling in the **Suggestions** list and click the **Change** button.

3. PowerPoint corrects the error and moves to the next one. If the flagged word is correct as is, click **Ignore** to skip this instance of the word (or click **Ignore All**).

4. PowerPoint continues flagging errors; change or ignore them as necessary. When PowerPoint indicates that the spelling check is complete, click **OK**.

End

INTRODUCTION

Any text in a slide that appears with a red wavy line under it indicates a misspelled word or a word that isn't in the Office dictionary. This enables you to immediately see whether a word you typed is misspelled. In addition, you can use PowerPoint's Spelling dialog box to check for errors in your presentation.

No Usable Suggestions?
If none of PowerPoint's suggested corrections is the one you need to correct an error, you can correct the word yourself. Click in the **Change to** list box, type the correct word, and click the **Change** button.

Checking from the Beginning
You don't have to be at the beginning of a presentation when you check for spelling errors. If you start in the middle of a presentation, PowerPoint automatically continues at the beginning of the document.

Enhancing PowerPoint Presentations

You can insert many elements—such as tables, clip art, and other objects—into your presentations to help keep the audience's attention and interest in the information you are presenting. In addition, you can add special features such as animation effects, transitions, and action buttons to enhance your presentation.

Your PowerPoint presentation file contains everything you need: an outline of your presentation, your slides, audience handouts, and even your speaker's notes. You can prepare this file to give at a presentation using the Pack and Go feature. This allows you to give your presentation on a computer that doesn't have PowerPoint installed.

You can even rehearse the timing of the presentation to make sure it isn't too long or too short. You can also print your outline, speaker's notes, and audience handouts to use and distribute. And, you can publish your PowerPoint presentation to the Web.

Inserting Slide Objects

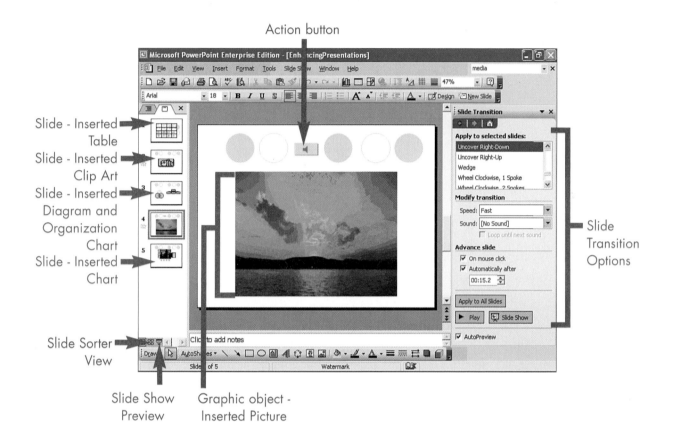

Action button

Slide - Inserted Table

Slide - Inserted Clip Art

Slide - Inserted Diagram and Organization Chart

Slide - Inserted Chart

Slide Transition Options

Slide Sorter View

Slide Show Preview

Graphic object - Inserted Picture

Inserting a Table

Start

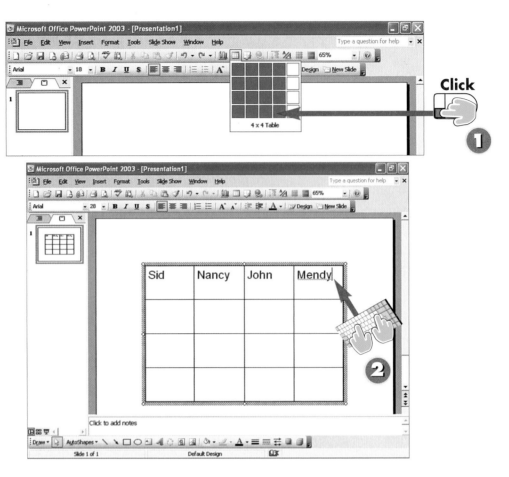

Click

1 Click the **Insert Table** button on the Standard toolbar and select the number of rows and columns you want the table to have (for example, **4×4**).

2 A table is inserted; click in it and type the text you want placed in the table. Use the Tab and arrow keys to move between the table cells, like in Excel.

End

INTRODUCTION

Sometimes you might need to add more to your presentation than just words. For example, you might want to display data or show relationships between numbers or totals. Creating a table in PowerPoint is one way to do this. You can insert a table directly into your slide and format it just as you would a Word table.

TIP

Adding Excel Worksheets
You can add Excel worksheets to your presentations as objects. To do so, open the **Insert** menu and select **Object** to open the Insert Object dialog box; then select **Microsoft Excel Worksheet** from the **Object Type** list (if you want to browse for a specific, already created worksheet file, select the **Create from File** option; otherwise, select **Create New**). Click the **OK** button.

Inserting a Chart

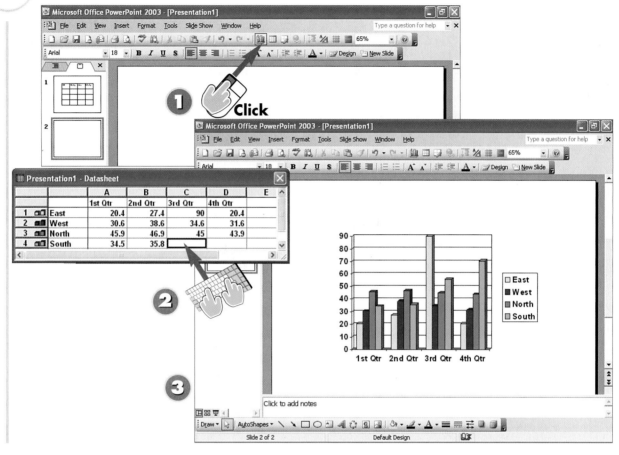

1. Click the **Insert Chart** button on the Standard toolbar to open a sample chart and Datasheet window.

2. Type the desired data in the datasheet, using the **Tab** and **arrow keys** to move between the cells, just like in Excel.

3. The chart automatically updates to reflect the data you type into the datasheet.

INTRODUCTION

Charts can be a great way to get your point across in a presentation because they present data visually. For example, instead of including a worksheet or table, you could use a graph that shows a comparison of your sales regions by quarter.

TIP

Adding an Excel Chart
To insert an existing Excel chart directly into your presentation, select **Insert**, **Object**. Then, select **Microsoft Excel Chart** from the **Object Type** list (make sure the Create New option is selected) and click **OK**.

TIP

Copying and Pasting
An alternative to typing all the information into your datasheet is to copy and paste it from your source (if you have a data source)—such as Excel, for example.

Inserting Clip Art

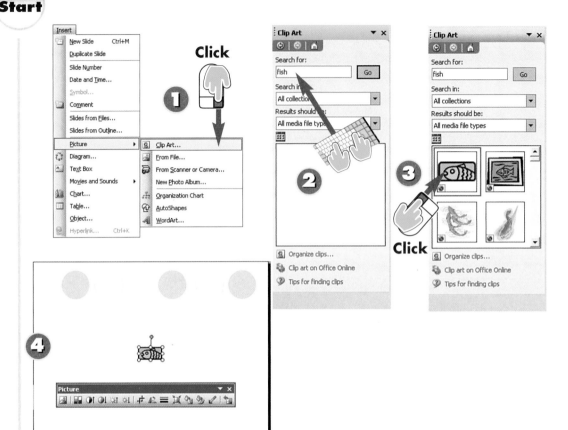

Start

Click

Click

End

1. Open the **Insert** menu and select **Picture, Clip Art** to open the Clip Art task pane.

2. Type a description for the clip art you are looking for in the **Search for** text box, and then press **Enter**.

3. If Microsoft has clip art that matches the description you typed, it is displayed in the Clip Art task pane. Click an image in the results list to insert it into your worksheet.

4. The clip art is inserted into your slide.

INTRODUCTION

With Microsoft clip art, you can choose from numerous professionally prepared images, sounds, and movie clips. You can move them around in the document and even assign text wrapping. (The first time you try to use Microsoft clip art, you might be asked to set up your collections and organize your clips. Be sure you do this.)

TIP

The Picture Toolbar
When you insert a picture, such as clip art, the Picture toolbar appears with tools you can use to crop the picture, add a border to it, or adjust its brightness and contrast.

TIP

Resizing and Repositioning Clip Art
You can resize and move the clip art anywhere on the slide. See p. 217 for more information about this.

Inserting a Diagram or an Organizational Chart

Start

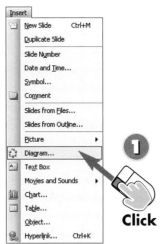

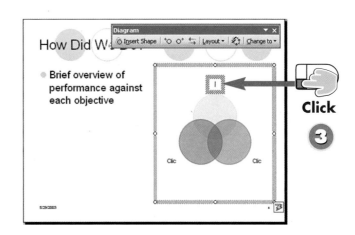

Click

3

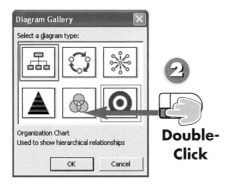

2

Double-Click

Click

1. Open the **Insert** menu and select **Diagram** to open the Diagram Gallery.

2. Double-click the desired diagram type—for example, **Venn Diagram**—to insert it into your slide.

3. Click to add text to the diagram as necessary.

End

INTRODUCTION

PowerPoint lets you insert a diagram or an organizational chart directly into your slides. You can insert the diagram or chart and then add the appropriate information in a manner similar to inserting a table and adding the data.

TIP

Inserting Organization Charts
You can open the **Insert** menu and select **Picture**, **Organization Chart** to insert an organization chart ready for you to input information.

Inserting a Picture from a File

Start

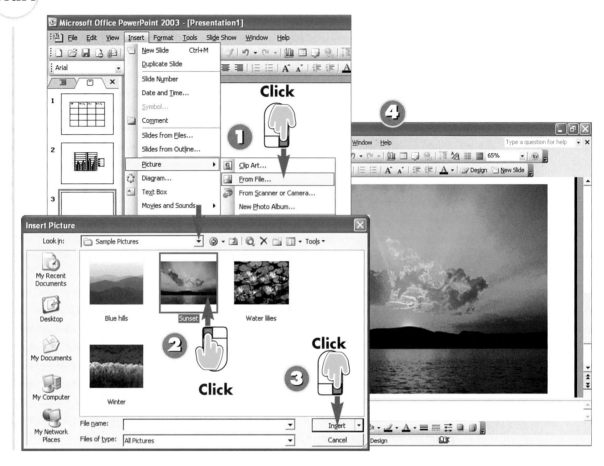

1 Open the **Insert** menu and select **Picture, From File** to open the Insert Picture dialog box.

2 Using the **Places** bar or the **Look in** drop-down list, open the folder that contains the file you want to insert, and click the file to select it.

3 Click the **Insert** button to insert the file into the slide.

4 The picture file is placed.

End

INTRODUCTION

With digital cameras and sharing pictures online becoming more popular, you'll most likely want to insert a picture file that you have saved on your computer into a slide in your presentation. You can easily insert all types of graphics files: Windows Metafiles, JPEG files, PNGs, Macintosh PICT files, Kodak Photo CD files, and many more.

TIP

Movies and Sounds
To insert movies and sounds into your slides, select **Insert, Movies and Sounds**. Then select Movie from Clip Organizer (select from the movie clips Office installed); Movie from File (select from your own movie clip files); Sound from Clip Organizer (select from the sound clips Office installed); Sound from File (select from your own sound clip files); Play CD Audio Track (select from your own music CD or downloaded audio track); or Record Sound (record your own sound clips).

Resizing or Moving Objects

Start

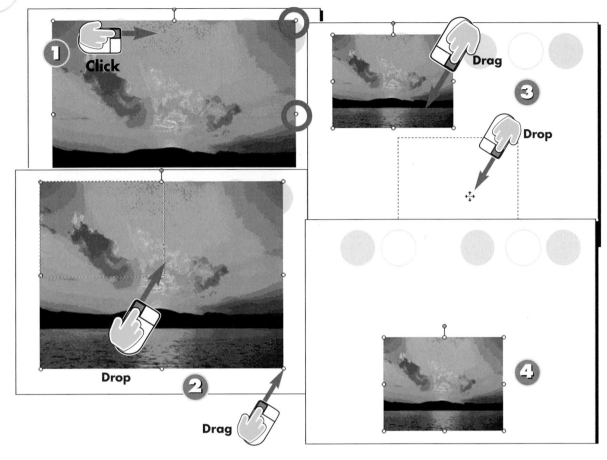

1 To resize an object, first click the object you want to resize. Sizing handles appear around the edges of the object.

2 Click and drag one of the handles inward to make the object smaller or outward to make it bigger; then release the mouse button.

3 To move an object, click the object and drag it to the spot where you want it to appear. Release the mouse button to drop the object in its new location.

4 The object is moved.

End

INTRODUCTION

You can easily move or resize objects—including text, art, tables, and charts—on a slide, or you can move them to another slide. In addition to resizing and moving objects, you can cut, copy, and paste them just as you do in Word (refer to p. 38 for more information).

TIP

Correct Proportions
Using the corner border handles to resize an object increases or decreases proportionately. If you use the side border handles, you increase the horizontal and vertical sizes separately, possibly making the object look disproportionate.

TIP

Rotating Objects
To rotate an object, double-click the object to open its Format dialog box. Select the **Size** tab and alter the **Rotation** angle so that it alters the displayed direction of the object—for example, by 90°.

Reordering Slides

Start

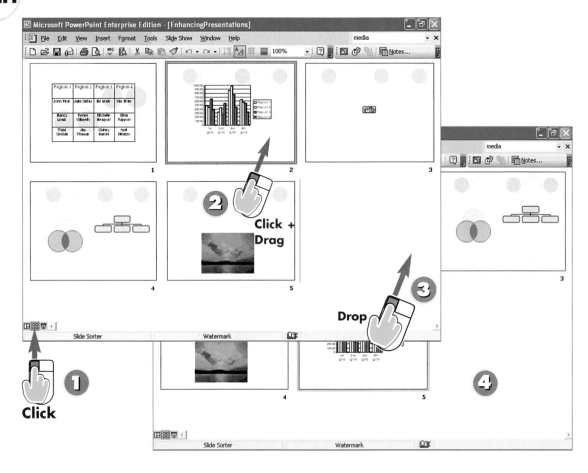

Click

Click + Drag

Drop

1 Click the **Slide Sorter View** button.

2 Click a slide you want to move and drag it to the desired spot in the order.

3 Release the mouse button to drop the slide in the new location.

4 The slide is moved and the other slides reorder.

End

INTRODUCTION

You can quickly and easily rearrange the order of your PowerPoint slides. For example, you might decide you want to place your graphical slides earlier in your presentation to draw the attention of the audience.

TIP

Undoing an Action
If you move a slide to the wrong location, click the slide and move it again. Alternatively, click the **Undo** button on the Standard toolbar (or press **Ctrl+Z**) to undo your last action of moving the slide.

Viewing a Slide Show

Start

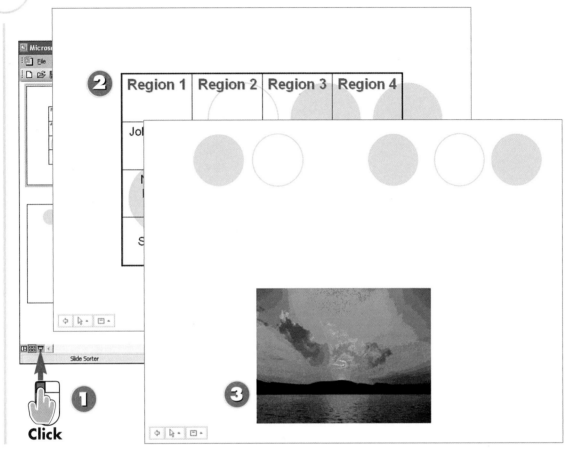

Click

End

① With your presentation open, click the **Slide Show View** button on the View toolbar.

② The first slide in your presentation is displayed; press the **spacebar** to display the next slide.

③ The next slide is displayed. Press the **Esc** key at any time to stop the slide show anywhere in the presentation.

INTRODUCTION

Perhaps the best way to test your PowerPoint presentation is to view the presentation onscreen. Your slides appear in vivid color and consume the entire screen (as they would in an actual presentation). You can use the mouse pointer, press the spacebar, or press the Page Up and Page Down keys to advance the slides. Pressing the Esc key returns you to Normal view.

TIP

Keyboard Options
To display the previous slide, press the **Backspace** key. To display a particular slide, press the number of the specific slide on the keyboard and then press the **Enter** key. To stop the slide show, press the **Esc** key.

Adding Slide Transitions

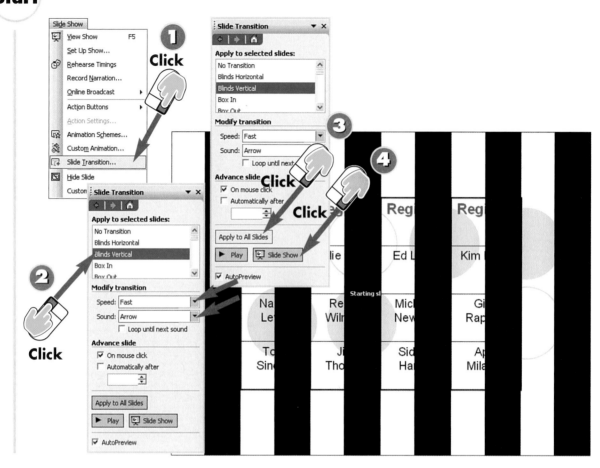

1 Open the **Slide Show** menu and select **Slide Transition** to open the Slide Transition task pane.

2 In the **Apply to Selected Slides** list, click the transition effect you want to use. You can modify the transition with the **Speed** and **Sound** lists.

3 Click the **Apply to All Slides** button to apply the slide transition to all slides in the presentation; otherwise, see the tip on this page.

4 Click the **Slide Show** button to see what the effect will look like on your presentation (move through it like you did in the previous task, "Viewing a Slide Show").

INTRODUCTION

Slide transitions can make your presentations look more professional and interesting. For example, having each slide appear to open like a vertical blind draws the attention of the audience. It's generally best to use only one type of transition in a presentation because using more can distract the audience from your message.

TIP

Additional Effect Options
If you want a special transition effect for a single slide, open the slide, select the effect, and select to apply it to the slide instead of to all slides. You can also change how you move to the next slide—for example, you can select On Mouse Click or Automatically After (you select the number of seconds).

Adding Animation Effects

Start

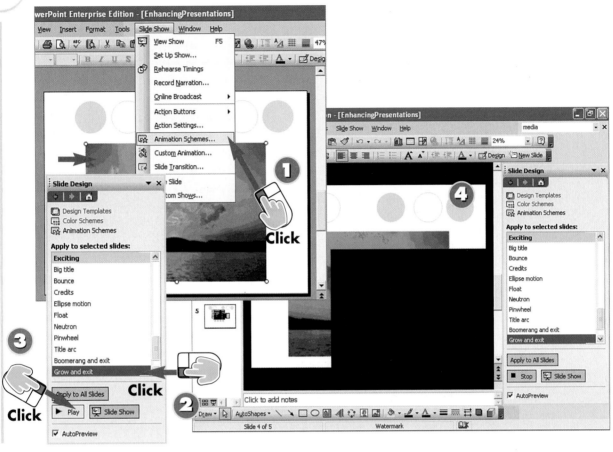

End

1 After you click the object to which you want to add a slide animation, open the **Slide Show** menu and select **Animation Schemes**.

2 The Slide Design task pane opens with the available animation schemes displayed. Click the effect you want to apply to the object.

3 Click the **Play** button.

4 View this effect as it appears in the slide area.

INTRODUCTION

In today's multimedia world, text and graphics sometimes aren't enough to keep an audience's attention. PowerPoint's animation effects, or *schemes*, can bring presentations to life, making it hard for people to ignore information. You can apply animations to draw attention to especially relevant information. For example, you could make a picture you don't want your audience to forget appear slowly on the slide. Keep in mind that effects on slides that aren't beneficial to the presentation can distract your audience instead of adding emphasis in a positive way.

TIP

Applying Effects
The types of animation effects you can apply depend on the type of object to which you are applying them. In addition, not all effects are installed by default, so you might need the Office installation CD to add some effects to your presentations.

Adding Action Buttons

Start

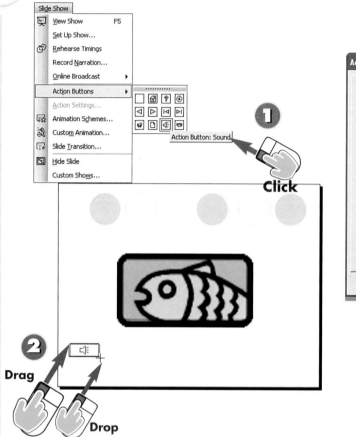

Click

Drag

Drop

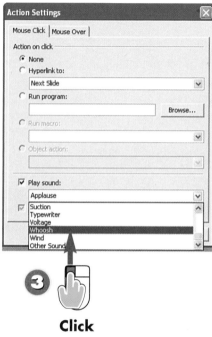

Click

1. Open the **Slide Show** menu, select **Action Buttons**, and select the **Sound** button from the list of buttons that appears (ScreenTips explain the sounds).

2. Click and hold the mouse button in the location where you want to add the action button to the slide. Then drag it to the appropriate size and release the mouse button.

3. The Action Settings dialog box opens. Click the down arrow next to the **Play Sound** field and select the sound you want to associate with the action button.

INTRODUCTION

Action buttons are elements you can add to your PowerPoint presentations to provide information or draw attention to your presentation. For example, you can add an action button that makes a sound when you click the button during the presentation. You can set up any type of action to be associated with the action button: opening a document, linking to a URL, or even playing a sound or movie clip. In this task, you learn how to add an action button to a slide and configure that action button to play a sound when it is clicked.

TIP

Independent Actions
Each action button should be independent of other objects on your slides. Action buttons do not work properly if you group them.

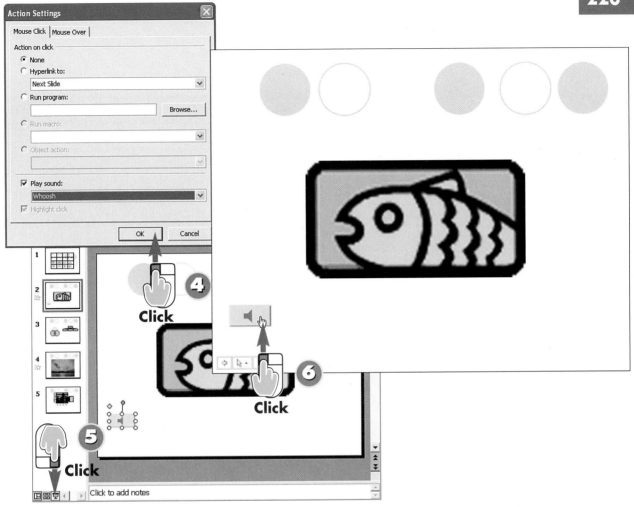

4 Click **OK**.

5 To try the action button, begin by clicking the **Slide Show** button.

6 Click the action button to hear the sound. When you're finished, press the **Esc** key to return to Slide view.

End

Multiple Action Buttons
TIP
You can place several action buttons on a slide. For example, you can create one that makes a sound, one that takes you to a Web site, and one that pops up visual information for the audience.

Adding Hyperlink Buttons
TIP
Adding a hyperlink button to your presentation can be a convenient resource for information. For example, if someone in the audience has a question about where your information came from, you could click a hyperlink button and immediately go to the Web site where you obtained your information (assuming, of course, that your PC is connected to the Internet during the presentation).

Preparing the Presentation for Another Computer

Start

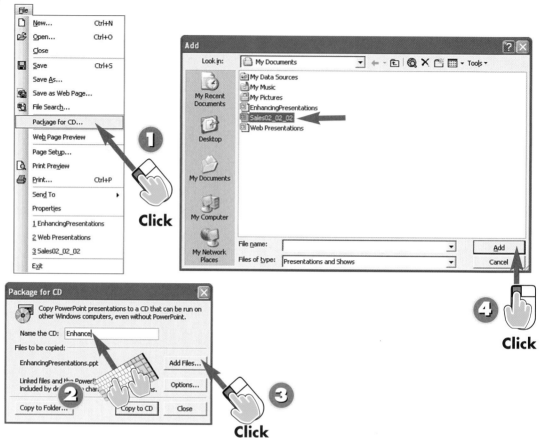

1. After you've opened the presentation you want to pack, open the **File** menu and select **Package for CD**.

2. The Package for CD dialog box opens. Type a name for the CD you want to create (maximum 16 characters) in the **Name the CD** text box.

3. Click the **Add Files** button to open the Add dialog box, where you select additional files you need for your presentation—linked files are included by default.

4. Select a file to include, and click **Add**. PowerPoint returns you to the Package for CD dialog box. Repeat steps 3 and 4 until you've selected all the files you need.

INTRODUCTION

You might need to use someone else's computer to give a presentation. Fortunately, you can create a CD of your presentation and use it to view the presentation from any computer—even one that does not have PowerPoint installed. The PowerPoint feature that enables you to do this is called *Package for CD*.

TIP

CD Options

You'll want to include on the CD any files linked to your presentation, along with the PowerPoint Viewer. Fortunately, these items are included by default. If you don't want to include them on your CD, click the **Options** button in the Package for CD dialog box and use the Options dialog box that opens to deselect them. Also, always check the Embed Truetype Fonts option; otherwise, the presentation will not look right if the fonts you use aren't on the presentation computer.

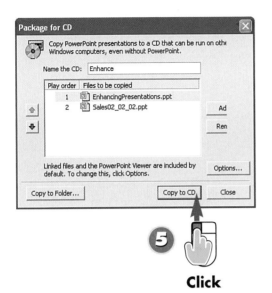

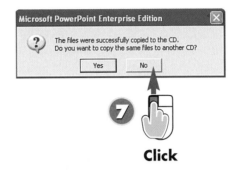

Click
⑤

Click
⑦

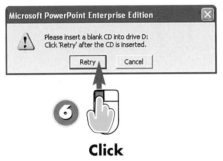

⑥
Click

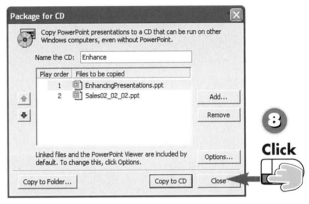

⑧
Click

⑤ When all the files you need appear in the play list, click the **Copy to CD** button.

⑥ If you haven't yet inserted a blank CD into your computer's writable CD drive, PowerPoint prompts you to do so. Insert a blank, writable CD in the drive and click **Retry**.

⑦ PowerPoint displays its progress as it copies the files to CD and notifies you when the process is complete. To copy the files to another CD, click **Yes**; otherwise, click **No**.

⑧ PowerPoint ultimately returns you to the Package for CD dialog box; click the **Close** button.

End

Altering the Play Order
You can alter the order in which selected files are played by clicking a file in the play order in the Package for CD dialog box and then clicking the up and down arrows on the left side of the dialog box to move the file up or down in the order. To remove a file from the list, click the file and then click the **Remove** button.

Copying to a Folder
If you prefer to copy the presentation to a folder (for example, on a network), click the **Copy to Folder** button in the Package for CD dialog box. This comes in handy if you need to use a different computer to copy the files onto CD.

Rehearsing a Presentation

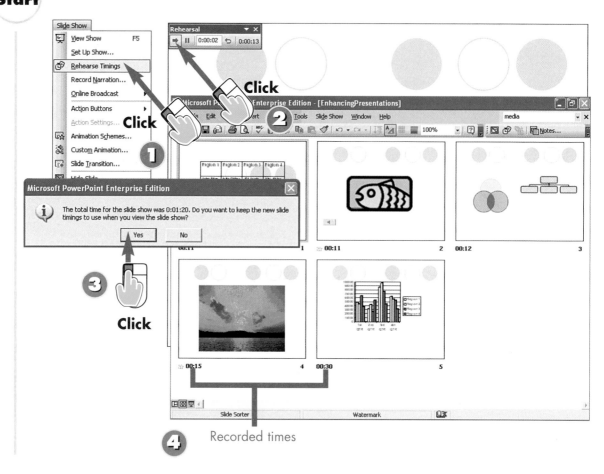

Recorded times

1. After you've opened the presentation you want to rehearse, open the **Slide Show** menu and select **Rehearse Timings**.

2. Rehearse your slide show, clicking the **Next** button on the Rehearsal toolbar to move through each of the slides as you would perform them.

3. When you finish rehearsing the slide show, PowerPoint asks whether you want to record your slide times. If so, click **Yes**.

4. PowerPoint displays these times in Slide Sorter view.

When people create presentations, they usually have a specific time limit they need to stick to. Instead of using your watch and trying to time the show yourself, why not let PowerPoint do the work for you? If you need to stop and make some notes, you can pause the time recorder. If you get off to a bad start or need to repeat the rehearsal, you can click the Repeat button. When you get to the end of the slide show, PowerPoint asks whether you want to record the slide times; if you do, Slide Sorter view shows recorded times with each slide.

Canceling the Rehearsal
You can click the Close (×) button on the Rehearsal toolbar to cancel a rehearsal and resume working in the presentation.

Printing a Presentation

Start

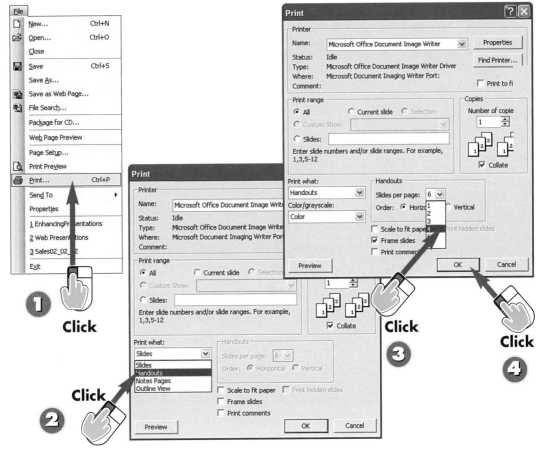

Click ①

Click ②

Click ③

Click ④

① After you've opened the presentation you want to print, open the **File** menu and select **Print** to open the Print dialog box.

② Click the down arrow next to the **Print what** field and select a printing option (for example, **Handouts**).

③ Click the down arrow next to the **Slides per Page** field and select the number you want (for example, **4**). (This option is available only if you print handouts.)

④ Click the **OK** button to print the presentation. Alternatively, click the **Preview** button to see what the printed presentation will look like.

End

INTRODUCTION

In PowerPoint, you can print copies of your slides, handouts for your audience, notes pages, or the outline. For example, you might want to print copies of your presentation so the audience can follow along, print your presentation in Outline view for your boss to review, or print speaker notes for yourself.

TIP

Additional Printing Options
In the Print Range area of the Print dialog box, you can select to print all slides, the current slide, or specific slides. In the Copies area, you can select the number of copies to print or have PowerPoint collate the slides.

Getting Started with Outlook

Microsoft Outlook is an email client, an appointment calendar, a journal, and several other tools all rolled into one personal information management (PIM) application. Outlook is similar to a three-ring organizer with folders that you might tote around during your business day.

With Outlook, you can keep track of email, daily appointments, and meetings. Whether you are working on an individual computer or computers linked in workgroups, you can use Outlook to contact people, prioritize your work, and manage your time. You can easily access all these features using the Outlook bar—with it, you can see items in your calendar, tasks, contacts list, and even mail folders.

Outlook mail folders let you read, create, and send messages. When you receive a message, it goes in your Inbox. When you create and send a message, it goes in your Outbox until you actually connect to the Internet. After you have connected to the Internet and sent the message, Outlook puts a copy of the message in your Sent Items folder.

To use Outlook's email features, you need to have access to the Internet. You might have an account with an online service (for example, America Online), with a local Internet service provider (ISP), or in a corporate setting where you have to log in to the network to gain Internet access. In any case, you should connect to the Internet to perform the tasks in this part, although to understand the tasks, you don't need to.

Using Email

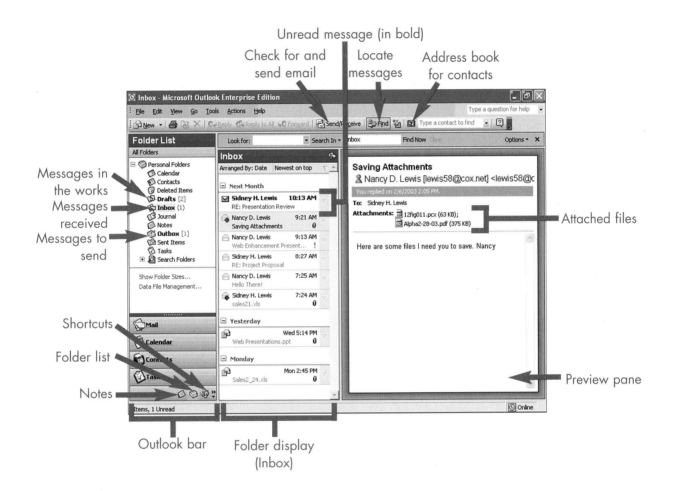

Unread message (in bold)

Check for and send email

Locate messages

Address book for contacts

Messages in the works

Messages received

Messages to send

Shortcuts

Folder list

Notes

Attached files

Preview pane

Outlook bar

Folder display (Inbox)

Moving Around in Outlook

Start

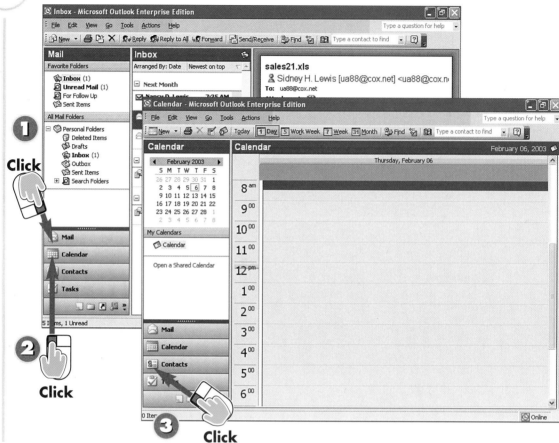

Click

Click

Click

1 Click **Mail** on the Outlook bar to view the default Mail options.

2 Mail options are displayed. To view the default Calendar options, click **Calendar** on the Outlook bar.

3 Calendar options are displayed. To view the default Contacts options, click **Contacts** on the Outlook bar.

TIP

Outlook Bar
You can decrease the Outlook bar display buttons so that you can see more options available to each Outlook task. Click the heavy blue bar above the Mail button and drag it larger (up) or smaller (down) to view more or less of the Outlook bar buttons.

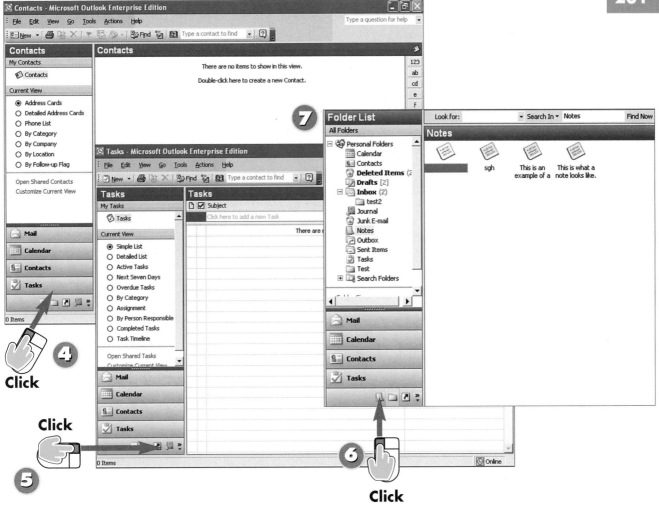

Click

Click

Click

4. Contacts options are displayed. To view the default Tasks options, click **Tasks** on the Outlook bar.

5. Tasks options are displayed. To view the default list of Outlook options, click **Folder List** on the Outlook bar.

6. The Folder list is displayed. To view the default Notes options, click **Notes** on the Outlook bar.

End

Compact Folder Files

When you start to accumulate hundreds of emails saved in Outlook, it can affect your computer's performance (slow it down). One thing you can do is compact your folder files. To do so, click the **Data File Management** link (you might need to scroll down in the Folder List) to open the Outlook Data Files dialog box. Then, click the **Settings** button to open the Personal Folders options. In this dialog box, click the **Compact Now** button to shrink the size of your personal folder file on your hard drive.

Changing Your Email Preferences

Start

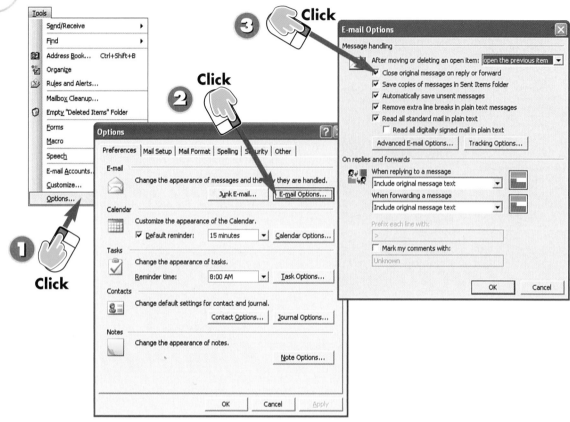

1 Open the **Tools** menu and select **Options** to open the Options dialog box to the Preferences tab.

2 Click the **E-mail Options** button to open the E-mail Options dialog box; the current settings are the Outlook defaults.

3 Click **Close Original Message on Reply or Forward** so anytime you reply to or forward a message, the original message window will automatically be closed.

INTRODUCTION

After you get used to working with email, you will find that you have individual preferences you associate with the emails you send to and receive from others. For example, when replying to a message, some people don't like to have the original message as part of the email (the default is to display the original at the bottom of the reply). As another example, you can have all the email you receive appear as regular text if you don't want to view message formatting. Test drive Outlook's various email preferences to see what you like best.

TIP

Other Options
You might have noticed that the first Options dialog box contains buttons to change the options for the Calendar, Tasks, Contacts, Journal, and Notes. You can click these buttons to review the Outlook defaults and make changes as you like.

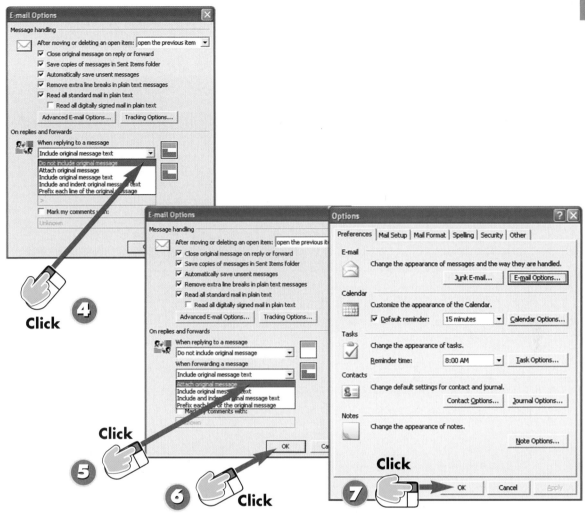

Click ④

Click ⑤

⑥ **Click**

⑦ **Click**

④ Click the down arrow next to the **When Replying to a Message** field and choose how you want the original message handled.

⑤ Click the down arrow next to the **When Forwarding a Message** field and choose how you want the original message handled.

⑥ Click the **OK** button in the E-mail Options dialog box to accept your changes.

⑦ Click the **OK** button in the Options dialog box to apply your changes and return to working in Outlook.

End

Mail Setup
Click the **Mail Setup** tab on the Options dialog box and set up additional email accounts by clicking the **E-mail Accounts** button. For example, suppose you have a temporary email account on Yahoo.com that you want to periodically check; you can instruct Outlook to check for email on this account each time you send or receive messages (or immediately, if you have the Send Immediately When Connected option checked in the Options dialog box). In addition, the Send/Receive button enables you to specify which email accounts are checked when, and in what order.

Spelling
The Spelling tab on the Options dialog box enables you to request that your emails be automatically spell-checked before your email is sent (after you click the Send button). This is a convenient feature you should always select.

Creating an Address Book Contact

Start

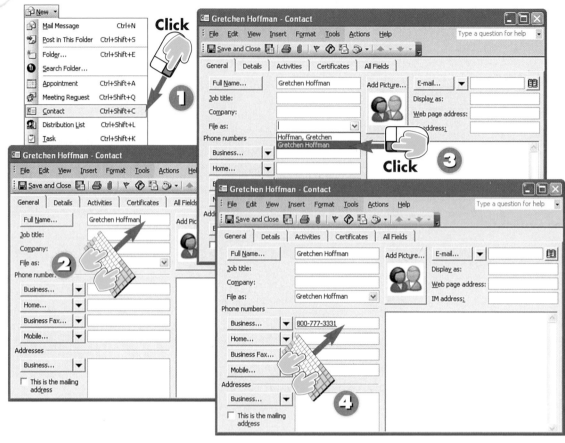

1. Click the down arrow next to the **New** button on Outlook's Standard toolbar and select **Contact** from the menu that appears.

2. An untitled contact window appears. Type the contact's name in the **Full Name** text box; the window's title bar is updated to reflect the name you typed.

3. Click the down arrow next to the **File As** field and choose how you want the contact name to appear (last name first or vice versa).

4. In the **Phone Numbers** area, type any phone numbers you have for the contact in the **Business**, **Home**, **Business Fax**, and **Mobile** fields.

INTRODUCTION

Using Outlook's Address Book, you can store information about all your business and personal contacts, much like you would with a paper-based address book. After you enter all your contacts—that is, the names, addresses, phone numbers, and email addresses of your friends, family members, and business contacts—into Outlook's Address Book, you can use this information to send email, create mailing lists, and more.

TIP

Deleting a Contact
To delete a contact, click the **Contacts** button in the Outlook bar to switch to Contacts view, click the contact to select it, and then click the **Delete** button on the Contacts toolbar.

Click

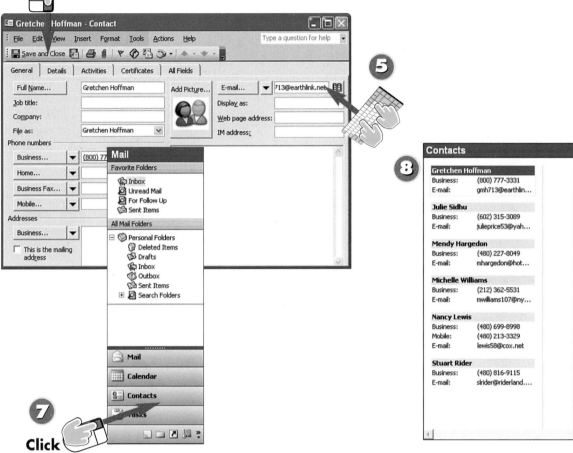

Click

(5) Type the contact's email address in the **E-mail** field.

(6) When you finish entering information about the contact, click the **Save and Close** button on the Contact window's toolbar.

(7) Click **Contacts** on the Outlook bar to see a list of your current contacts.

(8) Your list of contacts appears. To add more contacts, repeat the steps in this task.

End

Opening the Address Book
To open your address book to review all your contacts, click the **Address Book** button on the Standard toolbar. (The button looks like a book lying open flat.)

The Details Tab
The Details tab of the Contact window allows you to add more specific information about a contact. For example, you can include Department, Office, Profession, Manager's Name, and Assistant's Name information.

Adding a Contact Picture
You can click the Add Picture button—which looks like the head and shoulders of two people—to display an image file. The Add Contact Picture dialog box opens, and you can select a filename to which to link.

Creating and Sending an Email Message

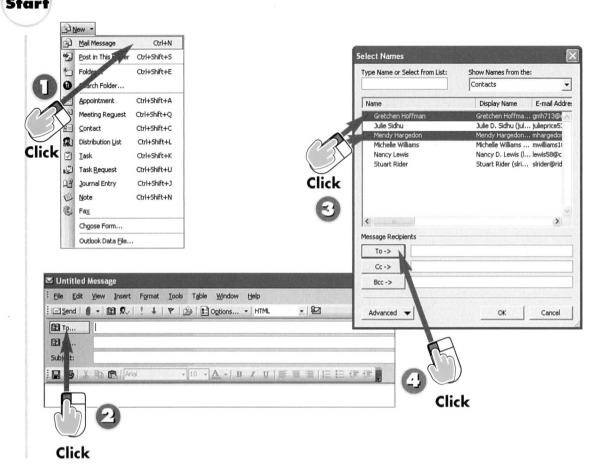

1. Click the down arrow next to the **New** button on Outlook's Standard toolbar and select **Mail Message** from the menu that appears.

2. An untitled message window appears. Click the **To** button to open the Select Names dialog box. (Or, type the recipient's email address in the **To** field and go to step 6.)

3. The Select Names dialog box opens. In the **Name** list, click the name of the person to receive your message. To select multiple names, **Ctrl+click** each name.

4. Click the **To** button to place the selected name in the message window's To field.

INTRODUCTION

Creating and sending email messages will likely be the task you perform most often in Outlook. Fortunately, creating a new message is easy. You can attach files to your messages (covered later in this part), specify the level of a message's importance, and choose different recipients from your Outlook Contacts list.

Using Cc and Bcc
In addition to containing a To field, message windows also contain Cc (carbon copy) and Bcc fields. Enter a recipient in the Bcc field if you want her to receive the message without the primary recipient's knowledge.

Changing the Message
You can change the text in the To, Cc, Bcc, Subject, and Message fields at any time before you send your message. Simply click in the desired text area and type the correct information.

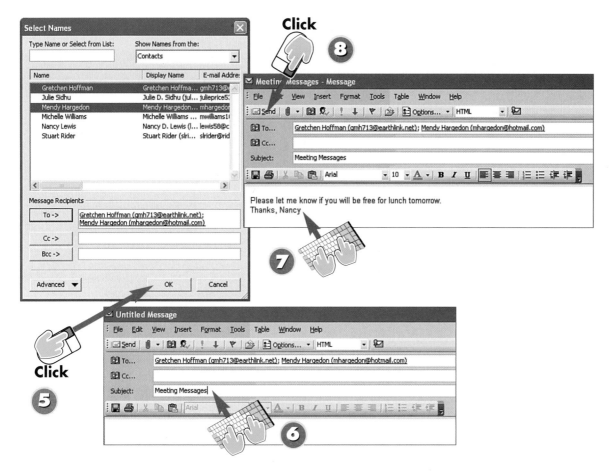

Click

8

Click

5

7

6

5. The selected recipients are added to the To field in the Select Names dialog box; click **OK** to add the names to the To field in the message window.

6. Click in the **Subject** area and type a brief but descriptive subject for your message.

7. Click in the body of the message window and type your message.

8. Click the **Send** button to send your message.

End

Checking For and Reading Email Messages

Start

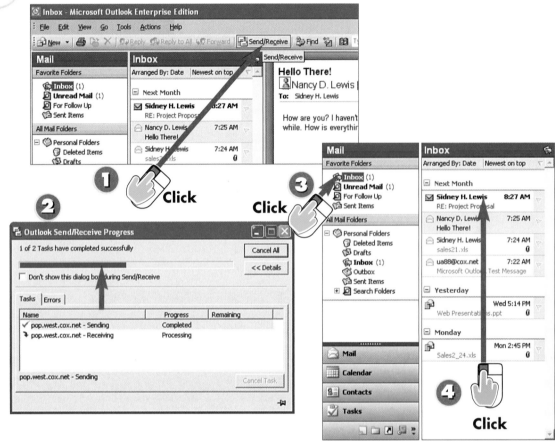

Click

Click

Click

1 Click the **Send/Receive** button on the Standard toolbar to send any email currently in your Outbox and receive email from others.

2 A dialog box that tracks the progress of the Send/Receive process appears briefly as Outlook checks all your email addresses for outgoing and incoming messages.

3 If the Inbox isn't already open, click the **Inbox** folder on the Outlook bar to display any new and old messages you have received (and haven't yet moved to another folder).

4 Unread messages appear in bold text. Click a new message you would like to read. To open the message in its own window, double-click the message.

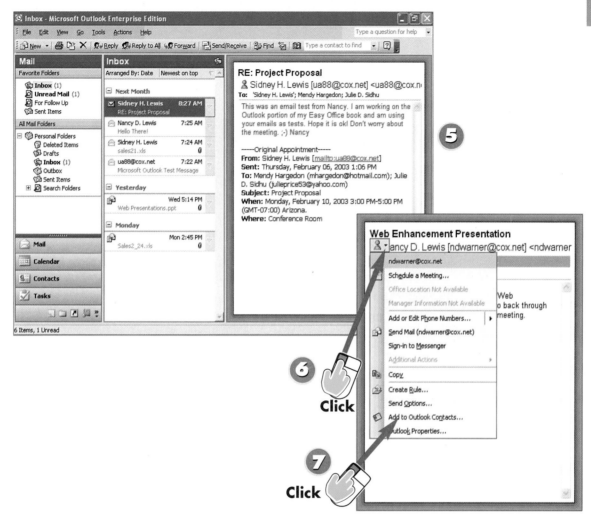

Click

Click

5 The contents of the new message are displayed in the Preview pane.

6 Click the **Sender Name** smart tag to view a list of options.

7 Optionally, select **Add to Outlook Contacts** to add the message's sender to your contacts list.

End

Reading Message Attachments
You can open and review any files that are attached to messages you receive while you are in Outlook. Double-click the attached file's name, and Outlook asks whether you want to open or save the file. If you opt to open the file, the file opens in the application in which it was created; if you don't have that application installed on your computer, Outlook asks which program you want to use to try to open the file. For more information about handling attachments, see the next task.

Saving Email Attachments

Start

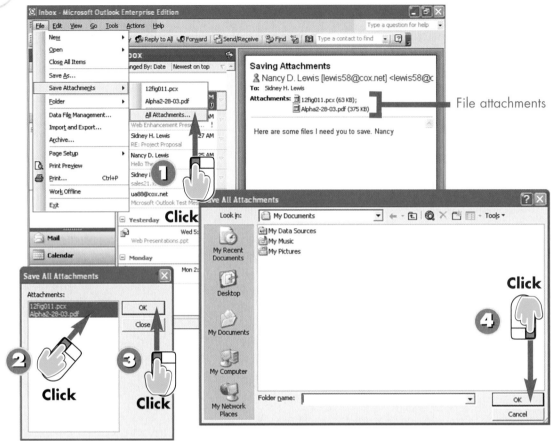

File attachments

Click

Click

Click

Click

End

1. With a message containing one or more attachments displayed in the Preview pane, open the **File** menu and select **Save Attachments**, **All Attachments**.

2. If the email message contains multiple attachments, the Save All Attachments dialog box opens. In the **Attachments** list, click the names of the files you want to save.

3. Click the **OK** button.

4. Locate and open the folder in which you want to save the attachment(s), and then click the **OK** button.

Single Attachments
The File, Save Attachments submenu lists the files attached to the selected message. To save specific files, select that file's name in the **File**, **Save Attachments** submenu.

Replying to an Email Message

Start

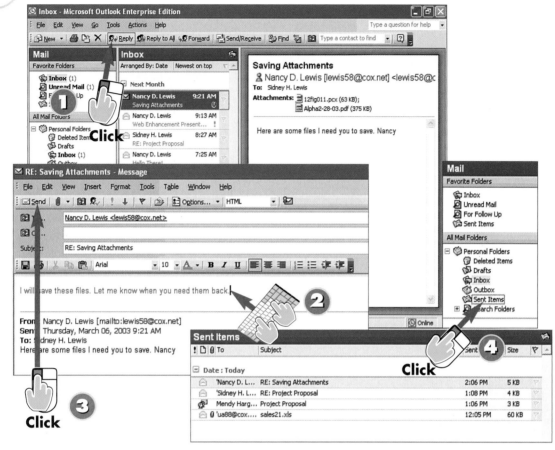

Click

Click

Click

Click

① Select the message to which you want to reply from the Inbox, and then click the **Reply** button on the Standard toolbar.

② A message window opens with the To and Subject fields complete. Type the body of your reply in the message window.

③ Click the **Send** button to send the message.

④ Click the **Sent Items** folder to see whether the message was sent. (This works only if you have your email preferences set to send messages immediately.)

End

INTRODUCTION

When you reply to a message, the To field of the message you send is automatically addressed to the sender of the original message (you can add or delete recipients as needed) and the Subject line contains the original message's subject preceded by **Re:** to indicate that your message is a reply.

TIP

Replying to All
If you receive a message that was also sent to other people, you might want to respond to the sender as well as to the other recipients. To do so, click the **Reply to All** button in step 2 and then type and send your message as normal.

TIP

Saving to Draft
If you try to close a message window before you send it, you can save it in the Drafts folder. To access it later, click the **Drafts** folder in the **Personal Folders** list. You might need to expand the list of All Mail Folders.

Forwarding an Email Message

Start

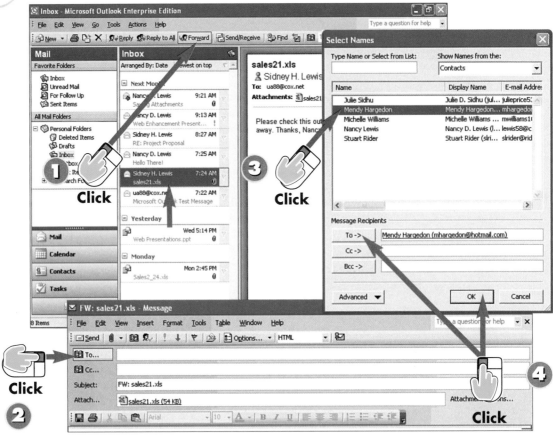

Click

Click

Click

Click

1 Select the message to forward from the Inbox, and click the **Forward** button. A message window containing the original message's subject and contents opens.

2 Click the **To** button to open the Select Names dialog box, or type the recipient's email address in the message window's **To** field and skip to step 4.

3 In the **Name** list, click the name of the person whom you want to receive the message (to select multiple names, **Ctrl+click** each name you want).

4 Click the **To** button, and then click **OK** to add the selected name(s) to the message window's To field.

INTRODUCTION

Suppose a message you've received would be pertinent to another individual. In that case, you can forward the message to that person. It's usually a good idea to add a sentence or two to the message that explains why you're forwarding the message.

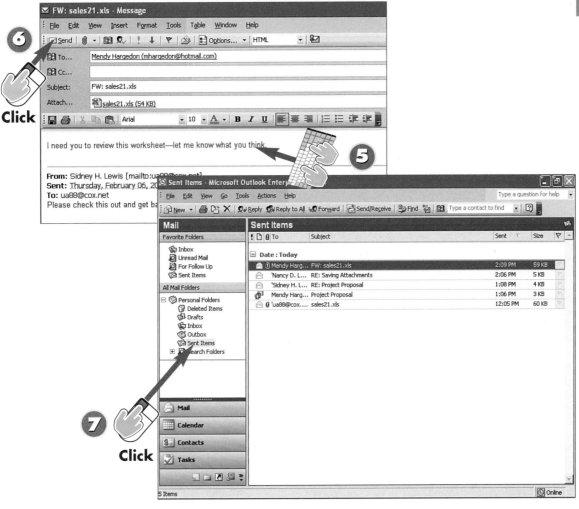

5 Click in the body of the message window and type your message.

6 Click the **Send** button to send your message.

7 Click the **Sent Items** folder to see whether the message was sent. (This works only if you've set your email preferences to send messages immediately.)

Altering Information
You can alter the information in the forwarding message window by selecting the text and deleting it or typing over it. For example, you might want to alter the Subject line to be more understandable to the person to whom you are forwarding the message.

Save to Draft
If you aren't ready to send a message you are writing—for example, if you're pressed for time and want to add more later—click the message window's **Close** (×) button. Outlook asks whether you want to save the message. Click **Yes**, and the message is saved in the Drafts folder. To access it later, click the Drafts folder in the Personal Folders list. You might need to expand the list of All Mail Folders.

Attaching Files to an Email Message

Start

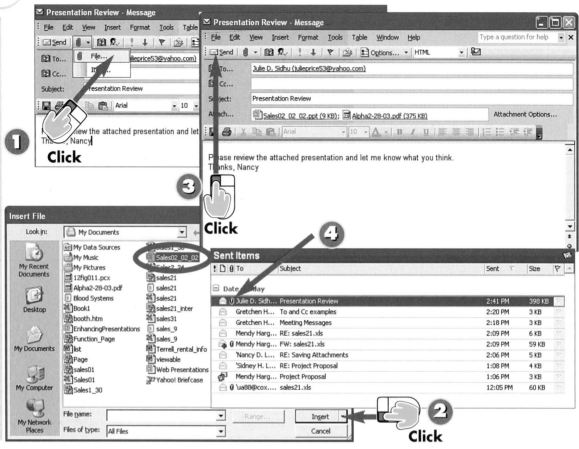

Click

Click

Click

End

1. Click the **Insert File** button (the one with a paperclip on it) on the message window's toolbar and select **File** from the menu that appears.

2. The Insert File dialog box opens. Locate and select the file(s) you want to attach to your email message; then click the **Insert** button.

3. The file is attached. Click the **Send** button to send the message as normal.

4. The sent message displays a paperclip icon next to the recipient's name in the Sent Items folder.

INTRODUCTION

Suppose you're working on a project with a co-worker and want to email her a document that contains an updated version of the project schedule. In that case, you simply "attach" the document file to the email message; then, when the recipient receives the email, she can open the attached file on her own computer.

TIP

Dragging Attachments
Another way to attach a file to an email message is to click and drag a file from your computer (for example, from the My Documents folder in an Explorer Window) and drop it on your email message.

TIP

Forwarding Versus Replying
Suppose you receive an email with an attached file. If you reply to that message, the attachment in the original message is not attached to the reply message. If you *forward* the message, however, the attachment remains.

Deleting an Email Message

Start

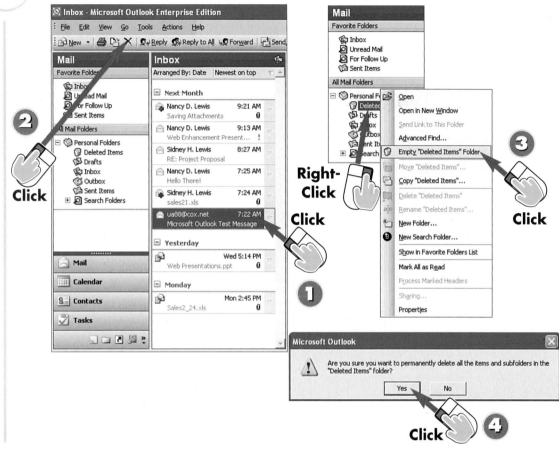

Right-Click

Click

Click

Click

1. Click the message you want to delete; it can be in any Mail folder.

2. Click the **Delete** button on the Standard toolbar. (Alternatively, press the **Delete** button on your keyboard.)

3. Deleted messages are placed in the Deleted Items folder. To empty this folder, right-click and select **Empty "Deleted Items" Folder** from the shortcut menu that appears.

4. Click the **Yes** button to permanently remove the messages in your Deleted Items folder from your system.

End

INTRODUCTION

As you receive more and more email messages, you might decide to delete any messages you no longer need. For example, you might want to delete the Welcome message Microsoft sends you the first time you use Outlook. You can delete messages in any folder.

TIP

Restoring Deleted Items
If you decide you want to keep the deleted message *before* you empty the Deleted Items folder, you can click the message in the Deleted Items folder and drag it into a different Mail folder.

Finding an Email Message

Start

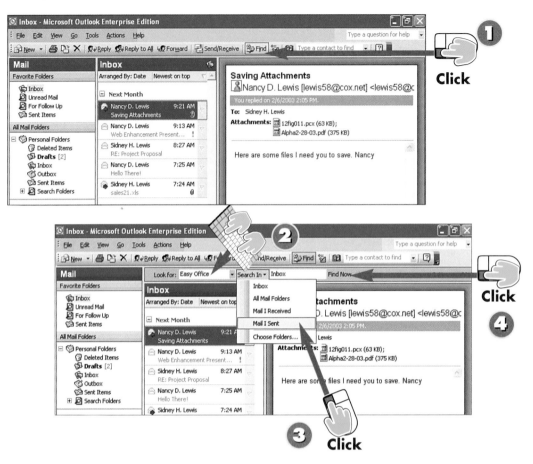

Click

Click

4

Click

3

Click

1 Click the **Find** button on the Standard toolbar to open the Find toolbar.

2 Type a keyword(s) in the **Look for** text box. This is the word that Outlook will search for in the Subject line and body of your messages.

3 Click the **Search in** button and select the Mail folder or folders you want to search. Select **Choose Folders** to search in a folder you created yourself.

4 Click the **Find Now** button; any matches are displayed in the Folder display area.

INTRODUCTION

Suppose you've received an email message that contains information you need, but you cannot remember which message it was. You do remember, however, some keywords that appear in the message. In that case, you can search for messages that contain the keywords you remember using Outlook's Find feature.

The Default Folder

TIP

Whichever Mail folder is currently open is the folder the Find feature searches by default. If you want to search in a different folder, be sure to select it in step 3.

Click **Click**

7 6

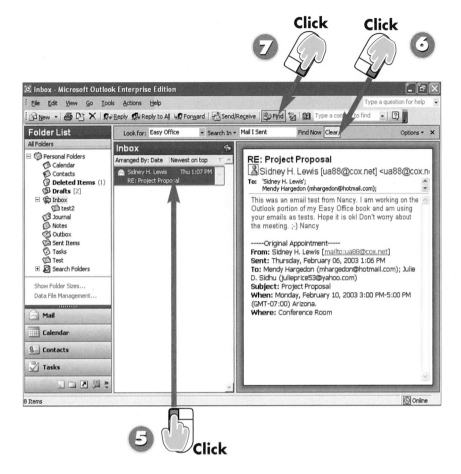

5 **Click**

5 Click one of the found messages to open it in the Preview pane.

6 To clear the search you just performed, click the **Clear** button. The search results are replaced by the contents of the folder that was open when you began the Find operation.

7 Click the **Find** button on the Standard toolbar to close the Find toolbar.

End

Advanced Find Options
If you don't find the message on your first try, try an advanced find. Click the **Options** button on the Find toolbar and select **Advanced Find** from the menu that appears. Then, narrow the scope of your find with more selection criteria.

Scheduling an Appointment

Start

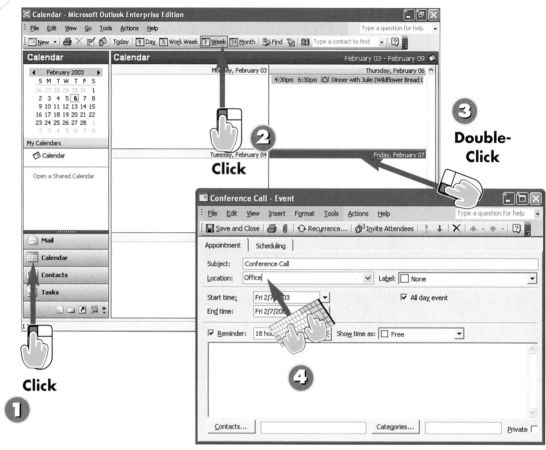

① If necessary, click **Calendar** in the Outlook bar to switch to Outlook's Calendar feature. Today's schedule is shown by default.

② Click the **Week** button on the Calendar toolbar to view your weekly schedule. (You can also click the Today, Day, Work Week, or Month views.)

③ Double-click the day on which you want to schedule an appointment to open an Event window.

④ Type a subject and location for the event in the **Subject** and **Location** fields (the subject you type immediately appears in the Event window's title bar).

INTRODUCTION

In the Outlook Calendar, you can switch the view from today's schedule to the schedule for a different day, a week-at-a-glance, and a month-at-a-glance. You can schedule appointments and events—such as meetings, doctor appointments, and conferences—in any of these Calendar views. You can even move the appointments and events around and set up Outlook to send you reminders for appointments so you don't miss them. If you need to immediately go to today's calendar display, click the **Today** button on the Standard toolbar. This takes you to today's date, no matter which view you are in.

TIP

Organizing Your Calendar
To see suggestions about how you can better organize your calendar, click the **Organize** button on the Standard toolbar (it looks like blocks falling into place, to the left of the Address Book).

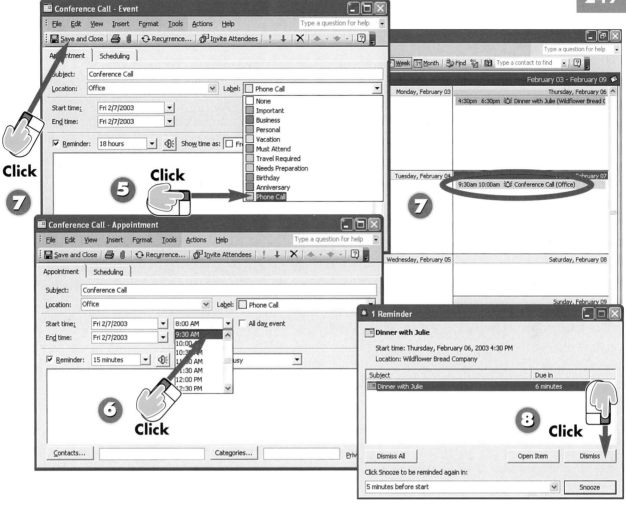

5 Click the down arrow next to the **Label** field and select the type of event you want to schedule—for example, select **Phone Call**.

6 Click the down arrow to the right of the second **Start Time** field and choose a start time for the event; do the same in the **End Time** field.

7 Click the **Save and Close** button in the Event window's toolbar; the event is displayed in your Outlook Calendar.

8 Outlook reminds you 15 minutes before the appointment. Click **Dismiss** to accept the reminder, **Snooze** to be reminded later, or **Open Item** to change the event information.   **End**

TIP
Long Appointment Description
If the description of your appointment is too long to read in the Week or Month view, simply move the mouse pointer over the appointment; the complete description appears in a ScreenTip.

TIP
Removing an Appointment
To remove an appointment, click the appointment to select it and then click the **Delete** button on the Standard toolbar. Of course, if you delete the wrong appointment by accident, you can always open the Edit menu and select Undo to restore it.

Scheduling a Meeting

Start

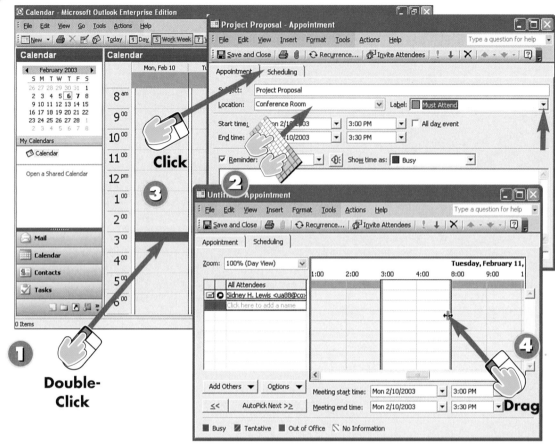

Click

Double-Click

Drag

---

1. With the day on which you want to schedule your appointment visible onscreen, double-click the desired appointment time to open the Untitled Appointment window.

2. Type a subject and select the location for your meeting in the **Subject** and **Location** fields. Then click the **Label** field down arrow and select a label for the meeting.

3. Click the **Scheduling** tab in the Appointment window.

4. To set the meeting duration, click the bar in the timeline. Or, select the start and end times from the **Meeting Start Time** and **Meeting End Time** drop-down lists.

INTRODUCTION

Outlook's Meeting Planner enables you to plan a meeting from start to finish with other attendees. You specify the attendees, determine a meeting time, check for any schedule conflicts, and even schedule a room. You also can send an email to the other attendees, inviting them to the meeting.

TIP

Meeting Times
If you didn't select the meeting time on your calendar before you opened the Meeting dialog box, you can set the meeting time on the Attendee Availability tab by selecting the start and end times.

TIP

Recurring Meetings
If a meeting you want to schedule occurs at the same time each week, click the **Recurrence** button on the Appointment window toolbar. The appointment will appear on your calendar at the same time and day each week.

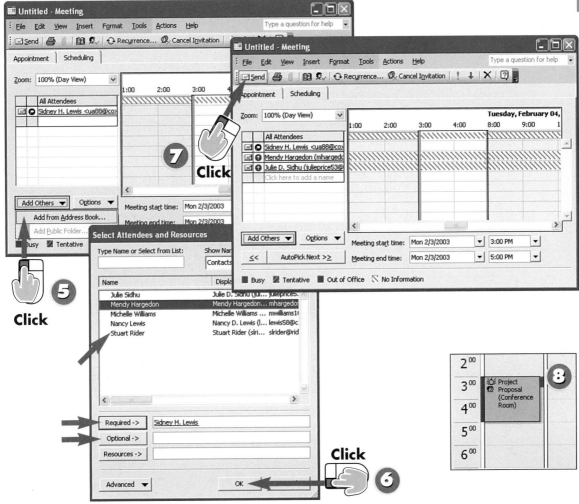

5. Click the **Add Others** button and select **Add from Address Book** to open the Select Attendees and Resources dialog box.

6. Select the required contacts in your Contacts list, and click the **Required** button. Then select the optional contacts and click **Optional**. Click **OK**.

7. Click the **Send** button to send emails to all the attendees on the list.

8. The meeting appears in your Outlook Calendar view.

End

Meeting Icons

In Calendar view, select the meeting's date on the current month calendar and then click the **Day** button on the Calendar toolbar. Notice that the meeting is scheduled, with a Meeting icon (two people) next to it.

Meeting Responses

Many workplaces set up Outlook so that recipients of meeting requests can choose to accept, tentatively accept, or decline your meeting request. These responses come back to you as email messages. When a recipient accepts or tentatively accepts, Outlook automatically puts the meeting on that person's calendar.

Adding Tasks to a To-Do List

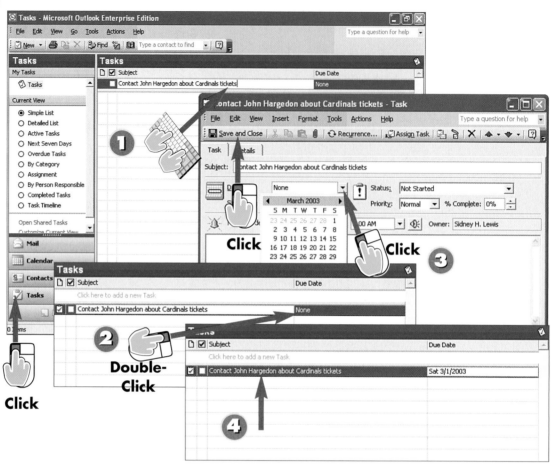

1 Click **Tasks** in the Outlook bar to switch to Outlook's Tasks feature. Then, type a new task in the **Click Here to Add a New Task** box.

2 Double-click the task's **Due Date** field to open the Task window.

3 Click the down arrow next to the **Due Date** field and select a date. If necessary, do the same in the **Start Date** field. When you're ready, click **Save and Close**.

4 Outlook adds the task to your Tasks list, complete with the due date you specified.

End

Creating Notes

Start

Click

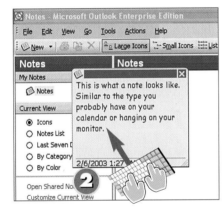

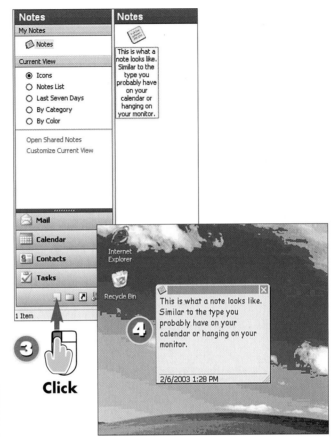

Click

1. Click the down arrow next to the **New** button on Outlook's Standard toolbar and select **Note** from the menu that appears to open a blank sticky note.

2. Type the text for your note in the Note box.

3. Click the **Notes** button on the Outlook bar to see all the notes you have created.

4. Notes you haven't closed by clicking the **Close (×)** button in the Note box's upper-right corner also appear in your workspace.

End

INTRODUCTION
You can use Outlook's Notes feature to jot down ideas, questions, reminders, directions, or anything else you would write on paper. You can leave Notes visible onscreen as you work.

TIP
Changing Note Colors
Click the **Note** icon in the upper-left corner of the note and then select **Color** from the menu that appears. Select a different color (blue, green, pink, yellow, or white) to represent different types of notes.

TIP
Editing Notes
To open a note in Note view, double-click the note. To resize an open note, drag the lower-right corner of the note. To delete an open note, click the Note icon in the upper-left corner of the note and select Delete from the menu that appears.

Creating a Journal Entry

Start

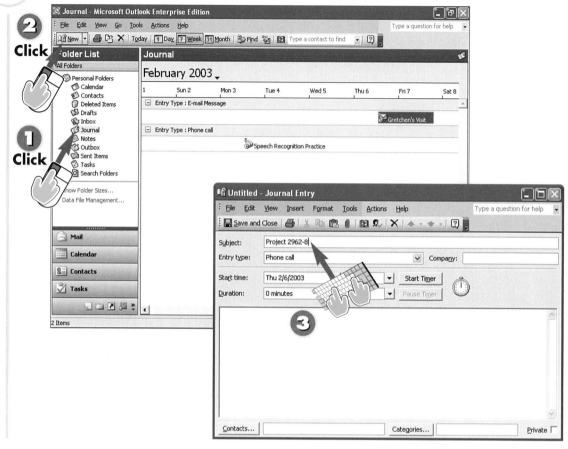

1. Click the **Journal** icon on the Outlook bar Folder list. (If this is your first time using Journal feature, Office will walk you through a setup process; just follow the prompts.)

2. Click the **New** button on the Standard toolbar to open the Journal Entry window.

3. Type a subject for the journal entry in the **Subject** text box.

TIP

Entry Types
Specifying the entry type is very important because this is how the Journal feature tracks your entries. For example, if you select Microsoft Word, the Journal feature tracks the amount of time and documents you work on.

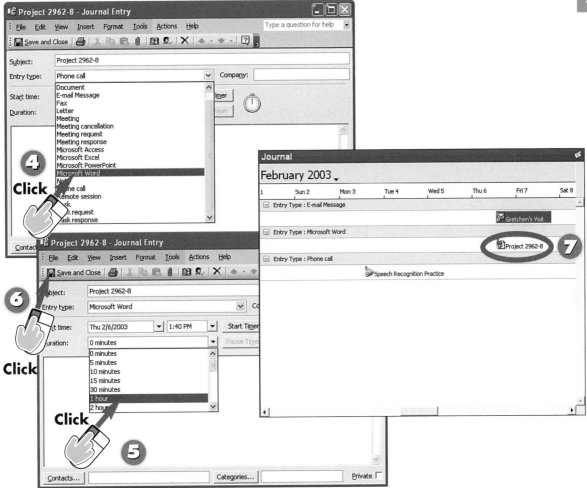

Click the down arrow next to the **Entry Type** field and select the kind of task you're performing.

Click the down arrow next to the **Duration** field and select the amount of time you've spent performing the task.

Click the **Save and Close** button to save the journal entry and return to the Outlook Journal view.

The journal entry is added.

Deleting a Journal Entry
To delete a journal entry in Journal view, right-click the journal entry you want to delete and select **Delete** on the short-cut menu.

Timer Buttons
If you have not yet performed the task you are recording in your journal but are just about to start, click the **Start Timer** button in the Journal Entry window and begin working. When you're finished working, return to the journal entry and click the **Stop Timer** button to record the time in the Duration field.

Advanced Office and Web Features

Throughout this book, you have learned about features in Office that help you accomplish tasks and make your work easier. This final part takes you a step further so that you can copy and link with other documents, import and export, and even automate repetitive tasks with macros.

Numerous Office features can make working with the Internet and the Web easier and more convenient. This part covers general Office Web features, which can be used in Word, Excel, and PowerPoint. We even show you how to get Outlook into the act.

You can view your Office documents in a browser to see how they will look if you put them on a Web page. You will learn how to save a Web page as an Office document and open it in an Office application. You can add URLs and all kinds of hyperlinks to your documents. In addition, you can edit, assign ScreenTips to, and remove hyperlinks using the Hyperlink dialog box. You can even add email hyperlinks and send your documents as email messages. If you aren't sure what all these things are, keep reading and working through the tasks.

To use the Web and Internet features in Office, you need to have access to the Internet. You might have an account with an online service, with a local Internet service provider (ISP), with a local cable company, or in a corporate setting where you have to log in to the network to gain Internet access. In any case, you should connect to the Internet to perform the tasks in this part.

Working with Hyperlinks

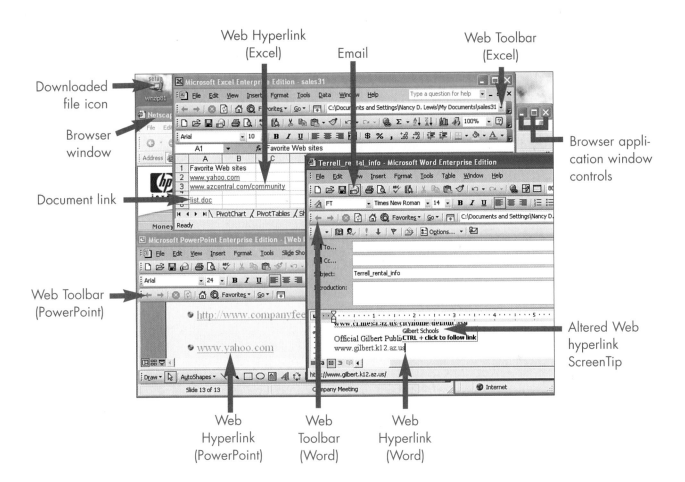

Web Hyperlink (Excel)

Email

Web Toolbar (Excel)

Downloaded file icon

Browser window

Document link

Browser application window controls

Web Toolbar (PowerPoint)

Altered Web hyperlink ScreenTip

Web Hyperlink (PowerPoint)

Web Toolbar (Word)

Web Hyperlink (Word)

Copying and Linking to Office Documents

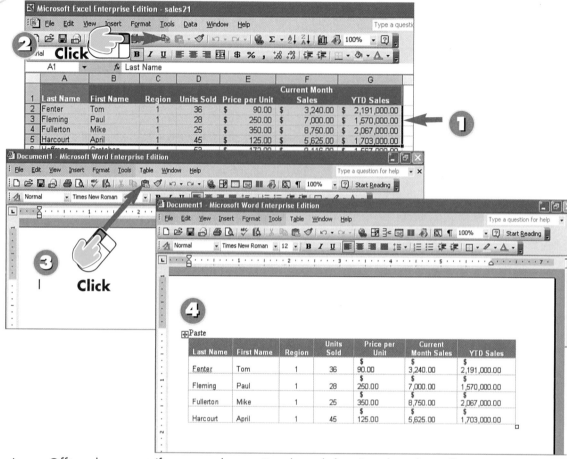

1. In an Office document (for example, an Excel worksheet), select the cells you want to copy or link to in another document (for example, a Word document).

2. Click the **Copy** button on the Standard toolbar.

3. In a new, blank Office document (here, a Microsoft Word document), click the **Paste** button on the Standard toolbar.

4. The cells are copied (not linked) into the Word document.

Until now, you have learned about the many ways you can copy and paste items in your documents. This task takes you a step further by showing you how to copy and *link* to other Office documents—for example, between Excel and Word, as outlined in this task. When you paste data, the data becomes part of the new location and is no longer representative of any changes made to the original location. When you link data, the link can be updated so that any changes to the original location will display in the new location.

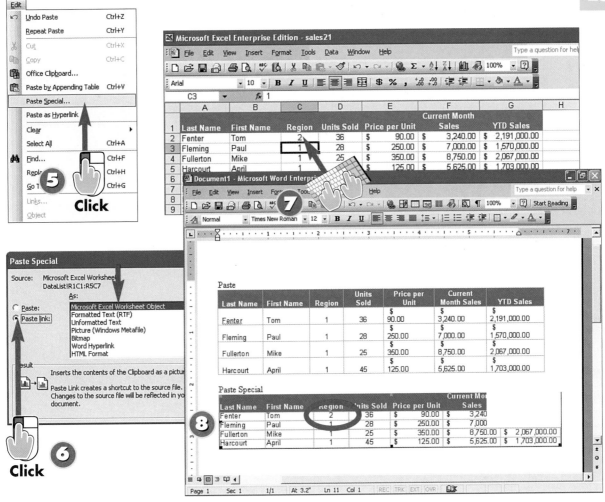

5 To link the data (not copy), click in the document where you want the data to appear; then selct **Edit**, **Paste Special** to open the Paste Special dialog box.

6 Click the **Paste Link** option button and, in the **As** field, select **Microsoft Excel Worksheet Object**. Click **OK**; the cells are linked (not copied).

7 Switch back to your Excel worksheet and edit the contents of one of the cells you copied (in this case, I changed Tom Fenter's region to **2**).

8 Switch to the Word document and see that the cell content was updated in the linked cells but not the copied cells.

End

Automating Repetitive Tasks with Macros

Start

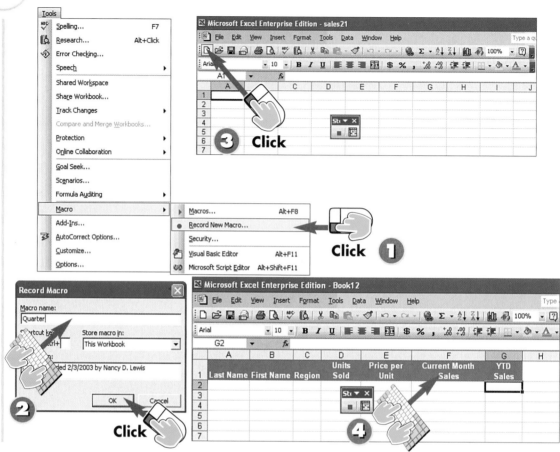

1. Open the **Tools** menu and select **Macro, Record New Macro** to open the Record Macro dialog box.

2. In the **Macro Name** field, type a descriptive name for the macro—something you will easily remember (for example, **Quarter**)—and click **OK**.

3. Office begins recording your actions; all actions will be performed by the macro when it is run. In this case, click the **New** button to create a new workbook.

4. Add and format any text that you want automatically placed in each new workbook the macro creates.

INTRODUCTION

If your job requires you to use your computer to perform repetitive tasks, you can probably use Office to create a macro to automate those tasks. For example, suppose you frequently create quarterly workbooks. You could create a macro that automatically opens a new blank workbook and adds the appropriate column heading information, as outlined in this task. You can create macros that accomplish just about any task in any Office application—without knowing anything about programming. You simply use Office's macro-recording feature to record the actions of a particular task; then, when you run the macro, Office performs these actions for you.

Macro Security

TIP

Before you run a macro, make sure you know who a macro is from and that it is a trusted source. To be extra careful, select **Tools**, **Macro**, **Security** to open the Security dialog box. Make sure the security level is set to High.

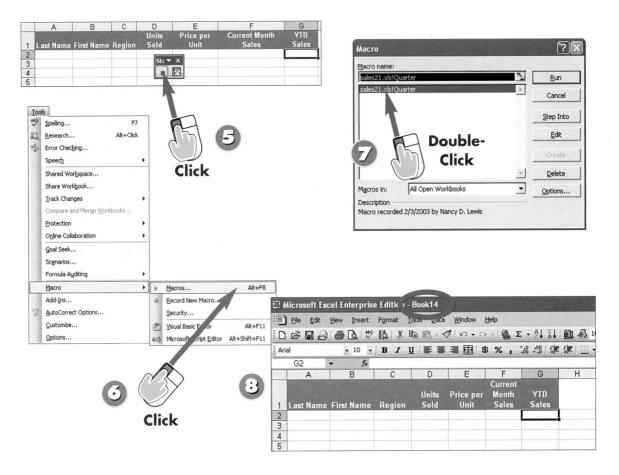

5. When you've completed all the actions you want the macro to perform, click the **Stop Recording** button.

6. To run the macro you created, open the **Tools** menu and select **Macro**, **Macros** (or press **Alt+F8**) to open the Macro dialog box.

7. Double-click the macro's name to run it. (Notice that the macro's name contains the name of the workbook you were using when the macro was created.)

8. Office runs the macro—in this case, automatically creating a new workbook and adding and formatting the text you specified.

Everything Records

Keep in mind that when the macro is recording, everything you do is recorded. For example, if you page down through a worksheet, that will happen when you run the macro later.

Adding Macros to Your Toolbars

You can add macros to your toolbars to make it easy to launch them. To do so, click the **More Buttons** arrow on the right side of the Standard toolbar and then click the **Add or Remove Buttons** command. Select the **Commands** tab on the Customize dialog box, and select **Macros** from the **Categories** list. Then select the macro for which you want to create a button in the Commands list.

Saving Data to Use in Another Application (Exporting)

Start

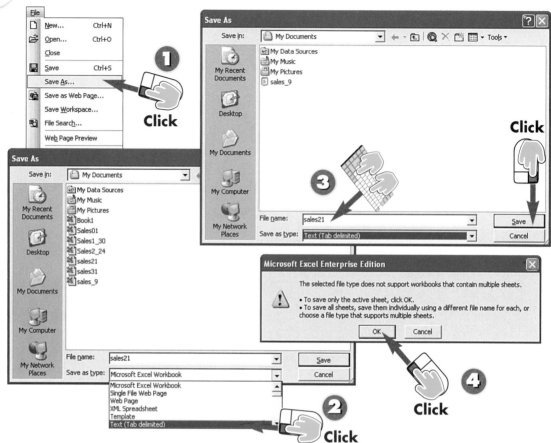

1. With the file that contains data you want to save for export, open the **File** menu and select **Save As** to open the Save As dialog box.

2. Click the down arrow next to the **Save As Type** field and select **Text (Tab Delimited)** from the list that appears.

3. Type a name for the file in the **File Name** field (or keep the current workbook name) and click the **Save** button.

4. Excel notifies you that only the active worksheet—not the entire workbook—will be saved in the manner you've specified. Click **OK**.

INTRODUCTION

You might decide that the data you've entered into one Office application would be useful in another one. For example, you might want to upload the regional sales data you've entered into Excel to an Access database that has more extensive reporting tools or use it in a Word mail merge. Thanks to Office's exporting capabilities, you can. In this task, you learn how to save your Excel worksheet data in a tab-delimited format that other applications can use and to see what that data looks like in Word. *Delimiters* are the items that separate one field of data from the next, and they can be tabs, semicolons, commas, spaces, or other types.

TIP

Exporting Formatting
When you create a tab-delimited file for use in other applications, the data in the cells is the important information you are saving to export. The formatting in the cells (bold, blue, italic) is not saved because it's not necessary to the data.

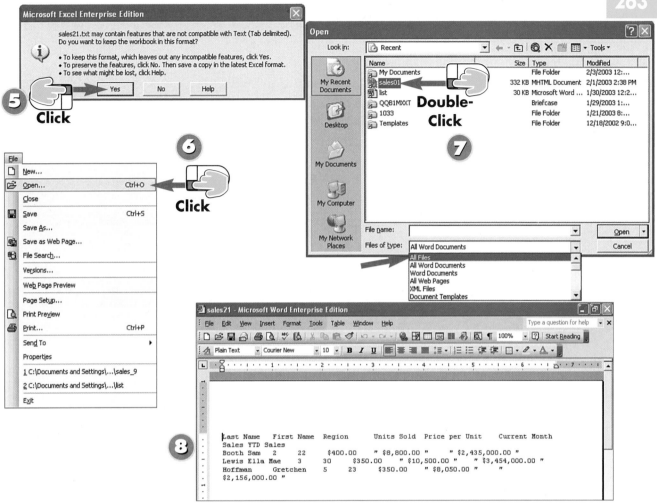

5 Excel warns you that the worksheet might contain some features (such as formatting) that cannot be retained when the sheet is saved in the new format. Click **Yes** to continue.

6 In Microsoft Word (start the application if necessary), open the **File** menu and select **Open** to view the Open dialog box.

7 Click the down arrow next to the **Files of Type** field, select **All Files** from the list, and double-click the filename you saved in step 4.

8 The tab-delimited file opens up in Microsoft Word.

Incompatible Features
Some examples of incompatible features are data formatting (color, font, and so on) and numeric styles (currency and the like). If the numeric styles can't be saved as a number format, they can be saved in quotes as text data instead of numeric data.

Calculations Lost
If there were any calculations performed in a cell to derive a number, only the actual number is saved—not the formula, function, or cell references. So, if cell F2 ($8,800.00) is actually =SUM(D2*E2), only the $8,800.00 is saved.

Using Data from Another Application (Importing)

Start

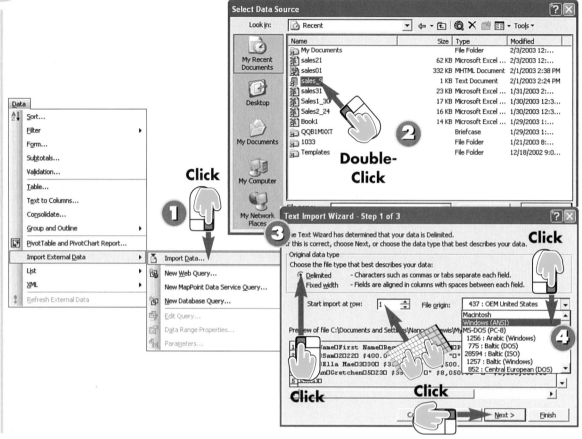

1 Open the **Data** menu and select **Import External Data**, **Import Data** to open the Select Data Source dialog box.

2 Locate and double-click the text file you want to import; Office launches the Text Import Wizard.

3 Click the **Delimited** option button (it describes the data in the file you are importing), and type **1** in **Start Import at Row 1** spin box (to import the entire file).

4 Click the down arrow next to the **File Origin** field and select **Windows (ANSI)** (the file originated on a Windows operating system platform). Then, click **Next**.

Another way to transfer data from one application to another is to *import* it. For example, you could import data from a Word document into an Excel spreadsheet; before you do, however, that Word data must be in a form that Excel can accept (namely, in a tab-delimited text file). In this task, you use the file you exported from Excel to Word in the preceding task to learn how to import data.

TIP

Delimiters and Qualifiers
Delimiters are the items that separate one field of data from the next; they can be tabs, semicolons, commas, spaces, or other types. *Qualifiers* are the items that qualify data as text; they can be double, single, or no quotes.

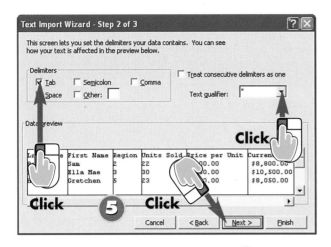

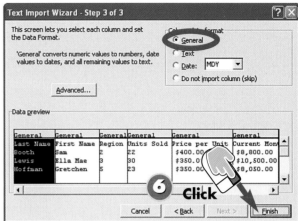

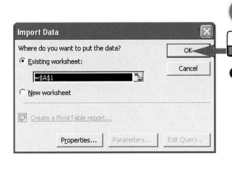

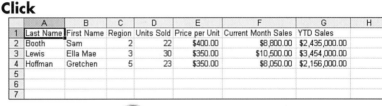

5️⃣ Under **Delimiters**, mark the **Tab** check box. Then, click the **Text Qualifier** field and select **"**. Preview the file in the Data Preview area; click **Next**.

6️⃣ Depending on your data type, select **General** (chosen here), **Text**, **Date**, or **Do Not Import Column (Skip)** in the **Column Data Format** area and click **Finish**.

7️⃣ Click the **OK** button in the Import Data dialog box to place the data in the existing worksheet beginning with cell **A1**.

8️⃣ The data is inserted.

End

Alternative File Locations

If necessary, click the down arrow next to the **Look In** field in the Select Data Source dialog box and select the folder that contains the file from the list that appears. To move up a folder level, click the **Up One Level** button on the toolbar. If you double-click a subfolder, its contents appear in the list of files and folders.

External Data Toolbar

The External Data toolbar opens automatically when you import data in this fashion. You can use the buttons on the toolbar or close the toolbar and work with the new data in your worksheet.

Surfing the Web with the Web Toolbar

Start

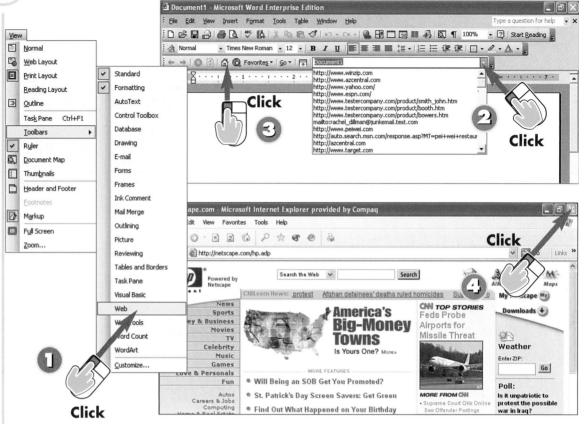

Click

Click

Click

Click

1. In any Office application, open the **View** menu and select **Toolbars**, **Web** to open the Web toolbar.

2. Click the down arrow next to the **Address** field to see Office documents and Web pages you have visited recently. If desired, click an entry in the list to visit that page.

3. To view your Internet start page, click the **Start Page** button on the Web toolbar.

4. Office launches a new default browser window, with your start page displayed. Click the window's **Close** button to return to the original Office document.

INTRODUCTION

Suppose you are working on a document and need to search for data pertaining to what you are writing about. Instead of opening your Web browser, you can simply use the Web toolbar in your Office application. You can use the Web toolbar in Office applications to open documents on the Internet; browse Web documents; jump to other documents, objects, or pages using hyperlinks; or even share your documents on the Web. If you have ever used a Web browser (such as Microsoft Internet Explorer or Netscape Navigator), this toolbar should look familiar. Keep in mind that you need to be connected to the Internet for this task; otherwise, Office will try to connect you after you use the Web toolbar buttons.

Searching the Web
Some of the best Web sites to search for information are **www.yahoo.com**, **www.google.com**, and **www.excite.com**.

TIP

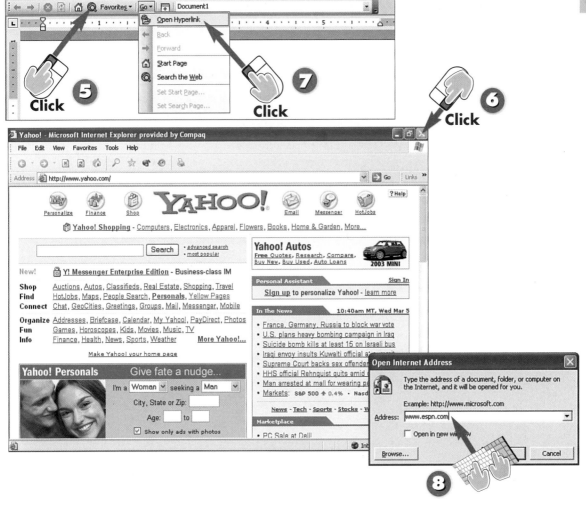

(5) To search the Web for information about a particular topic, click the **Search the Web** button on the Web toolbar.

(6) Office launches a new default browser window with a search engine page displayed; conduct your search as normal. When finished, click the window's **Close** button.

(7) If you know the Internet address (URL) you want to visit, click the down arrow next to the **Go** button on the Web toolbar and select **Open Hyperlink**.

(8) The Open Internet Address dialog box opens. In the **Address** field, type the URL you want to visit and press **Enter**; your default browser opens and displays the page.

End

Closing the Web Toolbar
Open the **View** menu and select **Toolbars**, **Web** to close the Web toolbar.

If you frequently visit a certain page, you can add it to your Favorites list, making it easier to access. To do so, open the page using the Web toolbar. Then click the down arrow next to the **Favorites** button on the Web toolbar and select **Add to Favorites** to open the Add Favorite dialog box. Click the **OK** button to accept the default page name (although you can assign any name you want to a Web page Favorites listing).

Saving a Web Page As a Text File

Start

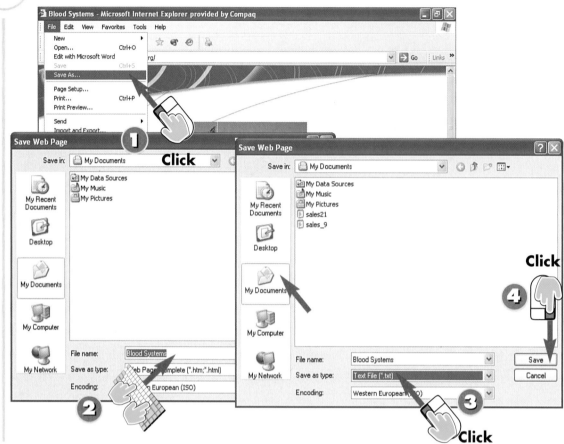

Click

Click

Click

1. After you've opened a Web page that you want to save as a text file, open the **File** menu and select **Save As** to open the Save Web Page dialog box.

2. If you don't like the default filename that appears, type a new name for the file in the **File Name** field (here, **Blood Systems**).

3. Click the down arrow next to the **Save As Type** field and select the **Text File** option from the list that appears. This saves only the text on the Web page.

4. Select the location in which you want to save the file—for example, in the **My Documents** folder—and click the **Save** button.

Suppose you find some information on a Web page that you want to save for future reference. Office lets you save the Web page as a text file that you can then open in an Office document.

Editing a Web Page

As an alternative to saving the Web page and working with it in an Office application, you can open the File menu and select Edit with Microsoft [Office Application] in your Web browser. This automatically opens the Office application that is best suited to edit that Web page.

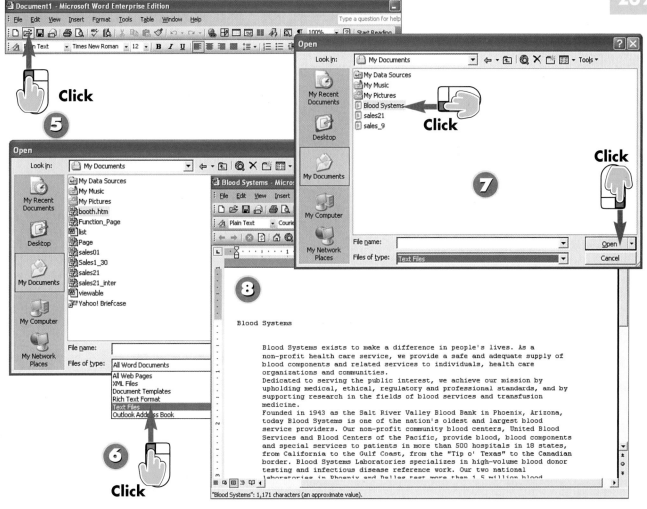

5 To view the file you just saved, click the **Open** button on the Standard toolbar in, for example, Microsoft Word.

6 Click the down arrow next to the **Files of Type** field and select **Text Files** from the list that appears.

7 Open the folder in which you saved the file in step 4 (in this case, the **My Documents** folder). Then click the file to select it and click the **Open** button.

8 The text file is opened.

Additional Save Options
In addition to saving a Web page as a text file, you can select how you want to save the Web page in the Save As Type area by selecting one of the following: Web Page; Web Archive; or Web Page, HTML Only. These options save not only the text, but also the graphics and other parts of the Web page so that they are intact when you open the file in an Office document.

Saving Documents As Web Pages

Start

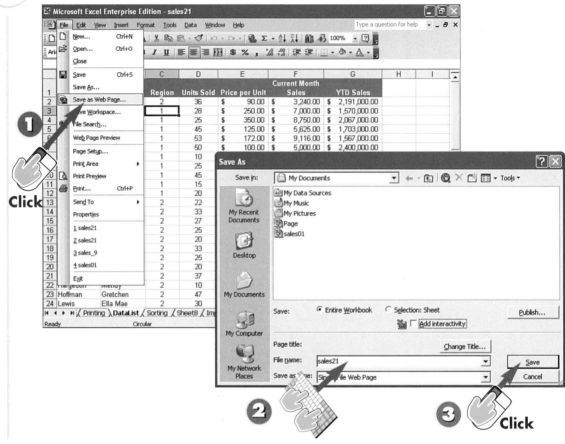

1 Click

2

3 Click

1. With the Office document you want to save as a Web page displayed onscreen, open the **File** menu and select **Save As Web Page** to open the Save As dialog box.

2. In the **File Name** field, type a descriptive name for the file you want to save (for example, **Sales21**).

3. Click the **Save** button. The document is saved as a Web page (that is, an HTML file), and the filename you assigned appears in the Web page's title bar.

End

Viewing Documents As Web Pages

Start

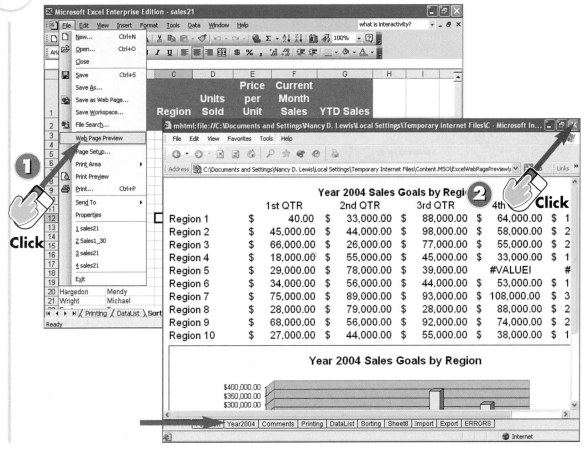

Click

Click

1. With the Office document you want to preview displayed onscreen, open the **File** menu and select **Web Page Preview**.

2. The document is opened in your computer's default Web browser. Click the **Close** (×) button in the browser window to exit and return to the original Office document.

End

INTRODUCTION

Office enables you to convert the documents you create using various Office applications into Web pages. At any time, you can view the documents you save as Web pages to see how they look.

Browser Buttons and Links

Notice that the Web browser acts just like it is displaying an active Web page. The document name is in the title bar, and the Explorer bar buttons are active.

Online Comments

If you have comments in a document that you publish to a Web page, you can move the mouse pointer over the comment indicator (the red bracket in the upper-right corner of the cell) to display the comment in a ScreenTip.

Adding Email Address Links to Documents

Start

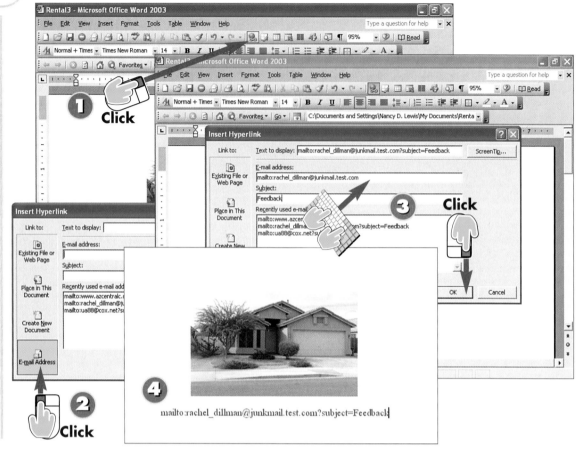

Click

Click

Click

End

1. Click in a document where you want to add an email address link (or select some text) and click the **Insert Hyperlink** button on the Standard toolbar.

2. The Insert Hyperlink dialog box appears. Click the **E-mail Address** option in **Link to** area.

3. In the **Address** field, type the desired email address. Type a subject in the **Subject** field, and then click **OK**.

4. When the link is clicked (while pressing **Ctrl** in Word), an email message window opens containing the email address and subject you typed in step 3.

Suppose you're creating a report for your customers to read, and you want them to email you as soon as they finish it to let you know their thoughts. In that case, you can add an email link to the document, which they can click to start an email message addressed to you.

mailto:
Notice that as soon as you type the @ symbol in the Address box in step 3, **mailto:** is placed at the beginning of the email address. This indicates that the link is an email link, not a Web address (URL).

Other Link Options
In addition to making text or cell data into an email link, you can click any other object and create a link. For example, you could make a piece of clip art, a chart, or a comment a link.

Typing Web (URL) Links Directly into Documents

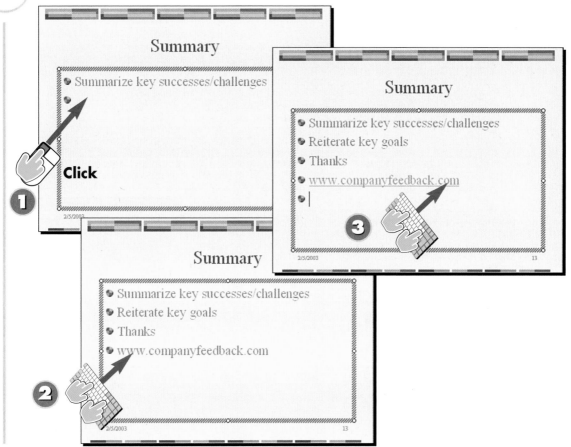

Click

1 Click in the document where you want to type a URL that will be the link.

2 Type the URL.

3 Press the **Enter** key; the URL automatically becomes a hyperlink. When this link is used, a browser window opens containing the page referenced by the URL.

End

A *URL* (short for *uniform resource locator*) is to a Web page what a street address is to a house—a unique way of identifying that page's location. Office enables you type URLs directly into your documents; when you do, Office automatically establishes a link to the Web page that the URL identifies. (If you're working in Excel, the process differs slightly; see the next task for details.) Anyone reading your document can then use this link to immediately view the page it references (see p. 277 to learn how). Links, also called *hyperlinks*, appear in a different color from regular text and are underlined, making them easy to identify. In addition to typing text into a URL link, you can also type email addresses directly in your documents to become links.

Removing Hyperlinks
If you are typing a hyperlink into a worksheet as an example and don't want it to be an active link, move the mouse pointer over the link, right-click, and select Remove Hyperlink from the shortcut menu.

Inserting a Web (URL) Link Directly into a Document

Start

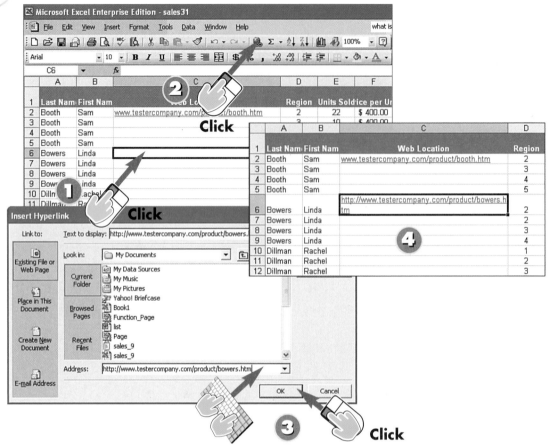

Click

Click

Click

1. Select the location in which you want to place a URL link.

2. Click the **Insert Hyperlink** button on the Standard toolbar to open the Insert Hyperlink dialog box.

3. In the **Address** field, type the desired URL, and then click **OK**.

4. The cell you selected in step 1 now contains a URL link. When this link is clicked, a browser window opens containing the page referenced by the URL.

End

As you learned in the preceding task, a URL is to a Web page what a street address is to a house—a unique way of identifying that page's location. Excel lets you insert URL links directly into your worksheets in much the same way you insert email address link.

Browsing the Web
If you cannot remember the URL you want to add, click the Insert Hyperlink button on the Standard toolbar to open the Insert Hyperlink dialog box. There, you can browse Web pages or use recent links to locate and add the correct address.

Other Link Options
In addition to making text or a cell into a URL link, you can click any other object and create a link. For example, you could make a piece of clip art, a chart, or a comment into a link.

Adding Document Links to Your Documents

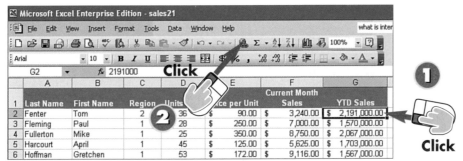

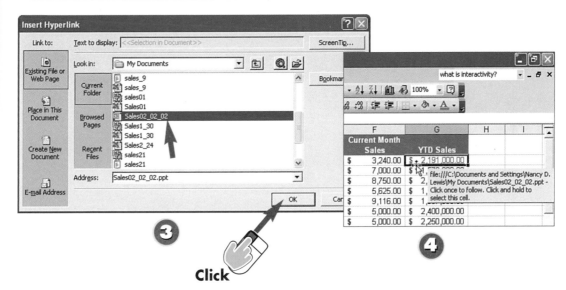

Click

① Click in the document where you want to add a document hyperlink.

② Click the **Insert Hyperlink** button on the Standard toolbar to open the Insert Hyperlink dialog box.

③ Locate and select the file you want to link to (it can be any type of file) and click **OK**.

④ The spot you selected in step 1 now contains a hyperlink; when you move your mouse pointer over the link, the location of the linked file is displayed in a ScreenTip.

End

Sometimes when you're creating an elaborate document, you'll want to add a link that takes you or the reader to some other pertinent file. For example, add a monthly report presentation link to your sales worksheet so that anyone reading the sales worksheet can use that link to immediately view the monthly report presentation.

Locating Recently Used Files

If the folder list in the Insert Hyperlink dialog box doesn't show the document you want to link to, click the **Recent Files** option to locate the document. If it has been a while since you last used the file you're looking for, click the down arrow next to the **Look in** field to find the folder in which the document is stored.

Changing a Link's Default ScreenTip Text

Start

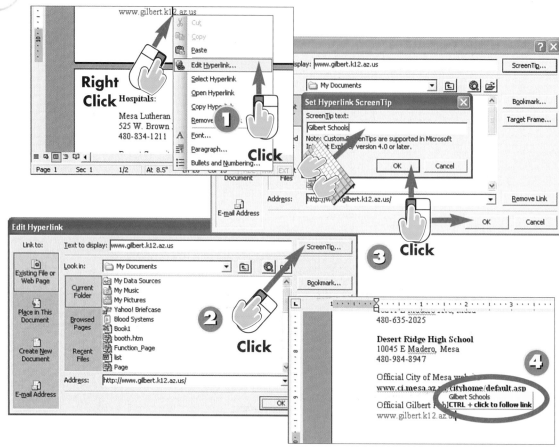

Right Click

Click

Click

① **Click**

③ **Click**

④

---

① Right-click a hyperlink and select **Edit Hyperlink** from the shortcut menu that appears to open the Edit Hyperlink dialog box.

② Click the **ScreenTip** button to open the Set Hyperlink ScreenTip dialog box.

③ In the **ScreenTip Text** field, type the text that the hyperlink's ScreenTip should display. Then, click **OK** in the Set Hyperlink ScreenTip and Edit Hyperlink dialog boxes.

④ Move the mouse pointer over the hyperlink; the new ScreenTip text is displayed.

End

Hyperlinked text is indicated by a different color, an underline, and a ScreenTip that is visible when the mouse pointer moves over the link. By default, the ScreenTip text is the document path, URL, or email address to which the link refers. You can change a link's ScreenTip by following the steps in this task.

TIP

Text to Display
In addition to altering a ScreenTip associated with a hyperlink, you can alter the hyperlink text displayed in your Office document. For example, you can have the **www.microsoft.com** hyperlink appear in your document as **Microsoft**. To do so, alter the contents of the **Text to Display** field in the Edit Hyperlink or Insert Hyperlink dialog box.

Linking to the Web in a Document

Click

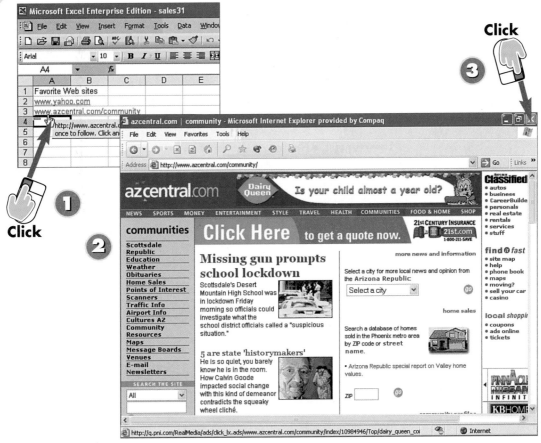

Click

Click

1. In Excel, simply click the link (in PowerPoint, you must be in Slide Show mode; in Word, you must hold down the **Ctrl** key while clicking the link).

2. Your default Web browser opens and displays the Web page.

3. Click the **Close** button on the document window to close the browser, or press **Alt+Tab** to toggle back to your original document.

End

INTRODUCTION

URL hyperlinks in your Office documents can be used by the people viewing those documents to immediately start their Web browsers and visit the Web page to which the URL link refers (assuming they are connected to the Internet already). The exact process by which this occurs, however, can vary slightly depending on which Office application you are using.

TIP

Using URL Links in PowerPoint
In PowerPoint, you need only click a hyperlink to view the link's associated Web page, but doing so works only when you are giving the presentation in Slide Show mode.

Updating a Link

Start

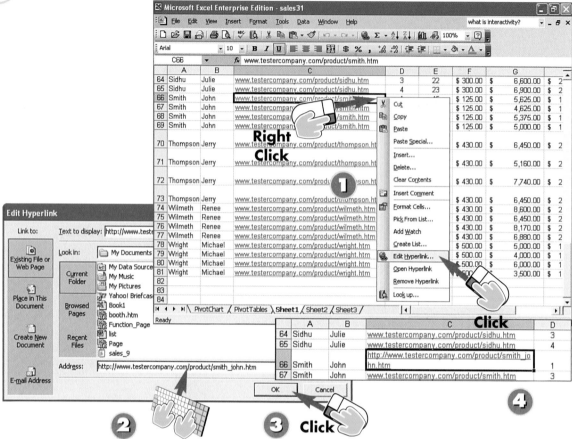

1. Right-click the hyperlink that needs to be edited and select **Edit Hyperlink** from the shortcut menu that appears to open the Edit Hyperlink dialog box.

2. Locate the page to which you want to link or, if you know the page's correct URL, simply type it in the **Address** field.

3. Click **OK**.

4. The link is updated.

End

Chances are, at some point you'll mistype a URL, email address, or document file location while creating a hyperlink and need to edit it. Alternatively, the URL, email address, or document file location associated with a hyperlink may change. Either way, you'll need to edit the hyperlink for it to function properly.

TIP

Clicking Hyperlinks
To edit a hyperlink in Excel, right-click the cell that contains the actual hyperlink. To edit a hyperlink in Word, simply right-click anywhere on the link. To edit a hyperlink in PowerPoint, you must either press **Ctrl** or **Shift** while right-clicking the link. In each of the Office applications, you then select **Edit Hyperlink** from the shortcut menu.

Removing a Link

Start

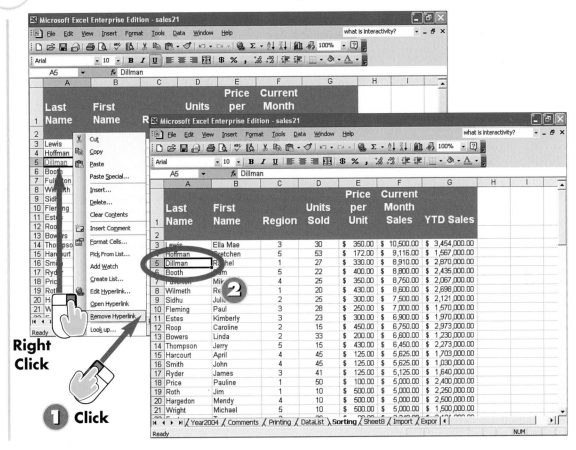

Right Click

1 **Click**

1 Right-click the hyperlink you want to remove and select **Remove Hyperlink** from the shortcut menu that appears.

2 The original link text remains but no longer acts as a hyperlink. (You can tell because the text is no longer underlined or a different color.)

End

If you refer to a particular URL, email address, or document file location in a document but don't want people to link to it, or if you decide you no longer want a particular hyperlink in your document, you can remove it. When you remove a hyperlink, the link text or object remains, but clicking it has no effect.

TIP

Using the Undo Command

If you remove a hyperlink but decide you want to put it back in your document, click the Undo button on the Standard toolbar; the hyperlink will be restored.

Sending a Document As an Email Message

Start

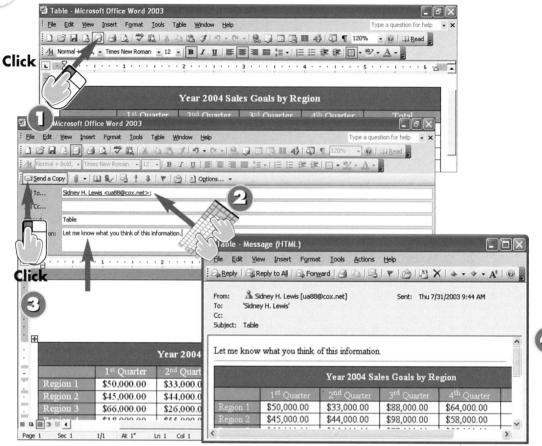

Click

Click

1. With the document you want to send displayed onscreen, click the **E-mail** button on the Standard toolbar to place the document in an email message window.

2. The Subject field contains the document's filename, and the document itself appears in the message body. Type the recipient's email address in the **To** field.

3. Type any additional text in the message body, and click the **Send a Copy** button to send the document.

4. When the recipient of your message receives and opens it, he can read the document directly in the email message.

End

Both Excel and Word have an E-mail button on their Standard toolbars that lets you immediately send a document as part of the body of an email. (PowerPoint's E-mail button, on the other hand, lets you send only a presentation document as an email attachment; see the next task for more information.)

Sending Documents
When you email from within Excel, you are asked to send the entire workbook as an attachment or send the current sheet as the message body. Click the **Send the Current Sheet As the Message Body** option button and click **OK**.

Canceling the Email
If you decide you no longer want to send the email, click the **E-mail** button on the Standard toolbar a second time to return to the document.

Sending a Document As an Email Attachment

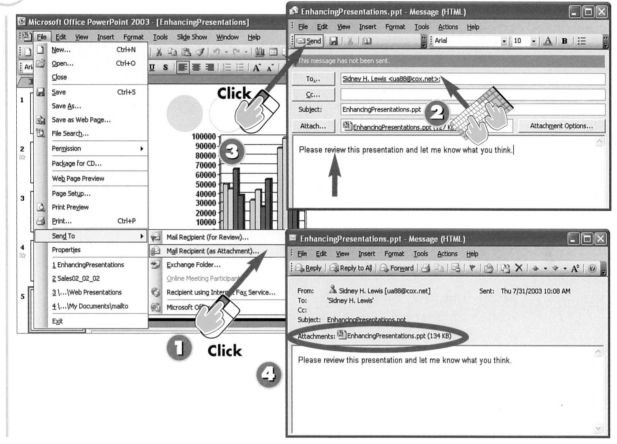

Click

1 Click

2

3

4

End

1. With the document you want to send displayed onscreen, open the **File** menu and choose **Send To**, **Mail Recipient (as Attachment)**.

2. The Subject field contains the document's filename, and the Attach field contains a link to the document. Type the recipient's email address in the **To** field.

3. Type any information you want in the body of the email message, and click the **Send** button to send the document as an attachment.

4. When the recipient of your message receives and opens it, she can open the attached document to view it.

If you want to get quick feedback on a document you are working on, Microsoft Office applications allow you to immediately send a document as an email attachment. The filename of the document is added by default to the Subject line in the email message, and the message becomes an attachment.

Canceling the Email

If you decide you no longer want to send the email message with the document attached, click the **Close** (×) button in the email document window. You will be asked whether you want to save the message. If you click Yes (and you use Outlook as your email program), the message will be saved in your Drafts folder; if you click No, the message will be deleted and you will be returned to the current document.

Glossary

A

active cell The selected cell in a worksheet. You can enter or edit text or data in the active cell.

absolute cell reference An entry in a formula that does not change when the formula is copied to a new cell. In certain formulas, you might want an entry to always refer to one specific cell value.

active document The document currently selected in the application you're using.

active window In a multiple-window environment, it's the window you are currently using or that is currently selected. Only one window can be active at a time, and keystrokes and commands affect the active window.

adaptive menu A menu that changes to show the commands you use most often.

alignment The way text lines up against the margins of a page. For example, justified text lines up evenly with both the left and right margins.

animation effect An illusion of movement during a PowerPoint slideshow that is accomplished by controlling how text is displayed.

attachment A file you attach to an Outlook item. For example, you might attach a worksheet to an email message and send the message and file to a co-worker.

AutoContent wizard A tool in PowerPoint that guides you through the steps of a proposed presentation and includes suggested content.

AutoCorrect A feature that corrects spelling errors as you type. You can also use AutoCorrect to enter particular phrases automatically.

AutoText A feature that automatically corrects mistyped text. You can also use AutoText to specify a string of characters that will automatically correct itself to a word or phrase. For example, Word comes with AutoText that automatically corrects "teh" to "the."

B

background A color or picture you can add to your Office documents or objects contained in them, such as tables, charts, or clip art.

browser A software program that lets you view documents on the Internet.

bullet An object, such as a circle or square, used to set off items in a list.

C

Calendar An Outlook feature that enables you to schedule appointments, meetings, and events. You can view the Calendar by day, week, month, or year.

carriage return When the cursor in an Office document moves to the next paragraph after pressing the Enter key.

cell An area in an Excel worksheet or a Word table that holds a specific piece of information.

chart   A graphic representation of data.

check box   A small box you click to enable or disable an option in a dialog box. If the check box has a check mark in it, the option is currently enabled; if it's clear, the option is disabled. Check boxes are not mutually exclusive; you can mark several check boxes in a group.

client   Software that uses resources available from other computers. For example, an email application client uses the resources available for running a mail server.

clip art   A predrawn illustration or graphics object you can insert into an Office file. Microsoft Office comes with a collection of clip art files you can use to illustrate your documents.

Clip Gallery   A collection of clip art, pictures, sound files, and video clips you can use to spruce up Office documents.

Clipboard   A location in Windows that holds information that is cut or copied. Items that are cut or copied are stored there and accessible with the Clipboard task pane.

color scheme   A set of eight coordinated colors you can use in your PowerPoint presentations.

column   (1)In a table, a vertical set of cells. (2)In a document, the vertical arrangement of text and graphics so the document looks like a newspaper.

conditional statement   A function that returns different results depending on whether a specified condition is true or false.

contact   A record of a person and that person's contact information, including her email address, phone number, street address, and any other personal details you choose to note.

context menu   *See* shortcut menu.

cursor   The location where you last entered text. This is a flashing bar in some applications.

data   The information you work with in an application, including text, numbers, and graphic images.

datasheet   A grid of columns and rows that enables you to enter numeric data into a chart.

data validation   The process of ensuring that data is accurately entered into a form for a data list.

default   The assumed option, behavior, or formatting that remains in effect unless you specify otherwise.

demote   To indent a line of text more than the previous line, indicating a lower level of importance.

dialog box   An information box that appears during the installation or use of an application and requires input from the user.

docked toolbar   A toolbar that is attached to one of the four sides of an application window.

document   A file you create with a program; a document can be saved with a unique filename by which it can be retrieved.

document map   A vertical display of the headings in a Word document. You can click an entry to move quickly to that part of the document.

document window   The window that controls the individual documents in an application window.

download   To transfer a file from the Internet to your computer from a Web page or an email attachment.

drag-and-drop   To move an object (an icon, a selection of text, a cell in an Excel worksheet, and so on) by selecting it, dragging it to another location, and then releasing the mouse button.

drop-down list   A list of choices presented when you click the arrow to the right of a field in a dialog box.

E

embedded object   An object that is physically included in the document to which it belongs. The source and destination files aren't linked, which means that when one object is updated, the other is not.

Endnotes   A Word feature in which a note number is placed within the document and reference information about the noted word or phrase is automatically placed at the end of the document.

export   To put the data in your application into a format other applications can use.

F

field   A place where you enter data in a data list or a data element on a form.

file   Information you enter in your computer and save for future use, such as a document or a workbook.

filter   A feature in Excel for controlling which records are extracted from the database and displayed in the worksheet.

floating toolbar   A toolbar that is not anchored to the edge of the window but instead is displayed in the document window for easy access. You can drag a floating toolbar to your Windows desktop.

font   The typeface, type size, and type attributes of text or numbers.

footer   Text or graphics that appears at the bottom of every page of a document or worksheet.

Footnotes   A Word feature in which a note number is placed within the document and reference information about the noted word or phrase is automatically placed at the bottom of the page.

format   To change the appearance of text or numbers.

formatting   Attributes of text and data that determine the appearance of information.

formula   In Excel, a means for calculating a value based on the values in other cells of the workbook.

formula bar   This is where Excel calculation and formatting elements are listed.

frame   A means for sectioning a window to enable it to show multiple documents. You can navigate each part of a frame separately.

function   A built-in formula that automatically performs calculations in Excel.

G–H

graphic   An image that can come in many shapes and sizes. Typical graphics include clip-art images, drawings, photographs, scanned images, and signature files.

group   To combine one or more objects to act as a single object, which you can then move or resize.

handles   The small black squares around a selected object. You use these squares to drag, size, or scale the object.

header   Text or graphics that appears at the top of every page of a document or workbook.

highlight   A band of color you can add to text by using the Highlight tool on the toolbar. In addition, when you select text to format or move, for example, you are selecting or *highlighting* the text.

hyperlink   Text formatted so that clicking it "jumps" you to another, related location.

I–K

I-beam   The shape of the mouse pointer when you move over a screen area in which you can edit text.

import   The process of converting and opening a file that was stored or created in another program. See also *export*.

indent   An amount of space that an object, usually text, is moved away from the left margin.

insert mode   A mode in which the new text you enter moves the text that was previously in the same location to the right.

insertion point   The blinking vertical bar that shows where text will appear when you type. The insertion point is sometimes called a *cursor*.

Internet   A system of linked computer networks that facilitates data communication services such as remote login, file transfer, electronic mail, and newsgroups.

justify   To align text so that it fills the area between the left and right margins.

L–M

landscape   The horizontal orientation of a page; opposite of *portrait*, or vertical, orientation.

legend   A way of understanding the elements in a chart and what they represent.

line spacing   The amount of vertical space between lines of text.

link   A connection between a linked object and a source object. If one of the objects is altered, the other is altered as well.

macro   A method of automating common tasks you perform in applications such as Word and Excel. You can record keystrokes and mouse clicks so that they can be played back automatically.

mail merge   A feature that enables you to combine information, such as names and addresses, with a form document, such as a letter.

margins   The space around the top, bottom, left, and right sides of a page. This space can be increased or decreased as necessary. This can also be the location where elements such as headers and footers are located.

mixed cell reference   A single-cell entry in a formula that contains both a relative and an absolute cell reference. A mixed cell reference is helpful when you need a formula that always refers to the values in a specific column but the values in the rows must change, and vice versa.

N–O

object   A table, chart, graphic, text box, or other form of information you create and edit. An object can be inserted, pasted, or copied into any slide.

Office Clipboard   A temporary storage area that holds multiple pieces of cut or copied text. You can paste items in the Office Clipboard into any Office document, in any order.

option button   A small white circle you click to choose an option in a dialog box. If the option button has a black dot in it, it is currently enabled; if it doesn't, it is disabled. Option buttons are mutually exclusive; you can mark only one option button in a group.

overtype mode   A mode in which the new text you type replaces the text that was previously in the same location.

P–Q

page setup   The way data is arranged on a printed page.

palette   A box containing choices for color and other special effects. A palette appears when you click a toolbar button, such as Border or Fill Color.

path   A map to the location of the folder that contains a file. For example, **C:\My Documents\Letters\ Mom.doc** means the document **Mom.doc** is stored in the **Letters** folder, which is stored in the **My Documents** folder (on the **C:** drive).

PIM   Personal Information Manager. Software (such as the Contacts folder in Outlook) in which you track information about contacts and keep notes on your interaction with those contacts.

Places bar   The vertical bar on the left side of the Open and Save As dialog boxes that contains buttons for frequently used folders.

pop-up menu   *See* shortcut menu.

portrait   The vertical orientation of a page; opposite of landscape, or horizontal, orientation.

presentation   A group of related slides you can create by using PowerPoint.

promote   To indent a line of text less than the previous line, indicating a greater level of importance.

R

range   A cell or a rectangular group of adjacent cells in Excel.

reference   A means for addressing something in a specified context. For example, in Excel, "A1" is a reference to the cell at column A, row 1.

relative cell reference   A reference to the contents of a cell that Excel adjusts when you copy the formula to another cell or range of cells.

Replace   A command on the Edit menu that you can use to automatically replace text with different text. This feature can also be used with special characters such as tabs and paragraph marks.

revision marks   The tracked changes you see onscreen.

row   A horizontal set of cells in Excel.

ruler   A tool for measuring distances of where objects are in relation to the page. Appearing horizontally across the top of a page and vertically along the side of a page in Word, rulers also display page margins and tab settings.

S

sans serif   Fonts that don't have "tails" on the letters (for example, Helvetica and Arial).

ScreenTip   A note that displays onscreen to explain a function or feature.

scroll arrows   The arrows at either end of a scrollbar that you can click to scroll through your document.

scroll bar   A long bar that lets you move through your document with the mouse. Word provides a vertical scrollbar on the right side of the window and a horizontal scrollbar along the bottom of the window.

scroll box   The small box on a scrollbar you can drag along the bar to scroll in either direction.

search criteria   Defined patterns or details used to find matching records.

select   To define a section of text so you can take action on it, such as copying, moving, or formatting it.

selection handles   Small squares around the edges of a graphical image that indicate the graphic is selected.

serif Fonts that have "tails" on the letters (for example, Times New Roman and Courier).

shortcut key A keyboard combination that provides a quick way to execute a menu command. For example, Ctrl+S is a shortcut key for the File, Save menu command.

shortcut menu A menu that pops up when you right-click an object. The options in this menu vary depending on the type of object you click.

slide A single document or page in a PowerPoint presentation.

slide show A visual presentation you can create with PowerPoint that uses text, graphics, and other effects. Use slide shows for business presentations, training presentations, and other tasks that require visual presentations.

slide transition A special effect used to introduce a slide during a PowerPoint slideshow.

sort A function that rearranges the data in a list so it appears in alphabetic or numeric order.

speaker notes Notes that help you document and give a presentation in PowerPoint.

status bar A place at the bottom of each Office window that tells you information about your documents and applications, such as whether you are in insert or overtype mode.

strikethrough A font option in which the text is marked out with a series of dash marks (for example, ~~strikethrough~~).

style A named collection of formatting settings you can assign to text. For example, the Normal style might use the Times New Roman font at 11 points with standard margins.

submenu A list of options that appears when you point at some menu items in Windows and in applications designed for use with Windows. A small, right-pointing arrowhead appears to the right of menu items that have submenus.

system tray The area on the right side of the taskbar that displays the programs loaded into memory for use.

T

tab An element that enables you to separate objects with a precise amount of space (such as 1"), which using the spacebar can't do.

tab stop An element you place in your ruler to allow you to add space and alignment between your tabs. For example, you could add a right, center, left-aligned, decimal, or bar tab stop.

table A series of rows and columns. The intersection of a row and column is called a *cell*, which is where you type text and numbers.

taskbar The bar on the Windows desktop (usually at the bottom of the screen) that contains the Start button at one end and the clock at the other. When a document is open, a button for it appears on the taskbar.

task pane   A vertical pane that usually appears on the right side of the application window and contains information and options associated with a particular feature. By default, task panes appear automatically when you perform certain actions.

TaskPad   In Outlook, a list of tasks that displays when you use the Calendar view.

template   Available in Word, Excel, and PowerPoint, a template provides predesigned patterns on which documents and workbooks can be based.

text box   A small box in a dialog box in which you can type text or numbers.

text wrapping   Text automatically flows to the next line without having to insert a carriage return using the Enter key.

theme   A consistent visual in a document that can include colors, icons, bullets, figures, background colors, and so on.

title bar   The bar across the top of a window that lists the name of the program and document that's open in the window.

toggle   A button or keyboard command you click or press once to turn an option on and again to turn it off.

toolbar   A collection of frequently used commands that appear as icon buttons you can click to activate.

transition effect   Movement that occurs between slides in PowerPoint to smooth the passing from one slide to another.

U–Z

URL   Uniform resource locator. A link to an addressable location on the Internet.

Web   Also known as the World Wide Web, it's a hypertext-based document retrieval system with machines linked to the Internet. This enables you to view documents, especially ones that are graphical in nature.

wizard   A specialized template that asks you questions about what type of document you want to create and then generates the document for you based on your answers.

workbook   An Excel document that contains one or more worksheets or chart sheets.

worksheet   In Excel, the workbook component that contains cell data, formulas, and charts.

Index

Q - R

index